Brazil's New
Racial Politics

BRAZIL'S
NEW
RACIAL
POLITICS

EDITED BY
Bernd Reiter
Gladys L. Mitchell

LYNNE
RIENNER
PUBLISHERS

BOULDER
LONDON

Published in the United States of America in 2010 by
Lynne Rienner Publishers, Inc.
1800 30th Street, Boulder, Colorado 80301
www.rienner.com

and in the United Kingdom by
Lynne Rienner Publishers, Inc.
3 Henrietta Street, Covent Garden, London WC2E 8LU

Library of Congress Cataloging-in-Publication Data
Brazil's new racial politics / edited by Bernd Reiter and
    Gladys L. Mitchell.
        p.   cm.
    Includes bibliographical references and index.
    ISBN 978-1-58826-666-8 (hardcover : alk. paper)
    1. Racism—Brazil. 2. Minorities—Brazil—Political activity.
3. Brazil—Race relations—Political aspects. I. Reiter, Bernd, 1968–
II. Mitchell, Gladys L., 1978–
    F2659.A1B74 2009
    305.800981—dc22

                                                        2009014226

British Cataloguing in Publication Data
A Cataloguing in Publication record for this book
is available from the British Library.

Printed and bound in the United States of America

∞   The paper used in this publication meets the requirements
          of the American National Standard for Permanence of
          Paper for Printed Library Materials Z39.48-1992.

    5 4 3 2 1

Contents

Foreword

Michael Mitchell

Brazil's New Racial Politics showcases new discussions of the Brazilian myth of racial democracy, but more important, it moves beyond merely unmasking that myth and addresses head-on the issue of racial inequality. The authors provide a window into the rich and broad perspectives currently being brought to bear on the continuing struggle for racial equality in Brazil. Because of this, and also because of its contribution to the body of social science work on racial inequality more broadly, the book deserves a wide readership. *Brazil's New Racial Politics* is not only an outstanding contribution to scholarly work in this field; it is particularly propitious in terms of its presentation of black-movement activism.

Brazil at the opening of the twenty-first century is not the same nation that it was in the 1950s and 1960s, or even in the 1980s and 1990s. Its newly discovered oil fields hold the promise of long-awaited energy independence; and its social policies, such as the *bolsa família* program and its AIDS awareness and prevention policies, have become models of public policy meriting serious study and even emulation. On the international scene, Brazil has made a credible claim to a seat on the United Nations Security Council. As well, Brazil as an emerging economic power has earned it inclusion in the powerful group that the World Bank calls the BRICs (Brazil, Russia, India, and China). Brazilians have accomplished enough in the past few decades to make the old joke about Brazil perpetually being the country of the future somewhat anachronistic. It is this changing situation that makes this book so valuable.

This volume arrives squarely in a period that social scientists refer to as one of *democratic consolidation*. Transfers of political power through competitive elections, the functioning of an independent and nearly transparent judiciary, and the subordination of the armed forces to civil rule all illustrate the extent to which Brazilian democracy has passed the point of imminent or even imaginable return to authoritarian rule. The Brazilian electorate, despite initial reluctance, voted to install a president from a clearly working-class background. Lula's reelection, mainly through the vote of the poor and working classes of the northeast, diluted the traditional dominance of the southeast and São Paulo over national politics. Nevertheless, weaknesses in Brazil's democracy persist, many of which greatly affect Brazilians of African descent, as several of the chapters in the volume convincingly point out.

It is within the context of a Brazil with a consolidated democracy that the contributors take up new issues, controversies, and political patterns and practices related to the still troublesome problem of racial inequality. Their starting point is no longer a debate about the myth of racial democracy. Rather, they begin with the assumption that this myth is a story from the past. Here the authors address controversies such as affirmative action, which has been energetically debated in Brazil since the 2001 United Nations Conference on Racism. They analyze the emergence of black politics, in which mobilizing around racial identity is significant. And they examine movement politics, both with regard to direct action protest and to the impact that racially oriented nongovernmental organizations have on the capacity of the black movement to sustain autonomy in the political arena.

The book allows the reader to follow an ongoing colloquy among its contributors. In this sense, a strictly academic tone gives way to dialogue. The contributors do not always agree with one another. What might have been a standardized discussion of like minds is, instead, a stimulating presentation of differing perspectives.

As Brazil has changed, so have the ways in which issues of race are articulated and understood. Thus, many of the seminal works on Brazil and race are useful today for a historical perspective, but not a comprehensive, contemporary view. That is why *Brazil's New Racial Politics* is not only critical, but timely. It is essential reading for all those interested in issues of race and politics today.

1

The New Politics of Race in Brazil

Bernd Reiter and Gladys L. Mitchell

Brazilian racism is not new, but this book, as the title indicates, examines new aspects of the racial politics of Brazil and presents a fresh perspective. The purpose of the book is to provide an overview of the emergent scholarship on black mobilization and agency in response to racism and color prejudice. It is also an attempt to capture the questions and problems triggered by a change in Brazilian "common sense,"[1] in particular a new sensitivity and awareness of the ways that racism structures Brazilian lives. The focus on black agency is one of the main characteristics of a new generation of Brazilian and Brazilianist scholarship, a scholarship more in tune with subaltern perspectives and thus able to offer new insights into Brazilian societal dynamics and their far-reaching political implications, especially with regard to a redefinition of Brazilian nationalism.

Unveiling Racism in Brazil

Racism in Brazil has been exposed systematically as early as the 1950s, when a group of distinguished scholars undertook an analysis of what then was internationally perceived as a "racial paradise." The UNESCO-sponsored research project, headed by Charles Wagley of Columbia University, counted on such valuable contributors as Marvin Harris, Luis A. Costa Pinto, Thales de Azevedo, Ben Zimmerman, and Harry Hutchinson, thus combining the insights of outstanding anthropologists and sociologists. Initiated in 1950, this broad research project gradually expanded to include even more scholars, such as Roger Bastide, Florestan Fernandes, Fernando Henrique Cardoso, and Octavio Ianni. By the 1960s, it was not only clear that Brazil was indeed far from being a racial paradise; it also became apparent that the whole idea of the racial paradise was a government-led nationalist project.

1

Yet despite the growing awareness that inequalities in Brazil could not be explained by class alone, the scholarship of the 1950s and 1960s was not coherent enough to dismantle the persuasive ideological construct of the Brazilian version of Jose Vasconcelos's "cosmic race,"[2] which reached back to the 1930s, and had, since then, been forcefully anchored into the Brazilian everyday reality by a series of vehement measures, including the use of a propaganda ministry under the Getúlio Vargas regime,[3] and through it, the widespread production of "historically correct" textbooks to be used in the growing number of Brazilian public primary schools (Dávila 2003). By the early 1960s, when the counterhegemonic discourse of some of the authors associated with the UNESCO project could have impacted the broader society and the government, the military ended democracy in Brazil and suffocated any attempt at producing the kind of knowledge that could have been used to mobilize parts of society for more justice and participation in politics as the military regime ended most voting. The scholars involved in critical studies of Brazilian society had to flee the country, and any attempt to continue researching Brazilian race relations came to an abrupt end.

In 1985, when the military regime finally collapsed, Brazilian social sciences had to start from where they were cut off twenty years earlier. Nevertheless, critical race studies came back with a vengeance, now equipped with the newly developed tools of more sophisticated statistical analyses that could count on a variety of new data, as the Brazilian state started to reintroduce skin color categories into its censuses and surveys. In 1967, the Brazilian Institute for Geography and Statistics (IBGE) created the Pesquisa por Amostra de Domicílios (PNAD) or *Penade,* as it came to be known among Brazilian researchers. The PNAD is a household-based survey tool that produced a myriad of new data on Brazil's social and economic reality. As a result, the ideology of the racial paradise came under increased attack, especially from a group of social scientists associated with the Rio de Janeiro–based Candido Mendes University, namely Carlos Hasenbalg, Nelson do Vale Silva, and Peggy Lovell, but also from a new crop of researchers at other universities, including the following operating out of the Federal University of Bahia: Nadya Castro, Antônio Sérgio Guimarães, Michel Agier, Luiza Bairros, and Vanda Sá Barreto, to name a few. These new voices added significantly to those that had spoken up against racism all along, particularly Cloves Moura, Lelia Gonzales, and Abdias do Nascimento.

Race-Conscious Scholarship, Statistical Data, and Black Mobilization

The analyses produced by this new generation of scholars left no doubt that ethnic background was an important variable in the explanation of Brazil's extreme inequalities in such central spheres of life as education, the labor market, job mobility inside firms, marriage, and even life expectancy. These scholars proved without a doubt that Brazilian blacks were worse off than their white countrymen and women. Furthermore, this inequality could not be explained by educational backgrounds or unequal income and wealth alone. Brazilian whites (and Asians) fared much better than Brazilian blacks and browns with similar educational backgrounds, who suffered from discrimination even if they had access to middle-class incomes. Money did not whiten after all, contrary to what Azevedo argued in 1954 (Azevedo 1996); nor was there a mulatto escape hatch benefiting brown people over black people as Degler (1971) had argued. This new knowledge was crucial for Brazil's newly emerging black-power movements, because it gave them the tools and arguments they needed to mobilize. After several attempts at mobilizing the Brazilian black population during the 1930s and the 1950s, they were silenced by the different manifestations of the Brazilian authoritarian state. Similar to the critical scholarship, black power in Brazil emerged invigorated from its internal and external exile. In 1978, when the military regime started to crumble, the Unified Black Movement (MNU) was created, thus providing a national framework for black activism for the first time. The data provided and analyzed by the new scholars from Rio de Janeiro and Salvador proved extremely instrumental for the goals pursued by the MNU and similar organizations. This link deserves further explanation, and allows us to explain the different uses of *race* in the literature, as well as in this book.

Race is an elusive category and provides an even more elusive way to forge a sense of collective belonging. Nobody is more aware of this elusiveness than Brazilian black-power activists. For most of the history of blacks in Brazil, Africans and their descendents had a strong sense of being different from their white slaveholders. This difference was forced onto them and used to hold them at the bottom of Brazil's social hierarchies, and it left no doubt that Brazilian whites had no intention whatsoever to accept the moral and legal equality of blacks, which held true well into the twentieth century. The sense of black identity was indeed so strong during most of the colonial period and slavery, which lasted until 1888, that African and Brazilian blacks of different ethnic and linguistic backgrounds and of different degrees of biological mixture repeatedly united to contest white supremacy and attempted to overthrow the system that held them at the bottom. On several occasions, Brazil barely escaped its "Haitian moment." As late as 1931, the radical Frente Negra Brasileira, the Brazilian Black Front, had a membership of about 200,000, mostly concentrated in the industrialized south (Davis 1999: 187). In 1936, however, the authoritarian government of Vargas outlawed the Black Front, together with all other oppositional political parties. The Vargas government sought to discourage any association that had the potential to endanger his project of national unity.

The risk of factionalism and even secession was so great during the 1930s that the Vargas government undertook extraordinary measures to forge a sense of nationality, national pride, and even a sense of what it meant to be Brazilian.

Among the most successful in this cause was sociologist Gilberto Freyre (1986). Freyre's writings on the Brazilian national character provided the ideological foundation upon which a unified nation could be constructed, and the Vargas regime left no means untouched to disseminate this ideology. Brazil would be a *racial paradise,* inhabited by one race, the Brazilian version of "cosmic race"—a tropical mulatto republic. Anybody daring to say differently was transformed into a naysayer and a reactionary. The concept of a racial paradise promised a solution to finally catch up to the developed world, even if—and especially because—Brazil had such a large mixed population.

To the black-power movement, this move proved devastating. Up until the 1930s, Brazilian blacks were forcefully united by the perverse power of racism and social Darwinism; after the 1930s, asserting one's blackness was transformed into an act of civic upheaval and antipatriotism and little by little, as the Vargas regime made sure that its version of the truth was accepted, asserting ethnic difference became an act of political incorrectness not only aimed against the state, but against mainstream society. Under Vargas, *race* was removed from textbooks, censuses, and from the official discourse about Brazil. The state thus produced the main and only official way to represent the country, and any Brazilian—black or white, mixed or indigenous—had no other choice but to accept that reality and to find ways of social mobility that explicitly took it into account. The core of the doctrine disseminated under Vargas was that no matter what their ethnic background, Brazilians are all mixed and hence *one.* Nevertheless, this was not an "imagined community," as Benedict Anderson (1991) suggests. Rather, it was a designed community, designed by the state and forced onto its people. The only one imagining, dreaming, and sometimes hallucinating such a community was the father of the idea, Gilberto Freyre.

The Vargas years severely delegitimized any attempt to forge a sense of racial solidarity among excluded blacks. Just as black-power movements regrouped during the 1950s and early 1960s, the state stepped in again, this time to avoid a potentially explosive bonding between labor and racialized groups. During the military regime, black-power activism became subversive and was subject to prosecution in the best-case scenario, but also to state-sponsored persecution, imprisonment, torture, and even death. The military regime also ensured that the category *race* would disappear again from the census, and it thus sought to curtail even the prospects for an emerging racial solidarity that would embrace and represent all those affected by the forces of racism and racialized exclusion. Categories, after all, are the building blocks of group consciousness (Brubaker 2004). Without numbers, mobilization is greatly complicated, as there can be no sense of a shared destiny if it is not known with whom, and with how many, this destiny is shared. Political activism is all but rendered impossible if there are no data and no existing categories other than being Brazilian.

This tenuous link between statistical categories, disaggregated data, and the forging of group identity and solidarity is precisely what made the studies of the 1980s and early 1990s so relevant. They provided the means and the tools upon which solidarity of the excluded could be constructed. With information on inequalities among different categories of people—differentiated by ethnic background, skin color, gender, age, region, educational background, and other demographic categories—the opportunities for ethnopolitical entrepreneurs to forge group solidarity and awareness tremendously increased. The data produced by scholars of the time left no doubt that Brazilian society had undergone a process of racialization; that is, certain groups had been systematically excluded and stigmatized based on their physical and cultural characteristics. It became apparent that no other factor had such a strong influence on one's life chances as the color of one's skin. Brazilian nonwhites are excluded from almost all spheres of life, including education, jobs, certain marriages, earnings, chances of job promotion, even life expectancy. Discrimination thus structures Brazilian life, and this discrimination is racist, because it targets nonwhites. Racism is thus responsible for creating a renewed sense of belonging to a group, the group of the discriminated, the exploited, and the excluded. The findings published by Carlos Hasenbalg, Nelson do Vale Silva, and Peggy Lovell during the late 1980s and early 1990s left no doubt about the salience of racism in structuring Brazilian social hierarchies and life chances, and they provided the crucial, race-specific information without which mobilization is impossible.

The Normalizing Power of Denying Racism

In 1999, when Michael Hanchard's collection, *Racial Politics in Contemporary Brazil,* first appeared, finding racism in Brazilian society was still a counterhegemonic endeavor, aimed not just against mainstream scholarship, but also against the official self-identification of the Brazilian state as well as a great part of its population, black and white alike. At the time, vehement reactions against Hanchard's scholarship were not entirely surprising. They were certainly revealing. Recognized international scholars, such as Pierre Bourdieu and Loic Wacquant (1999), took it upon themselves to accuse Hanchard of US imperialism. Many sectors of Brazilian society, especially the historically privileged, who had always been able to benefit from a system that had put them on top of social hierarchies based on the color of their skin and their real or invented European heritage, found a reverse racism in the fact that some scholars now accused them of being racists and maintaining a system that excluded almost half of the Brazilian population from equitable access to education, jobs, and social prestige. US scholars, used to the strict division of their own society and backed by powerful foundations, were misreading Brazilian realities that were more complex and multifaceted—so went the thrust of Bourdieu's argument. Other Brazilian scholars seemed to lament the political influence that this kind of scholarship had on Brazilian blacks, supposedly leading them to change their ways and embrace a US style of separatism aimed, in part, against Brazilian whites. Many Brazilian intellectuals, all of them white, thus sensed the end of what to them were "the good old days," hastened in by US blacks, who were introducing racial division into Brazil's racial paradise.

Yet the critics of this new scholarship of racial inequalities did more to reveal their own bias than to weaken the growing wave of race-conscious scholarship and black organizing that steadily grew in importance and influence during the 1980s and 1990s. On the scholarly side, all those standing up to defend the Brazilian status quo risked becoming political reactionaries, opposing actions to address the age-old inequalities of Brazilian society. Even worse, those accusing Hanchard and his colleagues of US imperialism raised resentment among the proliferating Brazilian black-power movements, because, apparently, they reproduced the paternalistic attitudes of the traditional power holders in Brazilian society, who have historically claimed to represent the country without ever representing its majority. Brazilian elites had achieved the impossible—through extremely cunning and vehement employment of the state apparatus in their own interests, they had transformed the poor and nonwhite majority into a minority. As a minority, Brazilian nonwhites were not only pushed and held at the margins of official Brazilian society, and thus left without any real political power; they were also kept at the margin of citizenship and transformed into second-class citizens whose preferences did not count as much as those of the European-descendent elites.

Once the majority was transformed into a minority, it became subject to what Michel Foucault, the French intellectual known for his wide-ranging studies including social institutions and power, has called the "normalizing gaze" of the powerful. Under this scrutinizing and measuring gaze, black and indigenous people become objects of anthropological inquiry, conducted by those who defined themselves as the inheritors of European culture and science—expat Europeans in wondrous tropical lands, inhabited by exotic peoples with strange habits. As decades of concerted effort to whiten the nation had failed, Brazilian state elites under Vargas were able to forge a nation where nonwhites were perceived as enriching ingredients to a dominantly European national culture. In the hegemonic imagery created in those times, blacks and indigenous groups became a sort of spice to the stew that made up the nation. To the white elites, this spice allowed them to define themselves as tropical people, thus providing them with a way to think of themselves at the same time as equals to white Europeans and those from the United States and, yet, as superior to them, due to the Brazilians' greater sensitivity, soulfulness, cunning, and flexibility—all inherited from the nonwhite contributors to the great Brazilian nation. To the white elites, who engineered this Brazilian nation, this was a perfect solution. It not only provided a way to compare positively to white Europeans and those from the United States and thus to escape the racial determinism that dominated thinking about race and its influence on development until the 1930s; it also blocked any effort to forge a sense of collective identity among all those that had potential grievances against the Brazilian state, and thus it undermined any mobilization of marginalized groups.

To nonwhites, this way of framing, perceiving, and selling the nation also seemed to offer some benefits, as it allowed escaping from the worst versions of racist doctrine and determinism of the time, namely all those theories that defined blackness as an unchangeable and unalterable human stain. The doctrine of the *mestiço* (mixed or half-breed) nation allowed for a gradual blending through a process of intergenerational whitening, even if this meant giving up one's culture and identity. Both black and indigenous people had given up much before without any reward, and Vargas's chimera seemed to compensate for all the suffering and sacrifice it demanded, with brighter days to come.

Times of Change

Nevertheless, the data produced during the 1980s and 1990s revealed that the dream of a color-blind society had not materialized, and all the sacrifice and the deferment of a happy ending in the future turned out to be nothing but wishful thinking. Brazilian nonwhites came to realize that their hopes of eventual compensation were in vain. Worse, all the sacrifice; the anxious effort to rid oneself of anything linked to Africanness, blackness, or indigenousness; the waiting and postponing only led to frustration. The research emerging in the 1980s and 1990s clearly demonstrated that Brazilian blacks, browns, and indigenous groups remained at the very bottom of social hierarchies. Worse, the stigma against anything nonwhite had not withered; hence nonwhites were not only left at the bottom of Brazilian society, but their sense of a shared destiny and community had been shattered by decades of false hopes of mulatto mobility.

The research conducted during the 1980s and 1990s provided ample evidence that the promise of a racial paradise had not been fulfilled. Providing hard empirical evidence for this failure proved cathartic. It not only inspired a new generation of researchers to examine Brazilian race relations; it also unleashed black-power movements. Black-power activists finally found in the hard numbers that these social scientists produced the substance and spark to mobilize all those frustrated with the dream of becoming mulattos. Hanchard's 1999 collection was not just a collection of the latest research on the effects of racism in Brazil; it also provided space for social activists and representatives of a new and growing race-conscious way of doing politics, represented best in the figure of Benedita da Silva, the first black, female senator, who once worked as a domestic servant.

To many observers, Brazil's participation in the 2001 International Antiracism Conference, held in Durban, South Africa, marked the beginning of a new era for thinking about Brazil. Much has changed since Hanchard published his collection, although certainly not enough for Brazil to come even close to the ideal of racial harmony that has been forcefully promoted for so long. In 2001, universities began to enact affirmative action policies for Afro-Brazilians. In 2003, a federal law was passed that requires public schools to teach African and Afro-Brazilian history. Currently, black-movement activists are pushing for affirmative action in employment because they became aware that Afro-Brazilian beneficiaries of affirmative action in universities continued to face discrimination in employment, even with a university education.

Brazil is living through another moment of its self-awareness as a nation. It is not just the growing awareness that racism is a real and serious problem impeding Brazil's path to a prosperous future. Much like the last days of Brazilian slavery, racism is currently being perceived as a shameful stain that needs addressing for the sake of saving the nation's pride. But with the edifice of the racial paradise crumbling, black organizing on the rise, and affirmative action in full swing, Brazil faces the question anew of how to read and understand itself. If Brazil is not a tropical mulatto paradise, what is it? If all the ideas about cordiality and color-blindness that have dominated minds and history books for generations are wrong, then the question of what is the truth becomes pressing. Brazil, in short, is in search of a new national trope—a new way of imagining itself. Brazil is at the crossroads. On one side is the possibility of joining what is commonly referred to as the West—a path opened by Brazil's status as an emerging market equal to or even more promising than China and India. On the other side lies the possibility to rescue some of the imagery of Latin America's difference—an idea much older than the doctrine of the mestizo nation, dreamed first by Simon Bolívar, the liberator, and José Martí, the great philosopher of the Latin American soul.

Again, social scientists and activists feed on each other to discuss the options and weigh different possibilities. Only this time, the historically excluded and their representatives take an active part in this discussion. Scholarship and activism are no longer elite affairs. They also no longer are purely national affairs as destinies and solidarities have long spread across national borders and produced intricate networks of understanding, cooperation, and sympathy. What unites the new voices in this discussion is their consciousness of being subalterns and their commitment to achieve positive change toward a more equitable and just society. Because of their greater internationalism, they are not sanguine about any nationalist model or racial regime that is readily available—least of all the models practiced in Europe and the United States.

The new social science scholarship about Brazil is aware that it cannot avoid dealing with race. It is also aware that the country is searching for new models and ways to represent itself—to itself and to others. A new Gilberto Freyre has yet to emerge, nor would it be desirable if one would appear. Instead, the current effort to rethink Brazil is more collective, more international, more self-aware and self-critical, and less elitist than anything that preceded it. The new voices speak from different social and geographical places, and they speak differently. There is no more space for chauvinism, no matter what kind. Scholars now have to reckon with activists and vice versa, as everybody is aware that knowledge is multifaceted and not the exclusive domain of university professors. If anything, the relationship between scholars and activists is symbiotic, as each needs the other for material, inspiration, and legitimization.

Yet the resulting discussion is not cacophonic, but rather marked by a careful and, more or less, systematic weighing of arguments, hypotheses, and possibilities. It is also not a narrow discussion, as the task in itself demands complex analysis. Sociologists, anthropologists, political scientists, and media and communication specialists all offer different viewpoints and angles of the same complex phenomenon that is Brazilian reality. Analysts of more geographically restricted problems are aware that the questions they raise are connected to broader issues and thus relevant to others facing similar problems, leading them to ask similar questions in other regions, or even countries. "The world is a ghetto," as Winant (2001) pointed out.

This Book

The time is ripe for another assessment of Brazil's racial politics. As we move beyond proving the existence and effects of racism, this book provides a snapshot of the current stage of the international academic discussion and the collective efforts and social movement actions to analyze, understand, and change Brazilian reality. They go hand in hand, and, as explained above, feed on each other, not to the detriment of positive science, but—to the contrary—to its enrichment, as they provide science with a strong sense of purpose and meaning. Current academic discussions about Brazilian reality are thus more than just scholarly exercises. They are strongly connected to the country's future, leaving no space for disengaged academic exercises or cynicism.

This sense of purpose radiates through all the contributions assembled in this volume. None of the contributors are just doing business-as-usual. They are all aware that they are participating in a greater project, where their voices bear the potential to impact the course of Brazil's future. Brazil, much like the United States, is as much a place of yet unfulfilled promise as it is a place formed by ideas of liberty, equal opportunity, and unity. Perhaps even more than any other country, Brazil is the country of the future, and after 500 years of conquest, colonization, discrimination, lack of opportunity, exclusion, and racism, Brazil is slowly but surely awakening to its own immense potential.

The selection of chapters was guided by our perception of this task of re-thinking Brazil. As mentioned above, sociology, anthropology, political science, and media and communication studies have all produced much relevant scholarship in this regard. We thus selected outstanding contributions from all these fields. Of course, any selection runs the risk of bias; ours results in selections influenced by our own convictions, beliefs, and familiarity with the subject. We sought to gather the clearest voices, addressing the most significant and representative topics currently discussed among scholars and activists of Brazilian reality and nationalism in general, and Brazilian race relations in particular. In addition, the focus of this volume is on the new politics of race in Brazil, which hints at our attempt to provide a space for recent scholarship in this field. Novelty, here, is not meant to represent any sort of avant-garde status. Rather, it represents our attempt to introduce to the broader audience the new approaches and findings about Brazil produced since Hanchard's assessment in 1999.

Three comments seem necessary. First, by focusing on Brazilian race relations, we are not narrowing the focus to a specific and particular problem among others of Brazilian reality. Instead, we contend that at this stage, discussing ethnicity, skin color, racism, as well as gender-related inequality is a sine qua non for anybody claiming to discuss social reality—Brazilian or not. It is no longer morally tenable or scientifically sound to discuss questions of social justice, equality, democracy, citizenship, education, politics, and human rights without considering race and gender. This is not a special task—and most certainly not the privileged task of those inflicted with the continued workings of racism and sexism. The practice of discrimination affects the object of such practice and its practitioner by dehumanizing both, an insight already developed in the eighteenth and nineteenth centuries by such authors as Kant and Hegel. By discussing Brazilian race relations, the contributors to this volume are all keenly aware that they are discussing the very substance of the social fabric that constitutes Brazilian society. The scope of this book, then, is of broad significance both for its empirical reach and for its methodological implications for the social sciences, as it seeks to anchor the discussion of race relations squarely in the center of other discussions of Brazilian realities. Skin color, after all, not only overdetermines its bearer and provides him or her with a highly relevant form of symbolic capital, or lack thereof; it is also one of the most immediate and consequential social markers structuring any society. Racialization is not a singular experience to the countries of the African diaspora; it is as much a phenomenon and a problem in all those societies that have long claimed to be homogeneous and free of racial problems. Brazil is only one case among many. It is, however, a very rich and telling case that allows the drawing of many conclusions beyond its national borders.

The second point is one of drawing analytical borders. We have opted not to include any historical accounts in this collection. This choice was not driven by any aversion we have to that field of study. We are, to the contrary, fully aware that history is currently being written and rewritten to fit the new requirements of the Brazilian people and their state. Nevertheless, a collection of historical accounts that reflects the current refabrication of Brazilian self-understanding and nationalism is a task that requires more historical distance. The discussions represented here are simply too new to permit such an endeavor.

The third point we need to clarify is our usage of the term *race*. We are fully aware of the risks of contributing to the reification of race as a social category by its repeated use. Race is, after all, an invention by the very social scientists that now seek to dismantle its power. We opted to still use this category because of the specific context of Brazilian discussions about social inequalities caused by skin color and perceived ethnicity. In the Brazilian context, progressive social forces are currently seeking to forge racial solidarity among discriminated people, who historically have been discriminated against because of their skin color and ethnicity. This category includes a large number of nonwhite people, or more precisely, people unable to successfully claim whiteness. To those progressive forces, the forging of a racial identity is the first step toward the creation of a racial solidarity, which would allow for the summing of enough political power to challenge the prevailing hegemonic structures of power in Brazil. Thus race represents a progressive agenda among historically excluded Brazilians as it offers the opportunity to forge enough racial solidarity and group identity to contest and conquer political power. Although we are aware of the extremely loaded etymology of the term and feel uncomfortable with most of its contemporary usages and connotations, we nevertheless find it important to reflect the state of its current usage in Brazil and thus opted for applying it in our book.

This book is structured the following way: Part 1, "Black Empowerment and White Privilege," introduces some of the new attempts and approaches to the study of racial inequality and black empowerment through racial consciousness in Brazil. It provides an example of some of the new problems that have come to the forefront of recent analyses, and it introduces some of the new questions that contemporary scholars have started to ask over the past few years. It examines how Afro-Brazilian identity has changed and how self-understanding depends on a person's social standing. Before delving into the complications of Afro-Brazilian identity and its political implications, in Bernd Reiter's chapter, "Whiteness as Capital," he deconstructs whiteness and the privileges it bestows on white Brazilians. Rather than focusing on the marginalization of Afro-Brazilians, Reiter examines the ways that white Brazilians are included. In studying whiteness and privilege, Reiter seeks to highlight the interdependence of exclusion and inclusion and of marginalization and the active defense of privilege. He offers new ways of studying Brazilian race relations and inequalities by shifting the analytical focus away from the victims of discrimination and exclusion, to the victimizers and benefactors. In doing so, he shows how white privilege goes unchecked in Brazilian society and contributes to poor quality democracy.

Gladys Mitchell's chapter on Afro-Brazilian color identification and black candidate preference demonstrates how black-movement activism may have influenced individual identification. Mitchell finds that Afro-Brazilians in Salvador and São Paulo who identify as black (*negro* or *preto*) are more likely to vote for black politicians than those identifying in lighter color categories. Not only does this suggest that ethnic voting exists in Brazil, but it shows that the common adage that *negros não votam em negros* (blacks do not vote for blacks) is completely wrong. Afro-Brazilians who embrace blackness do vote for black candidates. Black-movement activists have long encouraged Afro-Brazilians to embrace blackness and a black identification. Although most Afro-Brazilians continue to identify as brown (*pardo*), in 2007, Afro-Brazilians began to outnumber white Brazilians due to a higher number of Afro-Brazilians identifying as black. Only the future can tell if this will resonate in Brazilian electoral politics.

Angela Figueiredo reintroduces a new subject of study to the field of Brazilian race relations, namely the analysis of black middle and upper classes. This topic was first examined in the 1950s by Thales de Azevedo (1955) and has since been neglected. Addressing individualistic attitudes of middle- and upper-class Afro-Brazilians in Salvador, Bahia, Figueiredo finds that Afro-Brazilian entrepreneurs face racial discrimination and exclusion even though they have achieved social ascension, thus contradicting the widely held belief that in Brazil, *money whitens*. Figueiredo further finds that most of her interviewees have developed subtle ways to explain away the racial discrimination they routinely face, thus pointing to the high degree of normalization that racial discrimination has achieved in Brazil. When they do acknowledge it, they blame it on people having bad manners (*mal educado*). Furthermore, they do not act on it because they believe those who practice racism will suffer more than they will themselves, and they are not willing to become involved in legal matters. This implies that upwardly mobile Afro-Brazilian businesspeople may be less racially conscious or that their individualistic attitudes may influence the way they experience discrimination, making it less likely for them to identify racial discrimination.

In the final chapter of this section, Cloves Oliveira addresses the relatively new and unexplored field of race-conscious media studies. In his chapter on media treatment of São Paulo's first black mayor, Celso Pitta, he finds that despite the fact that Pitta sought a nonracialized identity, he was racialized throughout the campaign. Pitta was not connected with the black movement and did not run on a racial platform. Because former mayor Paulo Maluf supported him, the media attributed his electoral success to marketing, and he was often referred to as a marketing product. In addition, his opponent, Luiza Erundina, publicly called him a white thief (*safado branco*) who was not genuinely black. Interestingly, like those in the United States, Afro-Brazilian politicians face the challenge of racial authenticity as well as racism, making it difficult for them to fully achieve self-agency.

Part 2, "Affirmative Action Contested," takes on one of the most heated and debated topics in Brazil today. Ever since the Brazilian state first enacted affirmative action policies in 2001, broad sectors of Brazilian society have started to contest these policies, as they seem to threaten the very core of what it means to be Brazilian, namely to live in a society without a rigid color line. The two contributions we selected for this section discuss the different affirmative action policies enacted in Brazil, and they focus on the different reactions they have caused in different sectors of society. Furthermore, both contributors seek to explain why affirmative action is causing such vehement reactions among certain Brazilians, and they set out to analyze these reactions. To allow for a better comparative analysis, both authors focus their attention on the most contested affirmative action policy currently employed in Brazil, namely to regulate access to higher education.

Seth Racusen focuses on university affirmative action policies as an example of how it is difficult for Brazil to exit its existing racial order. He examines how universities seek to verify identity, while considering subjective identities in their process of identifying who should be entitled to privileged treatment. His "grammar of identity" concept acknowledges that there is a certain set of rules and understandings people use to describe themselves and others, and this varies in different contexts. Despite Brazil's complex system of identity, which is evident in the case that some self-identified white Brazilians have claimed a darker identity to benefit from the policy, Racusen believes implementing affirmative action in a fair way is possible. He promotes a layered approach in which Afro-Brazilians from public schools, whites from public schools, and Afro-Brazilians from private schools should be considered for university affirmative action.

In the other chapter in this section, Monica Treviño examines another aspect of this extremely contemporary debate, namely the support, and lack thereof, of affirmative action among Afro-Brazilians. Treviño pays special attention to the beneficiaries of this program and finds that nearly one-third of affirmative action beneficiaries do not agree with the program. Treviño thus concludes that the Brazilian black-power movement has paid too much attention to implementing this policy, but neglected to explain it enough to garner support for it. She finds that because of the taking over by nongovernmental organizations (NGO-ization) of the black-power movement, there has been less effort devoted to consciousness-raising among Afro-Brazilians, which is detrimental to changing negative perceptions of affirmative action and its beneficiaries.

Part 3, "The New Politics of Black Power," presents a discussion that has been on the agenda of scholars for some years; however, recent scholarship has been able to expand on and focus specifically on some of the questions previous scholars have asked. One of these foci is about the viability of cultural activism as a tool to achieve lasting change and improvement for the Brazilian black community. It is also about analyzing mobilization efforts by self-identified black women who have mobilized their communities without recognition in academic discussions. Keisha-Khan Perry's chapter offers a gendered and racialized account of black mobilization. Rather than attribute a lack of mobilization to racial hegemony or an excessive focus on culture, Perry acknowledges that black mobilization occurs in local communities such as the Gamboa de Baixo neighborhood, in Salvador (Bahia). Afro-Brazilians have been displaced in Salvador as some of its historic communities have been transformed into tourist attractions. Residents in Gamboa de Baixo recognize the historic importance of their communities, and women who have mobilized are fighting for clean water and other necessities in their community. In their efforts, they have recognized the challenges they face as poor black women and have embraced these identities rather than ignore them.

To many, recent cultural activism has contributed much to the raising of black pride and racial consciousness, thus contributing significantly to the formation of black group consciousness and racial awareness. Rap music in conjunction with NGO activism has produced, according to Sales dos Santos, much along these lines. This author finds examples of a very fruitful usage of culture to achieve social change. In his analysis of Brazilian rap music and the relationship between hip-hop cultural activism and NGOs, he finds that, to an extent, black-movement activism now takes place in NGOs and through rap artists. Rather than view NGOs as an impediment, Santos believes they serve as new agents of change in the Afro-Brazilian struggle. According to him, unlike traditional black-movement activists, who had a difficult time building relationships with the Brazilian state and its entities, NGOs facilitate such relationships, because they have professionalized black-movement activism. Furthermore, rap artists appeal to black youth through racially conscious lyrics that acknowledge that marginalization is due to both race and class, not simply class.

On the other hand, to Fernando Conceição, cultural activism does not lead to what is truly needed to improve the lot of Brazilian blacks, that is, the conquest of political power. To Conceição, cultural activism has done little to advance the position of Brazilian blacks, and much to consolidate the already existing stereotypes about them. Conceição's chapter thus focuses on Salvador's cultural movements and their relationships to politicians and nonprofit organizations. Written from the perspective of a longtime political activist, it allows us to witness the pitfalls of black cultural activism that dominates black organizing in Salvador, Brazil's black mecca. Conceição is skeptical about the potential of cultural activism and argues that cultural activism works to the detriment of political mobilization by consolidating the positions of Afro-Brazilians within social hierarchies and by strengthening the racist stereotypes about Afro-Brazilians commonly held by white Brazilians. He is also weary of the power of the cultural industry, which has already transformed much of black protest culture into yet another product to be uncritically consumed by the masses. The example of Salvador demonstrates, according to Conceição, that black cultural entrepreneurs who started their activism with an agenda of change and social justice have sold out to the powers of the media market, being transformed into agents that perpetuate, rather than challenge, the prevalent power structures that dominate Salvador in particular, and Brazil in general. Conceição finds that by becoming market entrepreneurs most of the leaders of black cultural movements he analyzes have replaced their loyalty from black-movement activists to politicians and nonprofit organizations, to profit from black economic misery. Once adapted to the market logic, these movements only discuss racial issues to the extent that it does not endanger their relationships with governmental entities and politicians. Rather than self-autonomy, they become entrapped in paternalistic and patrimonial relationships with white politicians. They are no longer the voice for the plight of Afro-Brazilians; rather, he argues, they are in part to blame for black exclusion and marginalization. He posits that rather than use alliances with those in power for the collective group, they seek individual advantage.

Finally, the part closes with Renato dos Santos's chapter on black mobilization through another nontraditional means, prevestibular courses. In his analysis of the prevestibular movement, that is, the movement of university prep courses offered for blacks and otherwise discriminated groups, Santos presents much evidence for the broad impact this movement had, not just on preparing the historically excluded to pass the university access exam (vestibular), but also in raising their racial awareness and pride in their cultural legacies. While these courses prepare poor and Afro-Brazilian students for college entrance exams, coordinators and administrative directors view these courses as an opportunity to teach about racial issues. This aids, according to this author, in sustaining the black movement.

In the conclusion, Reiter and Mitchell ponder the new scholarship introduced in this volume and its interactions and consequences for Brazilian black activism and race relations. As the contributions to this book amply demonstrate, Brazil is at the crossroads to redefine its foundational myth—the very element that allows Brazilians to self-identify as Brazilian and identify differently from other nations—Latin American, North American, and European. The current discussions do not allow for a prognosis for what will replace the myth of the racial democracy. They do, however, point to the fact that the times of racial democracy are over. The sheer amount of new reflections and analyses leaves no doubt about that. Brazil, so Reiter and Mitchell conclude, might finally be able to live up to its eternal promise to be the country of the future, precisely because it is finally willing and able to look critically upon itself. No problem can be fixed without acknowledging it first, and Brazil seems finally ready to let go of a long-established tradition of merely pretending to attack its social problems, a tradition so deeply rooted in Brazilian culture that it has produced its own expression—*para inglês ver* (done for the sake of satisfying the Brits). A Brazil ready to face its own problems and shortcomings, not worried anymore what other nations think of it, might finally be ready to tackle the many problems it faces. The problem most central to the reinvention of a better, more equitable, and fairer Brazil is the problem of racism; addressing it bears the potential of a general catharsis toward a brighter future for more Brazilians.

Notes

1. The construction and maintenance of a racist or exclusionary common sense is a widely used term in critical race studies.

2. Jose Vasconcelos was a Mexican philosopher who wrote *La Raza Cósmica* (The Cosmic Race) in 1925, promoting the idea of the peoples of the Americas becoming a mixed race and uniting not only racially, but ethically and spiritually.

3. Getúlio Vargas was president from 1930 to 1945 and 1951 to 1954, although much of that time he was, in reality, dictator.

Part 1

Black Empowerment and White Privilege

2

Whiteness as Capital: Constructing Inclusion and Defending Privilege

Bernd Reiter

Exclusion is mirrored by inclusion. Thus, instead of focusing on the mechanisms that produce and reproduce exclusion, in this chapter I analyze the mechanisms and strategies used by those historically included to defend their privileged access to crucial resources and a system of rights that upholds their status as first-class citizens in contrast to the second-class citizenship of the excluded. According to James Holston and Teresa Caldeira (1998: 276), in Brazil, "The protections and immunities civil rights are intended to ensure as constitutional norms are generally perceived and experienced as privileges of elite social statuses and thus of limited access. They are not, in other words, appreciated as common rights of citizenship." Whiteness functions as an important capital in the construction of social status because it overdetermines those able to claim it and it indicates an elevated position in the existing social hierarchies (Reiter 2009a: 5).

Discussing the ways that inequality is maintained and reproduced in Brazilian society is highly relevant to the discussion of Brazilian democracy, because although Brazil's political system is troubled, its social problems are by far worse and more consequential. In their treatment of Brazilian democracy, authors like Diamond (1999), Linz and Stepan (1996), Mainwaring (1997), and Mainwaring and Scully (1995) typically point to a weak party system and problems resulting from an unstable balance between parliamentary and presidential systems as the causes for unfinished democratic consolidation in Brazil. Although this approach has improved our understanding of the importance of institutional settings to achieve certain outcomes, such analyses only provide partial answers to the question of why Brazilian democracy has remained shallow, exclusionary, elitist, and plagued by a seemingly never-ending string of political scandals. The debate over which political institutional settings are more likely to improve the functioning of democratic systems runs the risk of confounding means with ends, because although institutions are important to provide incentives and channel expectations, they cannot guarantee a desired outcome.

By the same token, although states must be seen as important and partially autonomous actors, most authors following the pathbreaking work of Evans, Rueschemeyer, and Skocpol (1985) have overestimated state autonomy and neglected the relationship between autonomous states and the societies into which states are embedded. Evans, Rueschemeyer, and Skocpol (1985: 9) were certainly right when pointing out that "states conceived as organizations claiming control over territories and people may formulate and pursue goals that are not simply reflective of the demands or interests of social groups, classes, or society." Many researchers following this tradition, however, have transformed malfunctioning states into independent variables in their explanations of broader outcomes, such as the failing of democracies. By focusing on structure alone they have neglected the very raison d'être of structures, namely their function of reproducing processes.

Although Brazil's democracy undoubtedly suffers from the shortcomings of its political system, the gravest impediments to consolidating Brazilian democracy are not of a political, but of a social, nature. Weak state structures cannot explain the much broader problem of extremely distorted and skewed processes that characterize the daily interactions and communications that occur and characterize Brazilian society and the interactions between society and the state.

Accordingly, it is not the failing state that causes Brazil's democracy to fall short of its promises, but the extreme societal inequalities that distort communicative processes of Brazilian society and hence provide the Brazilian state with too much autonomy from the will and needs of its majority and not enough autonomy from the interests of a relatively affluent minority. Due to extreme inequality, distorting the quality of societal processes in Brazilian society, privileged groups have long captured the state and used it to advance their goals without feeling or effectively being accountable to the masses. I thus propose to test the usefulness of treating societal inequality as the independent variable for explaining Brazil's faltering democratic regime.

To achieve this goal, which implies a shift of optics, it becomes necessary to step beyond the disciplinary limits of mainstream political science and integrate the work of other social sciences, because it appears that many of the limitations of currently available approaches in political science result from a narrow scope of research that is not necessarily dictated by the need for stringency, but by accepted borders of the discipline. Imprisoned by disciplinary borders, many social scientists seek out empirical examples that help prove or falsify their discipline-based theories, instead of developing explanations and models that are able to take into account a more complex reality. In short, our aim as researchers should be to adapt our theories and explanations to reality, and not seek out segments of reality that fit into our conceptual frameworks. State autonomy and new institutionalism cannot provide reliable answers to all questions related to democracy and democratization. So instead of making reality fit the confinements imposed by mainstream political science theory, I seek to take adequate account of the different available theoretical frameworks for the analysis of a necessarily complex reality. Insights and theoretical frameworks borrowed from history and sociology have proven especially helpful for this endeavor. The work of German sociologist Niklas Luhmann (1996) on the general functioning of social systems provides the entrance point for an analysis of the nature of *embeddedness,* as well as the interactions between the political system and broader society.

Power in Brazilian Society

Understanding the impact of societal inequality on Brazilian democracy requires a detailed understanding of the centrality of inequality in structuring the daily routines and the quality of interactions and processes of Brazilian society and its everyday reality. I contend that inequality is indeed the main structuring force of Brazilian society. The core reason for this is that inequality is functional to the maintenance of privilege of historically privileged sectors of Brazilian society, a group I call *the included.* To capture the workings of inequality, one needs to focus on the historically included and the strategies they apply to uphold inequality, and through inequality defend their privileged access to crucial resources and rights. Focusing on the included also helps to correct a very common mistake of reification, routinely committed by social scientists. By constantly examining the excluded, sociologists and anthropologists, in particular, have contributed to creating them as a problem and have helped consolidate the erroneous idea that there is something wrong with the poor, the indigenous, blacks, or other historically marginalized groups.

To be exact, by focusing on the excluded, social scientists involuntarily help the included to escape analysis. They also risk becoming functional to the ongoing process of consolidating the idea that blacks, indigenous groups, women, homosexuals, and the poor are *Others,* whereas the included represent the norm. In my own empirical research, I consistently found nothing to be wrong with the excluded and a lot to be wrong with the included. A shift of focus away from the excluded and onto the included thus necessitates a shift away from an anthropological gaze focused on those historically constructed as Others and a redirection of focus onto the men and women who have the power to decide what counts as right or wrong, normal or deviant, beautiful or ugly, worthy or unworthy of social esteem, and who is to be considered an equal participant in the public sphere and who is not.[1]

A first implication, or maybe complication, resulting from this shift of optics is the question, *who are the included*? Everybody knows who the excluded are, but it is very difficult to find a good definition of the included. Political scientists have traditionally dealt with this problem by differentiating between social and political elites and the masses, or *the people,* by analytically separating the rulers from the ruled. Sociologists have long drawn sophisticated pyramids and "onions" to explain the inner divisions of societies, sometimes creating sophisticated diagrams constructed on the basis of income, wealth, status, and patterns of consumption.[2]

The problem with all these attempts, which becomes immediately apparent to anyone conducting empirical research, is that when asked, almost everybody self-identifies as belonging to the middle class. Almost no one ever self-identifies as belonging to the elite. Avoiding self-classification as belonging to the elite must be seen as part of a strategy to evade being classified and examined, and this strategy is a common repertoire among privileged groups. Doing so, included groups obfuscate their relative power and their elevated position in existent social hierarchies and avoid scrutiny and potential blame. To avoid comparison that might lead to being considered elite and therefore to being blamed for existing social and political problems, most members of included groups, instead of comparing their life situation to that of the majority of the country, apply a much broader domain for comparing their income, wealth, and general lifestyle. Among Brazilian elites, this domain habitually includes international comparisons to middle classes in much richer countries of per capita incomes on average ten times higher than Brazil, typically the United States or countries of the European Union (EU). Comparing themselves to US or European middle classes, included Brazilians avoid comparison with the national average and the situation of most Afro-Brazilians and native Brazilians. Hence, earning R$3,000 a month as a university professor is not a lot when compared to the salary of full professors in the United States, where per capita GDPs are approximately US$46,000; however, in Brazil, where the per capita GDP is approximately US$9,700 (in 2008, at purchasing power parity), earning R$3,000 per month (about US$1,500 in 2008) is reserved for a small elite. By using international, rather than national, comparisons, Brazilian elites thus reiterate a postcolonial frame of reference, as many included Brazilians are more familiar with the lifestyle of Europe or the United States than with the living conditions of blacks or indigenous groups in their own country.

The capacity to escape classification is unequally distributed in any society. The poor, stigmatized, and historically marginalized, in most cases, do not have the choice to opt out of a system that makes them the objects of inquiry and exposes them to the classifying and hierarchizing gaze of the included classifier. The phenomenon of avoiding self-classification as a member of the elite has three important analytical consequences. First, it points to the necessity to use subjective, instead of objective, categories of social stratification. Inclusion, just like exclusion, is not absolute, but relative to other groups in society, mainly the excluded groups, and becomes absolute in perspective. Inclusion is not an absolute phenomenon and must be understood and analyzed in relation to exclusion. Second, inclusion, just like exclusion, is multidimensional and must have, at the minimum, economic and cultural dimensions, and these two dimensions must be interrelated.[3] Third, inclusion is maintained on the interpersonal and subjective level and reproduced in daily interactions among different groups. I will elaborate on each of these three consequences.

In the absence of specific literature on inclusion, the vast literature on exclusion, inequality, and injustice provides initial insights. Judith Butler (1998: 41), for example, asks rhetorically, "Is it possible to distinguish, even analytically, between a lack of cultural recognition and a material oppression, when the very definition of legal 'personhood' is rigorously circumscribed by cultural norms that are indissociable from their material effects?" For Butler, the answer is no. In her essay, she explains that the cultural and material are indeed intimately intertwined. She traces this insight back to Marx's *German Ideology* (1846) and Engels's *Origin of Family, Private Property, and the State* (1884). Marx points to the connection of the mode of production that produces a certain and corresponding mode of cooperation and social organization.[4]

Much of Butler's critique takes issue with Nancy Fraser's distinction between injustices of distribution and injustices of recognition. Fraser (1998) argues that both kinds of injustices are equally serious, but that they operate differently. For Fraser, to be misrecognized means "to be denied the status of a full partner in social interaction and prevented from participating as a peer in social life—not as a consequence of a distributive inequity (such as failing to receive one's fair share of resources or 'primary goods'), but rather as a consequence of institutionalized patterns of interpretation and evaluation that constitute one as comparatively unworthy of respect or esteem (Fraser 1998: 141)." Accordingly, Fraser defines misrecognition as an "institutionalized social relation, not a psychological state" (Fraser 1998: 141). Fraser also points to the connection she makes between the symbolic and the material. For her, "the norms, significations, and constructions of personhood that impede women, racialized peoples, and/or gays and lesbians from parity of participation in social life are materially instantiated—in institutions and social practices, in social action and embodied habitus, and yes, in ideological state apparatuses. Far from occupying some wispy, ethereal realm, they are material in their existence and effects" (Fraser 1998: 144). This discussion is confusing in that it mixes epistemological with ontological claims, but no matter how the material and the cultural relate in real life, the Butler-Fraser debate clearly demonstrates that exclusion can be separated into two analytical dimensions for the sake of gaining a better understanding of how they work. It necessarily follows that inclusion can also be usefully divided into two separate analytical realms, namely as constituted by material and symbolic or cultural variables. I will first focus on the material dimensions of inclusion.

Material Dimensions of Inclusion

In the absence of data on inclusion, the vast amount of data and analysis of exclusion in Brazil provides important clues for constructing a working definition and an analytical framework for the included. Initial insights can be gained, for example, from a comparison of educational data. Data from the PNAD, the Brazilian household survey conducted annually, demonstrate that a consistent gap of nearly two years in schooling separates white Brazilians from black Brazilians during the years of 1993 and 2004 (Reiter 2009a: 56). Although educational levels in general have been slowly rising in Brazil, the gap that separates white from black Brazilians has remained the same. Along with skin color as a clear indicator for inclusion, these data also suggest that having completed at least twelve years of formal education sets one part of the population apart from the other. Being white and having completed at least twelve years of formal education are therefore strong indicators of inclusion. The fact that over 80 percent of Brazilians attend public schools alludes to the fact that attending a private middle or high school is reserved for only a select few and makes it a strong indicator of inclusion.

Another criterion to differentiate between included and excluded groups can be elaborated by comparing income and wealth disparities. According to the same source (PNAD), in 2004, 41.7 percent of Brazilian blacks and 19.5 percent of whites were poor. In the poorer regions, for example the northeast, 56.7 percent of all blacks and 44.6 percent of all whites were poor.[5] Being poor, that is, living with less than one-half per capita minimum wage per month, is therefore a condition that characterizes between 40 and 56 percent of all Brazilians. In other words, it is the Brazilian norm. Not being poor, accordingly, is a privilege in Brazil and represents not the norm, but the exception. Given that the average monthly per capita income in Brazil in 2004 was R$586 (less than US$280), it follows that all those earning more than R$600 per month are a minority and are likely to belong to the group of the included. In 2006, R$100 equaled US$48.

In a country with extremely high unemployment rates, especially when the percentage of the economically active population working in the informal sector is considered, having a regular job must be seen as another characteristic of the included. Research on the informal sector in the city of Salvador has demonstrated that about 40 percent of the economically active Bahian population works in precarious jobs of the informal sector. These jobs do not offer any job security, health coverage, unemployment, or retirement benefits.[6] Having a regular job that offers job security and benefits is therefore another indicator that characterizes the included.

Additional indicators to characterize the included can be gained from reversing data on *digital exclusion,* that is, the number of households with telephones and personal computers. According to the Brazilian Institute for Applied Research in Economics (IPEA) in 2004, 23 percent of white-headed households and 8 percent of black-headed households had a personal computer at home. Furthermore, 60 percent of black households and 40 percent of white households had no telephone. Accordingly, having a telephone serves as a criterion to characterize included sectors, and having a personal computer must be seen as an extreme privilege in Brazil, only open to a small minority of Brazilians.

One last material criterion to differentiate included from excluded Brazilians is ownership of a car. In 2005, 12 percent of Brazilians owned a car.[7] Given the average household size in Brazil of 3.73 persons per household, an average of 44 percent of Brazilian households owned a car in 2005. This information is complicated by very expressive regional differences in car ownership and by the fact that rich households may own more than one car. Despite these distortions, it is nevertheless safe to say that the majority of Brazilian households do not own a car. Not owning a car in Brazil subjects those affected to severe restrictions with regard to time-efficient mobility and access to certain exclusive regions (e.g., certain beaches).

These data permit making a first step toward analyzing who the included Brazilians are and what they look like. When focusing on material dimensions and comparing national averages, included Brazilians are likely to have a regular job offering job security and benefits (*com carteira assinada*), have more than twelve years of education, earn more than R$600 per capita per month, have a telephone at home, own a car, and they may own a personal computer. More likely than not, included Brazilians successfully claim to be white. Although this is a very crude assessment of inclusion that does not further differentiate among included groups, it provides a first step toward a more sophisticated analysis.

Symbolic Dimensions of Inclusion: Whiteness as Capital

In Brazil, whiteness is an extremely desirable characteristic and, as we have seen, a strong indicator for inclusion. Brazilian history is marked by state-led efforts to whiten the nation, which was seen as a necessary condition for achieving civilizational progress. But the national project of whitening ultimately failed, as not enough northern Europeans were willing to settle in Brazil to whiten the nation (Lesser 1999). In addition, Brazilian elites themselves had long been exposed to racial mixing, which by their own standards and, according to some European and North American visitors, endangered their prospects of catching up to the civilized European ideal.

Whiteness, anything but a biological reality, is used as a symbolic indicator of civilizing potential.[8] Lesser (1999) demonstrates that what it meant to be white shifted in Brazil between 1850 and 1950, but whiteness remained a cultural category, signifying superiority and well-deserved privilege. Brazilian elites openly discussed and compared the different degrees of whiteness of such potential immigrants as Arabs, Japanese, and southern Europeans, associating whiteness with aptitude (Lesser 1999). The idea of whiteness was therefore constructed and used as a form of capital, strongly associated with merit and progressive, developmental potential. But claiming to be white was not a viable option for all.

During the 1930s, Brazilian elites found a solution to the problem of reluctant whitening by embracing the doctrine of racial mixing, proposed by Freyre's influential work *The Masters and the Slaves,* first published in 1933. Freyre's work provided a welcome solution for the racially impure Brazilian elites who "wished to be white and feared they were not" (Stepan 1991: 45). The 1930s was a time of populism and nationalism, under the extended rule of Getúlio Vargas, who was president from 1930 to 1937, dictator from 1937 to 1945, and again president from 1951 to 1954. Freyre's work allowed for a strategy of incorporating Afro-Brazilians into the *imagined* Brazilian community instead of separating or isolating them. Placing them at the bottom of the social hierarchy, this integration demanded from Afro-Brazilians, and any other group that potentially stood in the way of Vargas's project of building one nation, a complete negation of cultural distinctiveness. For the nationalistic state, Freyre's vision offered a solution not only for integrating former slaves; it also provided the slightly nonwhite members of the newly emerging urban elites with a way to save their own status. As well, this form of integration blocked any kind of separate group formation and therefore was very functional in suffocating the formation of collective grievances even before they could arise. When Freyre's theories were transformed into official state doctrine, Brazil became a *racial democracy,* populated by only one race, namely the mulatto. Freyre's theories served the project of nation building under the Vargas regime, offering a founding ideology upon which the Brazilian elites could imagine themselves, as it allowed them to cope with the historical fact of far-reaching biological mixing without abandoning European cultural values, which served as the guiding values for themselves and the nation. It also undermined Afro-Brazilian solidarity and mobilization, as under such a system, upward social mobility had to be achieved through the assimilation of European values, manners, and aesthetics. In other words, through this move, Brazilian values and social hierarchies could remain monolithic and European despite the country's biological and cultural diversity. During the 1930s, Brazil became a tropical Europe.

After the 1930s, the corporatist political institutions that sustained Brazilian social and racial hierarchies were never effectively restructured, which would have allowed for a reconfiguration of traditional social hierarchies. Instead, the Brazilian military, joined by state elites, avoided such an attempt at restructuring with a military coup in 1964, when the threat of social revolution became imminent, carried by an emerging class-consciousness among urban workers of the industrial south. The military coup not only avoided social restructuring, it also blocked the formation of a separate group identity, in this case class-based (Erickson 1977). Instead, during military rule (1964 to 1985), Brazilian social hierarchies were perpetuated, as great parts of the Brazilian population remained marginalized from participating in political and civic life.

Although the analyses provided by Erickson (1977) and Wiarda (1981) do not address the racial dynamics that permeate the Brazilian social body, their analyses nevertheless allow for the conclusion that those at the top of the Brazilian social and political body used whiteness as a tool to legitimate their privileges. Afro-Brazilians remained at the bottom of social hierarchies and dark skin complexion remained a signifier of low status, making all blacks suspect of being poor and potentially dangerous. This perception of Afro-Brazilians is so deeply rooted in Brazilians' perception that it has escaped scrutiny. It has become one of the ways Brazilians make sense of their everyday reality. Simpson (1993), in her study about "The Mega-Marketing of Gender, Race, and Modernity," demonstrates how in Brazil a "normalizing" discourse continuously associates whiteness with merit and blackness with unworthiness and danger.[9] Simpson analyzes the career of Xuxa, an ex-playmate and ex-soft-porn star emerging in the 1980s, who later became Brazil's most famous TV star, hosting afternoon prime-time programs for children. Simpson argues that, "in her celebration of whiteness, Xuxa not only taps deep and jealously guarded feelings among Brazilians about race but also asserts the validity of a nearly universal ideological construction wherein the blond female is presented as the 'most prized possession of white patriarchy.'"[10]

Whiteness is a highly desirable good to all those that are able to claim it with success. Because of Brazil's long history of associating whiteness with civilizational potential, whiteness has developed into the strongest marker of elevated social status. It symbolizes education and holding a regular job. Additionally, most Brazilians almost automatically associate it with being middle-class, having money, owning a car, and having access to other private services, most importantly private education.

Relational Aspects of Inclusion

As stated above, inclusion is not only multidimensional, it is also relational. This insight goes back to Hegel's classic discussion of the master-slave relationship. According to social psychologist Henri Tajfel (Tajfel and Turner

1986), groups constitute themselves in relation to other individuals and groups. A sense of identity is fostered through the drawing of borders that separate those inside from those outside. This drawing of borders not only permits the effective separation of one group into two or more, it also constitutes each group with reference to the others. Tajfel's main dialectic insight was that one group can only exist by defining itself as different from another. Difference and identity are constituted together. The economist Fred Hirsch (1976) has added another component to this insight. In his book on the *Social Limits to Growth*, Hirsch points out that certain goods are relational. He refers to these as "positional goods" that can be defined as goods that derive their value not from their absolute position, but rather from their relative position to others. Hirsch argues in the case of education that if everyone has access to higher education, the effect of leading to better jobs is thereby neutralized. Job requirements simply rise, making higher investment necessary, giving the better-off an advantage over the less well-off. At the same time, the cost in terms of investment required to have the same outcome rise is a process he calls "screening" (Hirsch 1976: 41). When overall educational levels rise, a job formerly open to high school graduates now demands a college degree. The maintenance of the privilege of access resides in a better starting position. The traditional included are able to maintain their distance from the historically excluded by simply raising the value of the positional good. Historically excluded groups will therefore never be able to catch up. Under such circumstances, education becomes a means to create and protect social prestige, potentially losing all of its emancipatory potential and its functionality of producing knowledge. It becomes a sticker that is displayed as a marker of social distinction.

Hegel's and Hirsch's work alerts us to the fact that even though educational standards might grow in absolute terms, the historically included are likely to maintain the distance that separates them from the historically excluded. Under conditions of increased competition in very scarce markets, border maintenance becomes extremely important, because it provides the historically included with additional financial, social, and cultural capital. In short, inclusion can only produce the desired effect if it is contrasted with exclusion. Maintaining one's own inclusion therefore requires maintaining the exclusion of others.

French sociologist Pierre Bourdieu's (1984) theory of distinction provides an entrance point for conceptualizing whiteness as highly effective capital, functioning in a social space that is constituted in relation to other social positions, where each one uses the other for reference. Although Bourdieu ignores ethnicity and race entirely in his theory, his thoughts on gender point to a direction that allows further development. He argues that "the volume and composition of capital give specific form and value to the determinations which the other factors (age, sex, place of residence, etc.) impose on practices. Sexual properties are as inseparable from class practices as the yellowness of a lemon is from its acidity: a class is defined in an essential respect by the place and value it gives to the sexes and to their socially constituted dispositions" (Bourdieu 1984: 107).

In this way, whiteness constitutes a capital in addition to the other capitals Bourdieu detects, namely financial, social, and cultural. Their importance, however, does not follow a simple additive logic. One capital rather connects to the others and together they determine the social place an individual will hold in a society. This allows for some flexibility, as one capital can be used to partly compensate for the lack of another, although this flexibility is limited precisely by the grouped condition of the different capitals. In that way, as Bourdieu points out correctly, each single capital tends to overdetermine the social position of its carrier, as the presence or absence of each single one is perceived as being indicative of the presence or absence of the others. It is in this sense that whiteness overdetermines its carrier, bestowing on him a social position that might not be warranted. Because of the composite character of the different capitals, whiteness signals the presence of other capitals, even though they might not be present. Blackness, at the same time, signifies the absence of other capitals and equally overdetermines its carrier.

The resulting social position then becomes a social expectation and reflects back on the carrying individual. "The homogeneity of the disposition associated with a position and their seemingly miraculous adjustment to the demands inscribed in it result partly from the mechanisms which channel towards positions individuals who are already adjusted to them, either because they feel 'made' for jobs that are 'made' for them . . . or because they are seen in this light by the occupants of the posts . . . and partly from the dialectic which is established, throughout a lifetime, between dispositions and positions, aspirations and achievements" (Bourdieu 1984: 110). In other words, individuals tend to conform to the social positions they hold and to internalize the role expectations associated with these positions.

What matters, then, is not the objective position an individual holds in the social space, but the subjective experience of living with and through this position and rather having to uphold and defend it in daily interactions, or trying to change or masquerade it to escape the negative effects resulting from potential overdetermination. Defending or challenging one's social place is a daily struggle and bears very tangible consequences for one's capabilities to live life.

In sum, given that inclusion is relational and works on the subjective, rather than the objective, level, statistical data can only provide very basic approximations to begin with. The more important dimension of defining one's inclusion vis-à-vis the exclusion of others must operate on a symbolic level. To reproduce a social structure that secures privileges and advantages to one group and denies it to others, the maintenance of the border that marks inclusion and separates it from exclusion becomes extremely important. It therefore does not come as a surprise that Brazilian daily life is full of symbolic acts to fulfill this border-maintenance function. This is even more the case where racial capital is not clearly demarcated and, therefore, illusive for providing clear borders of belonging, as under conditions of uncertainty, people will be more anxious to demarcate their belonging to one group or the other.

State and Society

Once we have reached an understanding of the mechanisms and processes that characterize Brazilian society and dominate everyday reality, we are equipped to examine how these processes that lead to the reproduction of inclusion and exclusion affect Brazilian democracy. The last part of this chapter thus offers a reflection on the ways in which political systems interact, and are influenced by, the broader social system into which they are embedded. My main argument is that state autonomy only refers to the operational structures of states—their institutions and bureaucracy. Nevertheless, states can only reproduce the processes of broader society. The work of Luhmann (1996) helps clarify the relationship between societies and states and also sheds light on the nature and extent of embeddedness.

The main argument I seek to advance with this analysis is that it is impossible to have a democratic (political) subsystem embedded in an undemocratic broader societal system. The reasons for this impossibility are many, and they operate on different levels (individual, family, and group). From a systemic standpoint, any subsystem operates by using and transforming the processes from its environment. The basic operation of any system, according to Luhmann, is the reduction of complexity and the creation of internal sense by imposing ordering principles onto the different processes, or media, in Luhmann's terms. A political subsystem is operationally autonomous (or "autopoetic"), but subject to operate using the media it finds in its broader environment. The medium of society, according to Habermas (1984), is communication. In the case of the state, the main medium is power. Hence, a state can operate autonomously in any type of society by creating an internal structure (a bureaucracy) that allows it to reduce complexity; establish, through its internal structure, criteria able to create internal homogeneity; and maintain its own border. But again, the media, or processes, that are available to do so originate in its environment. The immediate environment of any political subsystem is the broader societal system, although it also contains other political systems, other societal systems, and, to some extent, an incipient broader political system of worldwide reach (there are, however, no signs of an emerging worldwide societal system). If the medium of communication, which structures the societal system, is skewed and distorted by extreme inequality and the distorting exercise of power, then the state is likely to reproduce this distortion. In other words, a political subsystem embedded in a society whose main structuring force is the reproduction of inequality will necessarily reproduce inequality in its own internal operations, as well as in the outcomes it produces.

Thus, to capture the workings, achievements, potentials, failures, and shortcomings of states, instead of focusing exclusively on the internal processes that together constitute its operational structure, one needs to focus on two additional elements. First is the nature and content of the quality of processes, that is, the media used for internal communication within the system. Second, one needs to include an analysis of the broader societal system and other subsystems constituting the environment into which the subsystem of the state is embedded to capture the whole picture. After all, the subsystem of the state constitutes itself by processing information from its environment, reducing complexity, and thus differentiating itself from its environment.

How can these rather abstract categories be applied to the analysis of Brazilian democracy? An analysis of the quality of processes that constitute Brazil's broader society is needed. If the processes that constitute a society are extremely skewed and inequality becomes the main structuring force of a society, then inequalities pollute the operation of the state system, which ends up reproducing them.[11] Understanding how inequality structures a society thus leads us to an understanding of the ways that states reproduce these inequalities. In the case of Brazil, if the struggle over access and privilege is the main characteristic of its broader society, the Brazilian state will necessarily reproduce the mechanisms and processes associated with this struggle, because although structurally autonomous, the state relies on the processes of broader society as core media for its functioning.

Indeed, the Brazilian state has been consistently plagued by political scandal ever since its redemocratization was completed in 1985. The main trait of these political scandals can easily be detected as a spillover of societal inequalities into the political system, which typically takes the form of establishing patron-client relationships. Clientelism thus became an endemic phenomenon of post-1985 Brazilian democracy, where political officeholders use their office not to serve the general public, but as a tool to establish their own membership in the group of the included. Once there, instead of perceiving themselves— and being perceived by the majority—as public servants, they become arbitrary administrators of privatized public goods. Once in office, state representatives, as well as higher-ranking bureaucrats, join the political class, a term that reflects their elevated status as belonging to a distinctive group. As members of the political class, or even simply as administrators of power, they reproduce their belonging to a privileged group by differentiating it from those that do not. Disrespect, clientelism, nepotism, and the like are thus manifestations of a problem that has much deeper roots and a much more diversified repertoire, which routinely includes manipulation, intimidation, infantilization, and co-optation of the historically excluded.

Conclusion: Inclusion, the Society, and the State

Taken together, the concept of inclusion has material and symbolic dimensions. Whiteness is a crucial element of its construction, as it overdetermines those able to claim it with success. Most importantly, inclusion functions in relation vis-à-vis exclusion, and, as such, it requires the maintenance of exclusion to be effective. Being effective refers to its ability to demarcate the social terrain of all the included. This terrain is homogeneous and depends critically on its border maintenance. If individuals that are not clearly identifiable as included penetrate its borders, inclusion runs the risks of losing its main function, namely to secure and defend privilege. The main importance of conceptualizing inclusion is that it allows for an analysis of the strategies used by historically privileged groups to maintain their inherited privilege. In addition to its analytical power, inclusion has an ontological dimension, because Brazilians actively apply strategies to reproduce inclusion through exclusion. The effects and outcomes of applying these strategies bear very real and tangible outcomes for all those affected by them. Inequality also penetrates the state, because states are structurally embedded in societies and rely on the processes, or media, produced in broader societies for their interaction, constitution of identity, and the creation of institutions. These institutions provide the structures that guide and channel the substratum of their agency, namely processes, or media, but they cannot change them. In the final analysis, the struggle over privilege characterizes the quality of daily interactions in Brazilian society, and hence distorts the quality of societal processes in broader society, as well as the processes that constitute the interactions within its political system.

Notes

1. I am, of course, influenced by Foucault's analysis of "Discipline and Punish" and his analysis of the different ways power influences our societal relationships.

2. Pierre Bourdieu (1984) undoubtedly advanced our understanding of the inner divisions of societies when he offered his own diagram of social distinction based on group-specific habitus.

3. The most helpful discussion about the interrelation between economic and cultural exclusion is also the most helpful for the discussion of inclusion, namely the seminal articles written by Nancy Fraser (1998: 140–149) and Judith Butler (1998: 33–43).

4. Engels wrote, "According to the materialist conception, the determining factor in history is, in the final instance, the production and reproduction of immediate life. This, again, is of a twofold character: on the one side, the production of the means of existence, of food, clothing, and shelter and the tools necessary for that production; on the other side, the production of human beings themselves, the propagation of the species" (quoted from Butler 1998: 41).

5. Being poor is defined by Brazilian convention as earning less than one-half a minimum wage per capita, i.e., less than R$175 (US$80) per month.

6. Luiza Bairros, Vanda Sá Barreto, and Nadya Castro, 1992.

7. Global Auto Report, August 2006, www.scotiabank.com.

8. Harris (1993), studying race relations in the United States, demonstrates how symbolical whiteness was constructed and used in the United States as a form of capital to justify undeserved privilege.

9. The concept of "normalization," developed by Michel Foucault (1995), refers to the elevation of whiteness to a standard against which other groups have to be measured. Selden (2000) uses a similar approach when writing about *Eugenics and the Social Construction of Merit, Race, and Disability* in the United States.

10. Simpson (1993: 8). Simpson's quote is from Dyer (1986).

11. Although inequality is inherent to the operation of power, and states necessarily reproduce inequality, states reproduce more inequality, the more a society is structured by inequality.

3

Politicizing Blackness:
Afro-Brazilian Color Identification
and Candidate Preference

Gladys L. Mitchell

We are approximately 62 million of the electorate, blacks (*pretos*) and browns (*pardos*); therefore blacks (*negros*) in an electoral college of 125 million [people] are eligible to vote in the elections this Sunday. Since half the population self-declares [as black], the elections should represent for us an opportunity to make profound changes to revert the historical situation of disadvantage (my translation).
— Dojival Vieira, *Afropress,* January 10, 2006

Alckmin attacks Lula and looks for black (*negro*) votes.
— Maurício Savarese, *Notícias UOL,* August 20, 2006

Both Dojival Vieira and Maurício Savarese refer to the 2006 Brazil-ian presidential election and imply that an ethnic vote among Afro-Brazilians is taking place. Dojival Vieira urges the Afro-Brazilian electorate to realize their voting potential as a powerful voting bloc. In *Notícias UOL,* Maurício Savarese assumes that such a voting bloc exists. More intriguing are the racial and color categories that refer to Afro-Brazilians. Savarese, using the racial category *negro,* treats them as a group; yet Vieira uses the separate categories brown and black, which indicate that Afro-Brazilians are not a unified racial group. This begs the following questions. Do Afro-Brazilians vote as a racial bloc? Is there a *raça negra*[1] (black race), and, if so, do they see themselves as a distinct racial group or as different groups separated by color? What are the political implications of self-identifying in different color groups?

My hypothesis is that Brazilians who self-identify as black will vote for black politicians more than those who claim lighter color categories. Although this seems intuitive, much of the earlier research has not shown differences in political behavior among Afro-Brazilians (Mainwaring et al. in Middlebrook 2000; Mainwaring and Scully 1995). It is likely that racially conscious Afro-Brazilians will vote for black politicians because they believe these politicians will support policies that benefit Afro-Brazilians as a racial group. Because color can be manipulated in Brazil, Afro-Brazilians of all colors can choose the *negro* identity; however, I propose that only racially conscious Brazilians who embrace blackness will choose this identity. This consciousness will be manifested in their candidate preference.

In 2006, an original survey on racial identification, racial attitudes, and political opinion was conducted in Salvador and São Paulo, Brazil. Included in the survey was a question on voting. Respondents were asked if they voted for a black politician. In Salvador, 62 percent of respondents voted for a black politician in the past and 38 percent had not. In São Paulo, only 31 percent said they voted for a black politician and 69 percent had not. It is likely that the percentage of Afro-Brazilians who voted for a black politician in Salvador is almost double compared to São Paulo because there is a higher percentage of Afro-Brazilians in Salvador. This means they have more opportunities to vote for Afro-Brazilian politicians. This is confirmed in my explanation of my findings.

Historical Context

Traditionally, Brazil was known as a racial democracy where color was not a salient political identity because of racial miscegenation. The Brazilian state did not impose an official policy of legal segregation against Afro-Brazilians; therefore mobilization efforts around racial issues were less likely. Despite no official segregation, Afro-Brazilians have mobilized around black identities because of social exclusion since the 1930s (Hanchard 1994). Many times Afro-Brazilian activists sought to create a more unified black identity, rather than identify in a range of color categories. Afro-Brazilian activists forged black identities that were inclusive of Afro-Brazilians of different colors. Despite these efforts, not all Afro-Brazilians were ready to claim such identities. In the late 1980s, black-movement activism gained saliency and discussions of racism became more public and were discussed at the national level. Moreover, beginning in 2001, affirmative action policies were enacted in Brazilian universities, and the policy was specifically aimed at Afro-Brazilians and economically disadvantaged students.

As the Brazilian state now recognizes Afro-Brazilians as a racial group, the question remains whether Afro-Brazilians identify as such. Can group identity be manifested in individual Afro-Brazilians' color identification? Are there political implications when Afro-Brazilians identify as the color black (*preto*) or the racial category (*negro*)? Despite that Afro-Brazilians make up nearly half of the Brazilian population, they continue to be underrepresented in electoral politics. Is this simply the result of the common adage that blacks do not vote for blacks (*negros não votam em negros*)? This chapter examines the role that identifying as black—an identity strongly promoted by black activists—plays in electing black politicians. Findings show that Afro-Brazilians that identify as black (*preto* or *negro*) are more likely to vote for black politicians than Afro-Brazilians that identify in other color categories. Below I give a literature review of Brazilian politics and Brazilian racial politics. Most of this literature is based on research conducted before the implementation of affirmative action in universities. It is arguable that Brazil's changing racial dynamics, where claiming black identities is more beneficial than in the past, has resulted in more Afro-Brazilians identifying as such. Considering these changing racial dynamics is especially important when examining the possible role that racial identities play in voting patterns in contemporary Brazil.

In the field of political science, there are three areas related to my research, yet they do not speak to one another. I hope to contribute to understanding in this area and to show how they are all connected. First, most research on Brazil is on the transition from authoritarianism to democracy and democratization (Ames 2002; Hagopian 1996) and political institutions (Mainwaring et al. in Middlebrook 2000; Mainwaring and Scully 1995). This research does not focus on the role Afro-Brazilians play as black-movement activists and as voting blocs. Furthermore, Mainwaring et al. (2000) do not find significant differences in political opinion between whites and Afro-Brazilians.

Second, key works that do examine race in Brazilian politics focus on Afro-Brazilian mobilization, Afro-Brazilian politicians, or Afro-Brazilian racial attitudes. Michael Hanchard (1994) successfully highlights the efforts of black-movement activists from the 1930s to the late 1980s. He also examines the role racial hegemony plays in preventing large-scale black mobilization. Ollie Johnson's (1998, 2006) research examines Afro-Brazilian representation in congress and the impact of Afro-Brazilian politicians at the national level. Michael Mitchell's (1977) scholarly work examines racial attitudes of black-movement activists and Afro-Brazilians affiliated with black-movement organizations. While these scholars have made important contributions to the study of racial politics in Brazil, they tend to focus on black-movement activists and Afro-Brazilian politicians rather than the Afro-Brazilian electorate.

Third, Brazilian scholars have studied Brazilian voters and the role race plays in politics. They all demonstrate the impact of race in Brazilian politics. Amaury de Souza (1971) uses data from the 1960 presidential election to examine ethnic voting. He finds that Afro-Brazilians, regardless of their class level, overwhelmingly supported the Brazilian Workers Party (PTB) compared to white Brazilians. He attributes this to the fact that during Getúlio Vargas's years in power, some Afro-Brazilians ascended socially and economically; thus middle-class Afro-Brazilians continued to support the opposition party, to which Vargas belonged. Poor Afro-Brazilians supported the PTB because it presented itself as the party of the poor. Nonetheless, Souza finds no significant differences between white and Afro-Brazilian voters in terms of electoral participation and political interest.

Focusing only on Afro-Brazilian candidates and voters, Ana Valente (1986) examines the 1982 elections in São Paulo. Political parties such as the Democratic Labor Party (PDT), the Party of the Brazilian Democratic Movement (PMDB), and the Workers Party (PT), all leftist parties, supported Afro-Brazilian candidates and were dedicated to minority issues. Black-movement activists encouraged Afro-Brazilians to vote for black candidates. Despite their desire for an ethnic vote, of the fifty-four Afro-Brazilian candidates running for office, only two were elected, and these two were not tied to the black movement and did not explicitly discuss racial issues. Valente recognizes that black-movement activists prematurely expected an ethnic vote. Similarly, Sales Augusto dos Santos (2000) examines Afro-Brazilian federal deputies' platforms when running for office. Most of them did not focus on racial issues because they thought this would isolate voters. This indicates that they did not think an ethnic vote could elect them to office.

In contrast to the 1982 São Paulo elections, where only two Afro-Brazilians were elected, Cloves Oliveira (1997) finds that a substantial number of Afro-Brazilian candidates were elected in Salvador (Bahia). For example, he finds an increase in the number of Afro-Brazilians elected to the city council from 1988 to 1992. Much of the increase was due to the number of council members from working-class backgrounds. Oliveira believes that a change in political recruitment by political parties also aided in this increase. Afro-Brazilians elected to the city council tend to come from working-class backgrounds compared to white Brazilians who tend to come from upper- and middle-income backgrounds.

Soares and Silva (1987) examine Rio de Janeiro's 1982 election of Leonel Brizola. Although their focus is on the effects of urbanization, social class, and party organization on the Brizola vote in various municipalities, they are also interested in the role of race. They find that the higher the proportion of nonwhites, the more votes Brizola received. Those claiming a brown (*moreno*) identity tended to vote for Brizola more than whites and blacks. Afro-Brazilians who claim a brown identity may be light or dark-skinned. Edward Telles (2004) believes that dark-skinned Afro-Brazilians who claim a *moreno* identity are expressing a form of whitening and that an ambiguous identity allows people who may not be able to call themselves white to avoid stigmatized nonwhite categories (Telles 2004: 98). Soares and Silva propose three possible reasons that blacks did not support Brizola as much as browns. One is that Brizola made an explicit appeal for *socialismo moreno* to attract Afro-Brazilian voters; however, it is possible that he isolated black voters as the appeal was for *moreno* socialism and not for black socialism. Second, most blacks live outside the Rio metropolitan area, where the party's organization was not very strong.

Third, illiteracy could have played a role in voter access, and blacks have the highest illiteracy rate of all color groups.

Cloves Oliveira (2007) has conducted the most comprehensive and outstanding scholarly work that examines the role of the media on the election campaigns of Benedita da Silva of Rio de Janeiro and Celso Pitta from São Paulo. Silva ran for mayor in 1992 and lost. Pitta ran for mayor in 1996 and won. They are both Afro-Brazilian; however, Silva is known for addressing race, gender, and class issues and is affiliated with the PT, a progressive political party. Pitta, in general, avoided addressing racial issues and was from a conservative political party; the Brazilian Progressive Party (PPB). It is clear that race played an important role in how the media depicted the two. This study also examines how implicit and explicit racial cues were used by a variety of candidates to galvanize support from Afro-Brazilians. This work is important in establishing the role of race in Brazilian electoral politics.

In sum, my research will add to three areas of research, which include democratization, Afro-Brazilian mobilization and underrepresentation in politics, and the role of race in electoral politics. Race plays a role in electoral politics, yet it is unclear what role it plays in political preferences of Afro-Brazilian voters. The general theme in previous literature is that there are no differences in political opinion between white Brazilians and Afro-Brazilians. Some scholars give evidence of Afro-Brazilian ethnic voting, while others do not. Nevertheless, electing Afro-Brazilian candidates to office continues to be a challenge. In addition, considering Santos's (2000) interviews, it appears that some Afro-Brazilian politicians do not believe they can be elected with an ethnic vote.

Afro-Brazilian Voting

There is little current available academic literature on voting patterns of Afro-Brazilians. Considering the last ten years, it is possible that Afro-Brazilian voting may be more solidified than in previous decades. Afro-Brazilians overwhelmingly voted for President Luis Inácio "Lula" da Silva. Silva was first elected in 2002 and reelected in 2006. He is Brazil's first president elected from the PT, the leftist political party. Many journalistic accounts of Lula's candidacy referred to a "black" vote indicating that, in fact, ethnic voting does exist in Brazil. This is so, despite that thirty years before, no one would have thought this possible and even scholarly research found little evidence of a black vote. Some Afro-Brazilian politicians today rely on a black vote, although most do not (Mitchell 2009). An example is Janete Pietá, a current Afro-Brazilian federal deputy, who claims that most of her voter support came from Afro-Brazilians.

With the recent election of President Barack Obama, the first African-American US president, it has been interesting to note how many Afro-Brazilians in informal conversations quickly claim that Brazil experienced a similar phenomenon with Lula's election. Some compared Lula and Obama as two people who experienced economic hardships. Lula is from Brazil's poor northeastern region and Obama is an African American whose family sometimes struggled financially. Others simply made the claim that Lula is not white, is racially mixed, or in some cases claimed he is black. The point is that Afro-Brazilians identified with Lula because of his class or, in some cases, his perceived racial background. Some politicians have gained support from Afro-Brazilian voters based on their class or ambiguous racial identity. What is the profile of Afro-Brazilians who vote based upon race? Considering that mainstream media believes that ethnic voting among Afro-Brazilians occurs, it is necessary to examine the saliency of identity in voting.

This study focuses on the cities of Salvador and São Paulo. Salvador is located in the northeast of Brazil, which is a poorer region, while São Paulo is located in the south, which is wealthier. Salvador is nearly 70 percent people of African descent, while São Paulo is nearly 30 percent Afro-Brazilian. The two cities are interesting sites of comparison as Salvador is often referred to as the cradle of Afro-Brazilian culture, while much black-movement activity has taken place in São Paulo.

Survey Data

I use original survey data collected in 2006. Upon recommendation of professors at the Federal University of Bahia and the University of São Paulo who are experienced in survey research, I chose the neighborhoods Federação, Peri Peri, and Itapoãn in Salvador, Bahia. These neighborhoods are socioeconomically heterogeneous and have a substantial percentage of Afro-Brazilians. Some of the campus of the Federal University of Bahia is located in Federação, and is a prestigious public university and has middle-class households in the neighborhood, but also there are low-income households. Itapoãn is also socioeconomically diverse, but has a large proportion of low-income households. Peri Peri is located in the periphery and is considered a suburb because it is located farther away from the center of the city. It is a low-income neighborhood. In addition, these neighborhoods were selected because it is relatively easy to find people of African descent.

In São Paulo, the neighborhoods chosen were Cidade Tiradentes, Casa Verde, Brasilândia, Campo Limpo, and Capão Redondo. Cidade Tiradentes is a low-income neighborhood that is located in the far east of São Paulo. Cidade Tirandentes has a number of nongovernmental organizations (NGOs), including hip-hop organizations that attract youth in the community. Casa Verde is in the northeast of São Paulo and is mostly middle-class. Campo Limpo is located in the southwest and is known for its large social divisions with *favelas* (shantytowns) located beside condominiums of middle- and upper-class households. Capâo Redondo is located in the south and is located on the periphery of the city. It is a low-income neighborhood. Maps of these neighborhoods were available at the Institute of Brazilian Geography and Statistics (IBGE) in São Paulo. After obtaining these maps, streets were randomly selected where university students conducted face-to-face interviews.

Interviewers used a skip number method, choosing every fifth house.[2] If the street did not contain enough houses, they went to every third house. I asked interviewers to conduct interviews only with people of African descent. If they knocked on a door and believed the person was not of African descent, they asked if anyone of African descent lived in the household. An interviewer might have classified a potential respondent as white, but if the respondent identified herself as a person of African descent, the interview was conducted. This ensures that the respondent, rather than the interviewer, determined the color identification. Respondents were selected who were of voting age.

Descriptive Results of Survey Sample

Respondents were asked to identify their color in both open-ended and close-ended questions. In the open-ended question, they could identify themselves in a color category with no choices given. In the close-ended question, they were asked to choose a census color category. The 2000 census categories were white (*branco*), brown (*pardo*), black (*preto*), yellow (*amarelo*), and indigenous (*indígena*). Yellow denotes people of Asian descent.

In Salvador, 52 percent of the respondents were male and 48 percent female. In São Paulo, 57 percent were women and 43 percent men. In both cities, the average age was thirty-three years old. In Salvador, respondents' ages ranged from seventeen to sixty-seven years old, and in São Paulo, ages ranged from sixteen to eighty-three.

In my surveys, in both cities, more Afro-Brazilians chose a brown color or racial category in the open-ended question than were classified as such by the interviewers. In Salvador, interviewers classified 102 respondents as brown (*pardo*), whereas 121 respondents identified themselves as brown (*mulato, moreno, pardo, moreno claro, marrom*). In São Paulo, interviewers classified 119 respondents as brown, whereas 143 respondents identified themselves as brown (*mulato, moreno, pardo, moreno claro, moreno escuro, moreno jambo, marrom*). I consider *marrom, moreno,* and *pardo* brown color categories. *Moreno claro* is light brown. *Moreno escuro* is dark brown. *Mulato* is mixed-race. Table 3.1 shows the results in absolute numbers of respondents identifying in the open-ended and close-ended questions and how they were classified by the interviewer. In my analysis, I focus on respondents' self-classification in the open-ended question.

Overall, the color and racial category most often claimed is black. Considering the open-ended color categories, the Afro-Brazilian sample in Salvador is

Table 3.1 Self-Identification of Color by Afro-Brazilian Respondents

Close-Ended (Census) Category		Open-Ended Color Category		Interviewer-Classified Census Color Category	
Salvador					
White (*branco*)	12	White (*branco*)	8	White (*branco*)	2
Black (*preto*)	208	Black (*negro, negão, preto*)	210	Black (*preto*)	230
Brown (*pardo*)	104	Brown (*mulato, moreno, pardo, moreno claro, marrom*)	121	Brown (*pardo*)	102
Other	6	Other	0	Other	0
São Paulo					
White (*branco*)	21	White (*branco*)	20	White (*branco*)	4
Black (*preto*)	141	Black (*negro, negão, preto*)	150	Black (*preto*)	191
Brown (*pardo*)	131	Brown (*mulato, moreno, pardo, moreno claro, moreno escuro, moreno jambo, marrom*)	143	Brown (*pardo*)	119
Other	0	Other	3	Other	3

Source: Mitchell 2006: original survey data.

made up of 2 percent Afro-Brazilians who identified as white, 62 percent who identified as black (*preto, negro, negão*), and 36 percent who claimed a brown (*mulato, moreno, pardo, moreno claro, marrom*) identity. Considering the open-ended color categories in São Paulo, 6 percent of Afro-Brazilians identify as white (*branco*), 47 percent identify as black (*preto, negro, negão*[3]), 45 percent identify as brown (*mulato, moreno, pardo, moreno claro, moreno escuro, moreno jambo,* and *marrom*), and 2 percent identify as other. In both cities, the number of blacks (*pretos*) that interviewers classified exceeds the number of self-identified blacks (*pretos* and *negros*). In contrast, the number of self-identified browns exceeds the number of browns classified by interviewers. In Brazil, there is a tendency to identify as brown because it acknowledges racial mixture, which is part of its national identity. Findings in this study indicate that Afro-Brazilians who identify as brown have fundamentally different political behavior from those who identify as black. As stated earlier, in my analysis, I consider the respondents' color identification in the open-ended color category because that is the category people freely choose as opposed to a census category. I note that these are the categories respondents chose for the survey, but in everyday life, color categories can literally change by the minute depending on a person's social situation.

Despite that in both cities 2000 census data show that most Afro-Brazilians identify as brown (*pardo*), in the survey sample most Afro-Brazilian respondents identify as black (*negro* or *preto*). Thus there is sample bias as the sample has a larger percentage of Afro-Brazilians claiming black identities than in the 2000 census. This is the result of the fact that the survey was carried out in neighborhoods where it is relatively easy to find Afro-Brazilian respondents and the fact that the census does not allow Afro-Brazilians to choose the *negro* racial category. The census only includes the color category *preto,* which usually refers to darker-skinned Afro-Brazilians. Despite sample bias, the survey is a random sample of Afro-Brazilians and is useful for examining trends in Afro-Brazilian voting preferences.

Regression Analysis of Voting for a Black Politician

For each city, I ran a regression analysis of voting for a black candidate as the dependent variable and color identification, age, education, and political party as independent variables.[4] I also ran a logistic regression to get predicted probabilities of voting for a black politician by self-identified color groups. Respondents were asked if they voted for a black (*negro*) politician and could choose *yes* or *no.* The respondents' color identification is the color they identified as in the open-ended question. I did not include those who self-identified as indigenous, Afro-descendent, or Brazilian. I grouped colors and racial categories as follows: white (*branco*), mixed-race (*mulato*), light brown (*moreno claro*), brown (*pardo, moreno,* and *marrom*), dark brown (*moreno escuro, moreno jambo*), the racial category black (*negro* and *negão*), and the color category black (*preto*). The educational levels are incomplete middle school, completed middle school, completed high school, precollege, and in college or completed college. The age categories are 16 to 25, 26 to 40, 41 to 54, and 55 or older. The political parties named by respondents are the Brazilian Democratic Movement Party (PMDB), the Socialism and Freedom Party (PSOL), the Workers Party (PT), the Green Party (PV), the Brazilian Social Democracy Party (PSDB), the Liberal Front Party (PFL), Progressive Party (PP), the Communist Party of Brazil (PC do B), Democratic Labor Party (PDT), Brazilian Socialist Party (PSB), and the Liberal Party (PL). The regression model shows that in Salvador, age is statistically significant at the 99 percent confidence interval (see Table 3.2). In São Paulo, color, educational level, age, and political party are all statistically significant variables (see Table 3.3).

The first major finding is that color identification is statistically significant in São Paulo, but not in Salvador. In Salvador, only age is statistically significant. As age increases, the more likely it is that Afro-Brazilian respondents in Salvador voted for black politicians. I expected differences in color identification to play a larger role in Salvador, which has a higher percentage of Afro-Brazilians. In São Paulo, the Afro-Brazilian population only comprises 30 percent of the total population. In Salvador, Afro-Brazilians are nearly 70

Table 3.2 Regression Analysis of Voting for a Black Politician in Salvador

Voted for a Black Politician	Coefficient	Standard Error
Color	.23	.16
Education	.18	.12
Age	.45***	.11
Political party	.11	.15
Constant	.32**	.14
N = 205		

Source: Mitchell 2006: original survey data.
Notes: *p < .10; **p < .05; ***p < .01.

Table 3.3 Regression Analysis of Voting for a Black Politician in São Paulo

Voted for a Black Politician	Coefficient	Standard Error
Color	.26**	.12
Education	.31***	.11
Age	.55***	.11
Political party	.40**	.18
Constant	.05***	.12
N = 211		

Source: Mitchell 2006: original survey data.
Notes: *p < .10; **p < .05; ***p < .01.

percent of the population. Because of such a high percentage of Afro-Brazilians, I expected color differences among them to impact their voting preferences. I also expected the lower percentage of Afro-Brazilians in São Paulo to lead to more group identity so that color differences would not impact voting preferences. This was not the case.

The second major finding is that a higher percentage of Afro-Brazilians in Salvador voted for black politicians than in São Paulo. I ran a logistic regression to get the predicted probabilities of voting for a black politician by self-identified color groups. In Salvador, the predicted probability of all color groups that voted for a black politician is higher than in São Paulo (see Figures 3.1 and 3.2). I believe this is due to two reasons. First, Salvador is nearly 70 percent Afro-Brazilian and color categories are more flexible than in São Paulo. In Salvador, depending upon a person's physical characteristics, their color identification can be darkened. Gilmar Santiago, who was director of the Municipal Department of Reparations in Salvador in 2004, identified several

Figure 3.1 Predicted Probability of Voting for a Black Politician by Color and Race in Salvador

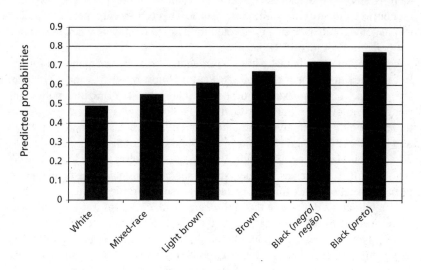

Color and racial categories of voters

Figure 3.2 Predicted Probability of Voting for a Black Politician by Color and Race in São Paulo

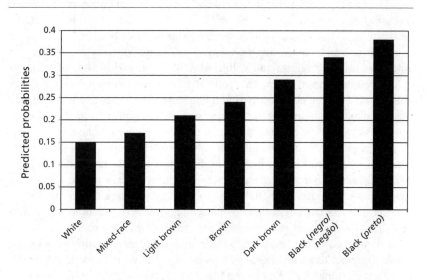

Color and racial categories of voters

politicians as *negro* because of their progressive views on racial policies. In contrast, because of the overwhelming percentage of whites in São Paulo, there is more of a black-white paradigm resulting in less room for a disjuncture between identifying whites and blacks. This is all to say that in Salvador, respondents could have said they voted for a *negro* politician, when in fact that politician did not identify as such.

Second, it is likely that a higher percentage of Afro-Brazilians run for political office in Salvador than in São Paulo. Unfortunately, I cannot compare recent data. To give an example of the fact that more Afro-Brazilian politicians run for local office in Salvador than São Paulo, I compare city council elections. The only readily available data I have are from Ana Valente's study of São Paulo's city council elections in 1982 and Cloves Oliveira's 1992 data on city council elections in Salvador. Valente uses the term *negro* to refer to all Afro-Brazilian politicians. In her study, she administered questionnaires to twenty-five candidates for city council who she identifies as *negro* (Valente 1986). Oliveira's data show that 436 *negros* and 79 *pardos* ran for city council (Oliveira 1997).[5] It is clear that Oliveira's data are more accurate than Valente's. Nonetheless, I use both Oliveira's 1992 data and Valente's 1982 data to roughly access and compare the number of Afro-Brazilians running for city council. A total of 515 Afro-Brazilians ran for city council in Salvador in 1992, and approximately twenty-five ran in the 1982 São Paulo city council elections. This gives credence to the idea that Afro-Brazilians in Salvador have a higher chance of voting for a *negro* candidate than in São Paulo because more Afro-Brazilians run for office.

The third finding is that in both cities there is an increase in the predicted probabilities of voting for a black politician according to color, from light to dark (white to black). In São Paulo, there is a positive relationship between color identification and voting for a black politician, education and voting for a black politician, and age and voting for a black politician. In both cities, as color becomes darker, the more likely it is that respondents vote for black politicians. This is a noteworthy finding because it indicates that racial identification plays a role in political choice, such as voting for a black candidate. This substantiates my claim that racial identification has political implications. Despite negative stereotypes in society (Sheriff 2001; Twine 1998), some Afro-Brazilians identify as black. Embracing blackness may be the result of black-movement activism that valorizes blackness or racial policies such as affirmative action that encourage Afro-Brazilians to identify as black. Black-movement rhetoric valorizes blackness, thus counteracting negative associations with blackness. Black-movement organizations are involved in a number of activities from protest marches in São Paulo to promote affirmative action policies for blacks (*negros*) to carnival groups in Salvador, Bahia, such as Ilê Aiyê. The lyrics and clothing of Ilê Aiyê reflect black pride and encourage Afro-Brazilians to embrace blackness.

The two categories for black are analyzed separately because *preto* is a color category, while *negro* is not. Rather *negro* is a politically charged racial category that denotes black. The predicted probabilities of voting for a black politician by respondents that identify as *negro* is higher than for those who claim the color categories white, mixed-race, light brown, brown, and dark brown. In Salvador, Afro-Brazilians who claim a black (*preto*) identity are 77 percent likely to vote for a black politician, those claiming a black (*negro*) identity are 72 percent likely, and the likelihood that an Afro-Brazilian claiming a white identity will vote for a black politician drops to 49 percent. This is a difference of 27 and 23 percentage points. In São Paulo, the likelihood of an Afro-Brazilian voting for a black politician who claims a *preto* identity is 38 percent. The likelihood for voting for a black candidate is 34 percent for those claiming a *negro* identity. This decreases to only 15 percent for Afro-Brazilians who self-identify as white. In São Paulo, Afro-Brazilians claiming black (*preto* or *negro*) identities are more than twice as likely as those claiming a white identity to vote for a black politician.

Color Consciousness and Black Candidate Preference

Holding educational level and political party constant, I find that an Afro-Brazilian in São Paulo who claims a white identity in the age category sixteen to twenty-five years of age is 7 percent likely to vote for a black politician. Nevertheless, an Afro-Brazilian claiming a black (*preto*) identity with the same characteristics is nearly three times as likely or 20 percent likely to vote for a black candidate. An Afro-Brazilian in Salvador who claims a white identity in the age category sixteen to twenty-five years old is 32 percent likely to vote for a black politician, holding educational level and political party constant. In contrast, an Afro-Brazilian who identifies as black (*preto*) with the same characteristics is 60 percent likely to vote for a black politician. This shows the stark difference in the probabilities of voting for black politicians depending on the self-identified color of Afro-Brazilians.

Political Party and Voting for a Black Politician

In São Paulo, an Afro-Brazilian affiliated with the PT in the age range sixteen to twenty-five claiming a brown identity is 12 percent likely to vote for a black candidate compared to an Afro-Brazilian claiming a black (*preto*) identity, who is 21 percent likely to vote for a black candidate. Contrarily, in São Paulo, an Afro-Brazilian affiliated with the PFL, a conservative party, in the age range sixteen to twenty-five, claiming a brown identity, is 7 percent likely to vote for a black candidate compared to an Afro-Brazilian claiming a black (*preto*) identity, who is 12 percent likely to vote for a black candidate. Although the trend that Afro-Brazilians identifying as darker colors remains, it is interesting to note the decrease in voting for a black candidate comparing a liberal party, such as the PT, and a conservative party, the PFL. This is likely the result of the PT being a more racially inclusive party because of its support of racial policies. Nevertheless, conservative parties have been open to Afro-Brazilian politicians, and in the past, PFL had widespread support due to Antônio Carlos Magalhães.

Education and Color

To highlight the role of education, I hold age and political party constant and examine the role of education in those claiming black (*preto*) identities. In São Paulo, education is very significant, considering that an Afro-Brazilian claiming a black (*preto*) identity with the highest level of education is more than twice as likely to vote for a black politician as an Afro-Brazilian claiming a black identity with the lowest level of education. An Afro-Brazilian claiming a black (*preto*) identity with the highest level of education (in or completed college) is 62 percent likely to have voted for a black politician, compared to an Afro-Brazilian with the lowest level of education (incomplete middle school), who is only 25 percent likely to have voted for a black politician.[6]

Preto and Negro Voting

The highest predicted probability of voting for a black politician in both cities is among *pretos*. As I pointed out earlier, *preto* is a color category that denotes the color black, rather than a racial category. Nonetheless, I believe it has political significance especially in a country where blackness is not valorized in the Brazilian media and daily life. In addition, Afro-Brazilians can willingly choose a nonblack category, and they often choose the brown category. I believe that *pretos* tend to be more racially conscious of their blackness than those claiming nonblack identities. For this reason, they are more likely to support black politicians than Afro-Brazilians that identify as other color categories. John Burdick's (1998) ethnographic research gives evidence that *pretos,* more so than *negros assumidos,* recalled personal experiences of racism. Burdick defines *negros assumidos* as those who later accepted a black identity but have not always identified as such. Unlike Burdick, I do not believe that Afro-Brazilians who claim the *preto* category see themselves as doomed to choose that category. In their recognition of racism, they are conscious of their race, and rather than buy into the myth of racial democracy—that discrimination is simply because of their class—they genuinely believe it is also due to their color and actively choose a color category accordingly.

Although there are differences between *pretos* and *negros,* they are both black identities and should be understood as such when examining racial consciousness. Claiming a black identity is a powerful example of how race is politicized. These data point to the fact that in both Salvador and São Paulo, black-movement leaders and activists have a potential voting bloc among black racially conscious Afro-Brazilian voters.[7] I believe *pretos* have a slightly higher predicted probability of voting for black politicians than *negros* because they identify as a stable and continuous color group that has faced racial discrimination and recognize it as such. *Negros* or *negros assumidos* may have identified in other color categories before personal experiences of racism or because of black-movement activity that led them to change their racial identification to *negro*. As census data show, the percentage of those claiming *preto* identities has remained relatively constant. This has only recently changed. Today, Afro-Brazilians outnumber white Brazilians due to an increase in the number of Afro-Brazilians identifying as *preto* (Werneck 2008).

In sum, Afro-Brazilians in Salvador and São Paulo who claim black identities (*negro* and *preto*) are more likely to vote for black politicians than those who claim lighter colors. Black-movement activists, hip-hop groups, and cultural groups such as Ilê Aiyê in Salvador, Bahia, valorize blackness and have been influential in Afro-Brazilians' embracing blackness. Embracing blackness is not an idle choice. My data demonstrate the political implications of embracing blackness. Such a finding is especially important considering that Afro-Brazilians now outnumber white Brazilians. The implication is that as Afro-Brazilians continue to embrace black identities, there will be an increase in the number of elected Afro-Brazilian politicians. Thus Afro-Brazilian underrepresentation is not simply due to the fact that blacks do not vote for blacks or that Afro-Brazilians in general do not vote for Afro-Brazilian political candidates. Rather, underrepresentation is due to the fact that not all Afro-Brazilians identify as a black (*negro*) racial group. In claiming blackness by identifying as *negro* or as the color black (*preto*), Afro-Brazilians' color consciousness manifests itself in support of black candidates.

Notes

1. In an article published in *Época* on July 17, 2002, authors Gerson Camarotti and Guilherme Evelin referred to Afro-Brazilians as the black race, *raça negra*. The headline read: "The Black Vote: Lula has the preference of the electorate of the black (*negra*) race, with 49% of their votes, according to the Vox Populi survey."

2. The author thanks the following interviewers in Salvador and São Paulo: Gloria Ventapane, Rosana Carvalho Paiva, Magda Lorena, Ricardo Summers, Leon Padial, Talita Pereira, Jackeline Romio, Kledir Salgado, and Thabata Silva.

3. *Negão* literally means *big black* or *really black*. In Brazilian Portuguese, one can emphasize that an object or person is large by adding *ão* to the word; thus *negro* becomes *negão*.

4. I ran a regression with voting for a black candidate as the dependent variable and color identification, age, education, political party, and an interaction variable education and color identification. The interaction variable was not statistically significant.

5. Oliveira gained access to each registration card of city council candidates to obtain demographic information.

6. I interacted color and education. I ran a regression with voting for a black candidate as the dependent variable and the independent variables of the interaction variable color and education, education, color, political party, and age. The interaction variable was not statistically significant for the Salvador or São Paulo sample. In Salvador, the age effect went away. In São Paulo, age and political party remained statistically significant, but there was no longer a color and education effect.

7. Today in Brazil one can find products for *pele moreno e negro* (brown and black skin). These products include soaps and lotions. Once, shopping on the infamous Paulista Avenue in São Paulo, I looked for hand lotion and was recommended to try a product that was for black and brown skin. Such a product never existed thirty years ago in Brazil. Despite the fact that Brazil is known as a racially mixed nation, businesspeople have recognized and are taking advantage of the popularity of racial categories.

4

Out of Place: The Experience of the Black Middle Class

Angela Figueiredo

> With a little hesitation, they approach me, they look at me with curiosity or with compassion and then, instead of asking directly how it feels to be a problem, they say: In my city I know an excellent man of color. . . . I smile, or I show interest, or I reduce the heat of my rage, according to the occasion. With regard to the real question: How does it feel to be a problem? I rarely say a word.
>
> —W. E. B. Du Bois, 1999: 52

Historically, the structure of Brazilian society has been described as a social pyramid in which the majority of whites occupy the top, the majority of *mestiços* (mixed-race) occupy the middle, and blacks occupy the bottom.[1] In this perspective, racial differences are subsumed in class differences, and, consequently, racial prejudice was explained simply as a mere expression of this, that is, prejudice is the result of class. "In Brazil, scholars suggested that the Brazilian system of racial identification necessarily subordinated race to class. They tended to believe that the persistence of racial inequality was due to class antagonism" (Winant 1999: 113).

Many researchers tried to explain the position of the *mulato* in Brazil with the "mulatto escape hatch" concept as defined by Carl Degler (1971). Precisely since *mulatos* have been described as a group, analyses have been centered on individuals or on a small group of *mulatos* that experienced social mobility. The majority of researchers did not try to understand the strategies of social mobility used by *mulatos*. The arguments to explain the presence of few blacks and *mestiços* in high positions of social strata were that this simply reflected the disadvantages of the past, poverty, and the absence of education that inevitably resulted from slavery (Skidmore 1974: 12). In fact, few *mulatos* occupied a position between blacks and whites. The majority were next to the economic position of blacks.

As I demonstrated in another work (Figueiredo 2002), different contexts and racial dynamics resulted in the use of distinct strategies of social mobility for blacks in Brazil and the United States. Brazil is different from the United States because the first generation of the black middle class emerged inside of the black community, as the result of official racial segregation (Frazier 1975), and, later, it grew as a consequence of affirmative action policies (Evans 1995; Landry 1987). For a long period in Brazil, the small group of *mulatos* that ascended socially was mainly associated with a network of relations with whites. This situation was described as sponsorship—a mechanism through which black individuals of low socioeconomic class benefited from an individual or a white family of upper- or middle-class status. In the1980s, the Brazilian government modified the mechanism for attaining public jobs—which in the past were carried out through such mechanisms—by starting to have more public competitions. The stability, wages, and the benefits guaranteed with public jobs were important for the black middle class in Brazil (Figueiredo 2002).

The majority of the black middle class in Brazil are first generation. Most of them are children of manual workers who ascended socially through schooling. This means that the majority of them keep a distance from their families. This leads to a rupture with their familial origin. The objective of this chapter is to reflect on the experience of middle-class blacks in Salvador, a city with the largest black population in Brazil.

The Context

The number of blacks in the city of Salvador is noticeable to any observer. Nevertheless, this number is not represented in the racial distribution in the occupational structure. Nor does a substantial black population mean that there is a large middle class. Also, as for their participation in politics, the black population has, in fact, stayed at the edge of power in decisionmaking politics. There is a small percentage of blacks in elected office (Oliveira 1997).

This information comes as a surprise to a significant number of Brazilians, who still believe that in Bahia racial dynamics are different from what occurs in other states. According to Jéferson Bacelar (2001), Bahia underwent a period of economic stagnation postabolition, which was only modified in the 1950s with the establishment of the state-controlled oil industry, Petrobras. Despite that some believe social ascension of blacks was relatively easy in Salvador, there are no records affirming this, nor are there any sources that give an account that blacks' positions were elevated during this period.

In contrast, Bacelar's research shows that in Salvador, the maintenance of a racial hierarchy in the labor market during slavery and for work relations was still based on personal, and not contractual, relations in customary and traditional norms.

It is likely that since the 1950s in some Brazilian capitals, and since 1970 in Brazil as a whole, structural changes in Brazilian society occurred that affected the mechanisms or strategies of ascension used by blacks. It is important to note the transformations in the occupational structure as a result of industrialization and urbanization. At the same time, there was a relative democratization of public education. Nevertheless, these structural changes were not enough to create equal chances between whites and blacks. Despite the fact that blacks have benefited from the expansion of public education, they are still concentrated in the lowest levels of education.

The interest in the social ascension of blacks or the "integration of blacks in society's class structures" is not recent (Fernandes 1972, 1978). Nonetheless there has been little interest in understanding the social ascension of blacks in specific sectors of the labor market, as well as the strategies used in the process of upward mobility. In Brazilian academic circles, even in the social sciences, especially in anthropology, where excluded groups are studied, the debate concerning the black middle class is relatively recent. This is most likely related to the fact that so few blacks are engaged in social science research activities, where, in addition, academic interest has traditionally focused on problematic and excluded groups. Which class do blacks who have socially ascended belong to and have they been integrated into the system? What are the constraints provoked by one's social origin and color?

Like the African American middle class, the Afro-Brazilian middle class also faces exclusion. Middle-class Afro-Brazilians are looked upon with curiosity when they participate in middle-class social activities and with distrust when they try to acquire or enjoy the symbolic and social goods associated with people with high financial means.[2] Even if they possess these goods, there is a certain discomfort among the nonblack middle class, creating questions about the possibility of black people owning certain goods and having the financial means to pay for them, or of frequenting social spaces that are restricted to the middle classes.

All of this creates additional tension in the daily routines of black people with higher economic means, who are always perceived as "out of place," which is socially constructed and symbolically determined. In other words, they pay a high price for being "out of their place." This distrust with regard to middle-class blacks results, in my opinion, from some important factors. The first, which is also the most well-known, has to do with the negation and rejection of the existence of racism and racial prejudice in Brazil and, consequently, the emphasis on class-based prejudice. The second is the low percentage of blacks in elevated social status positions. The third is the social construction of blacks that always places them in economic and symbolic positions that are inferior to whites. The fourth is the socioanthropological construction of the black racial category in such a way that blackness becomes incompatible with enjoying goods associated with modernity. This means that there is a resonance or an interpenetration of the social constructions originally formulated in different places and by different agents, such as ideologies in social science and common perceptions that are in perfect accord with one's understanding about the "place of blacks" in Brazilian society.

In this chapter, I tackle questions about the meaning of social mobility and about the perspective of Brazilian blacks in the contemporary context. One of the most salient characteristics of the Brazilian black middle class is the fact that it is constituted, mainly, by individuals who are the first generation of those who socially ascended. That is, most of the time they are children of manual workers who did not inherit goods and property, and therefore survive exclusively on employment salaries. They have also not been socialized in a middle-class environment, which means that they have not incorporated the values and worldviews that define the *habitus* of the middle class.[3] We are thus dealing with a middle class of a subalternalized group, which, for this very reason, is unstable, incipient, and encounters many difficulties in securing and maintaining itself in this class position (Figueiredo 2003).

Methodology

Research was conducted in Salvador, Bahia, with thirty black employers who own companies involved in various businesses.[4] The sample was composed of individuals who are commonly identified as mulattos, dark mulattos (*mulatos escuros*), and blacks (*pretos*); 86 percent of those interviewed were men, married, and the great majority were above the age of 40. All of those interviewed were owners of companies with six or more regular employees. The variation in the number of employees was great, ranging from the minimal limit of 6 to 100 permanent employees and 400 temporary ones, such as the case of the owner of a construction firm. I interviewed subjects occupied in professions typical of Bahian culture, such as the *baiana de acarajé* (African-dish street vendor), to the owner of a taxi company. There were significant differences in terms of income, educational level, and type of business. All this contributed to a very heterogeneous group of interviewees.

Social Mobility and Insertion in the White World

Although there are differences in the results and the approaches of research conducted on the upward social mobility of blacks since the 1930s, the majority is unanimous in demonstrating that upward social mobility of blacks only happens through dependent social relations between blacks and whites—that is, to ascend socially, blacks have to be supported by whites, to be married to someone white, or to emulate in their dress code and way of speaking the ways of whites. With regard to *apadrinhamento* (formalized extended family membership produced by becoming a godfather or godmother), Azevedo (1996: 166) observes:

> It is important to register that, until this moment, the main channel of social ascension, through which a great number of black people and mestiços had acquired elevated status, is education in the double meaning of good manners and a high level of education, beyond the mores and conception of the dominant culture, which, ultimately, is a problem of acculturation. . . . One of the mechanisms that facilitates this integration is the protection and the aid that many godfathers and godmothers extend to their godchildren of color, educating them in their own houses, or, at least, finding them jobs or directing them to institutions of secondary and superior education and many times continuing to guide and protect them.

Bacelar finds that in the recent past, working in the public sector was indicative of the good relations that blacks and browns had with whites, unveiling the existing clientelism in hiring practices and the *apadrinhamento* of blacks by white families.

> To belong to the public service, even if in subordinate positions, already denoted some form of prestige, indicating, at least, good relations with the owners of political power . . . to the extent that this insertion was achieved through clientelism and apadrinhamento. (Bacelar 2001)

In this sense, the unequal relationship between blacks and whites in the past did not imply an absolute impossibility of access of blacks and *mestiços* to higher ranks in the social hierarchy. Nevertheless, the ingression occurred based on a structure of individual merit, where affection, the allegiance to those recognized as superior, and confidence in the maintenance of these criteria could transform an agent, who was poor and black, and qualify him or her to gain access to scarce cultural goods. As this distributive structure is dependent on investments on the family and affectivity levels, the process of distribution of symbolic goods tends to strengthen individualizing strategies among the agents of dominated people.

The modern context has significantly modified structures of power, as much through the appearance of a mixed economy and the expansion of the Brazilian state as through the relative democratization of education. With this movement, hiring in public service by means of open competition has been consolidated. This process will decisively impact the social status of those who, until now, hardly had access to higher education and, as a consequence, the possibilities to transform their social status and to assume a social status distant from those in their families.

The mechanisms used to recruit public servants were modified completely, with the criterion of selection by means of open public competition, because it was perceived as more democratic. This was based on the fact that it not only reduces the likelihood of discriminatory actions that occur in other sectors of the labor market, but also because it diminishes the importance of networks and social contacts, the famous indications that regulate access to work. Nevertheless, we are unaware of the promotion criteria within public service employment.

In previous research, I demonstrated that the strategies of upward mobility used by the group in question (liberal professionals) were high education levels, the association they made between public and private jobs, and resources that marked the trajectories of the majority of those interviewed (Figueiredo 2002). With regard to black entrepreneurs and employers with low education levels, the establishment of a business is made possible, in most cases, through resources from the resignation of a formal job, where unemployment benefits (FGTS) are used for the opening of their own businesses. Those entrepreneurs with higher educational levels typically initiate their own business by forming small societies, with proper resources that are not necessarily proceeding from unemployment benefits, but from personal savings. It is important to note that none of them were able to count on the support of family capital.

Independent of the mechanisms to achieve mobility, it is worth noting that the social ascension of blacks has been historically guided by the use of individual strategies. Those blacks that ascend are seen, almost always, as an exception to the rule, mainly represented in inferior stratas of the professional hierarchy. More recent research points to the importance of the family in social ascension (Teixeira 1998). Azevedo observed that "the social ascension of black individuals is frequent and easy to verify. As a group, however, people of color ascend with more difficulty" (Azevedo 1996: 164).

Although focused more on public sector jobs, these brief references aim at demonstrating how the strategies of social mobility used by blacks changed in the last few decades—given that in the past they were characterized by the dependent relationship to white individuals or families. It appears that the relationship to whites, which allowed for upward mobility, was the same that allowed for the entrance into the white world, if only at the margins. I argue that the use of more independent mechanisms of mobility—that do not necessarily involve a relation of subordination, subservience, and, consequently, the need to accumulate debt with someone—influences the perception of the meaning of social mobility, of prejudice, and of racial discrimination.

With reference to data concerning inequalities in access to education and income inequality between white and black workers, there still remains a strong belief that black middle-class members are seen and treated as whites. Thus, inside specific spaces where their status can be easily recognized, exemplified by the home and workplace, some blacks have achieved purchasing power that is comparable to that of whites. Nevertheless, it is possible to have a problem or misunderstanding that makes their economic and social position irrelevant and their racial status gain salience and the term *black* and other, more pejorative denominations prevail, often in the form of accusations. Moreover, when going beyond these restricted spaces of recognition, almost always these individuals are seen as blacks and are treated in the way blacks are treated in general in Brazil, that is, always with a certain degree of distrust. In my interviews, this occurs typically when respondents want to enjoy their elevated economic position, such as in the consumption of luxury goods and services.[5]

Pelé is constantly cited in the occasions where racial discrimination and the dichotomy between race and class in Brazil are discussed. Nevertheless, the treatment extended to Pelé does not result from his socioeconomic position, but from public recognition, especially from people normally considered racist. Pelé is considered a special black person; his success in his profession made him a symbol of soccer and of national identity. Therefore, he does not provide a good example.

Starting from this conclusion, I analyze the examples of those who mentioned they were victims of prejudice and racial discrimination.[6] It appears that belonging to the middle class, far from being an antidote against discrimination and racial stereotyping, exposes blacks to situations of increased vulnerability, given that whites predominantly occupy the social spaces they frequent.[7]

In this manner, they are forced to reflect on their ethnic-racial condition and the limits of Brazil's racial ideology. As I will argue, the realization of being black, as well as any attempts at producing a discourse of identity, appears in the adult phase and as a result of contact with the white world.

It is certain that the interpretations of discriminatory practices can vary, and it is perhaps a good indicator of an individual's social status; a poor person who is discriminated against can attribute the different treatment to the fact that she is badly dressed for the occasion, can blame the fact that she did not know how to express herself properly, and even the fact that she did not know how to act properly. Many times these people end up, in one way or another, assuming responsibility for their discrimination. Inversely, the majority of middle-class blacks know that they are well dressed, that they have income and, at times, enough education not to be treated inadequately on the basis of stereotypes that establish the "place of *negros.*"

The initial question about racial discrimination was "Have you ever suffered any type of racial discrimination?" Some said no because they were well-known in Salvador, but they cited examples of discrimination that occurred in other cities. Others said no, but cited cases involving other people close to them. A significant segment of the interviewed answered no at first; however, when the interviewer insisted a little more on the subject, the interviewees ended up mentioning facts they considered unimportant and routine, for example, the fact that they had been mistaken for workers of the company. This was not taken seriously if they had not affirmed themselves to be the owner, manager, or administrator; but even then, some people insisted, "I want to speak with the manager." This demand would come from a salesperson, product representative, or a customer.

Nevertheless, none of the interviewees answered to this situation, and instead presented it as embarrassing. They typically spoke about it in an ironic tone, because it happened so many times they no longer considered it relevant. The example of one interviewee is sufficiently illustrative: at the time of the commencement of her youngest sister, she, the sister, and a friend went to the building of a dressmaker, located in a prestigious area of Salvador; when entering the elevator, a lady asked them if they had a friend, like themselves, that could work for her. The sister, a physician, educated in one of Salvador's most recognized universities, the Federal University of Bahia, felt extremely offended, while the others laughed about the "mistake" committed by the lady. It became evident that they had perceived this situation as discriminatory; after all, they were mistaken as house servants. Nevertheless, they did not believe this was sufficient for taking further action.

Others are slow to perceive that the differential treatment they received was indeed discrimination, based on their race. (Anecdotal information is identified by the interviewees' first names only to protect their identity.) When invited to participate in a culinary course in São Paulo, one respondent states:

> It is a hotel in São Paulo, pretty, five stars. I had to be housed in this hotel. . . . I think they never had a black guest before in that hotel; blacks probably just sweep the floor. A black woman appears, all in high heels, and says that she will give lessons there, and nobody believed it. So when I arrived, my reservation was already made, I showed my ID to the receptionist, saying that I was Antônia, but he did not find my name in the computer, but I knew it was there. I acted very appropriately, but he made me look for the training room, the bastard, in that immense place, and I had to walk around, going up the elevator, down again, coming out in places that I didn't even recognize, and I ended up entering all these conference rooms that had nothing to do with my course. I arrived at ten and walked around for four hours, before I came back to the reception hall. I asked him again and nothing. He said: "This name does not exist; I have never seen this name." Already irritated, I said: "Can you call this number for me?" He took the telephone and put it on the balcony for me to call. That's when I realized that it was prejudice; until then I had not felt that it was prejudice; I thought that he was just bullshitting! (Antônia)

Let us look at another example:

> This thing happened to me, and I didn't even think it was prejudice; I thought it was just a misunderstanding. I entered a drugstore in Rio de Janeiro. I made purchases there, and when I was writing the check, the cashier did not understand my city code, which is 071 for Salvador. Then I gave her my entire number, and she called to check if it was correct, but she made a mistake and used the Rio area code. The woman on the phone said: "I never had a servant with this name." Then the manager came and asked me "Ma'am, what is your

phone number?" I said, "My number is 071 . . . ." When I gave them my number, the manager was already terrified, because he thought I might think that this was discrimination. Never! I always knew it was a misunderstanding. (Dinalva)

This statement is rather odd. Before telling the facts, the interviewee affirms that what happened in the hotel incident was a misunderstanding. After that, she speaks of the incident that happened in Rio de Janeiro and says that the employee of the drugstore, when calling to confirm the phone number, heard the following reply: "I never had a servant with this name." Was it an interpretation of the interviewee or did the employee ask for the name of the servant? Then the manager appears, who already enters the scene "terrified, because he thought I might think that this was discrimination." In all instances of the story, direct and indirect references to racial discrimination appear—direct, in the case of the manager, and indirect, when the interviewee is mistaken as a house servant.

People who practice racial discrimination are always viewed as people with bad manners or as misinformed, but are never perceived by the interviewee as racists.

If somebody discriminates, I see that this person is not prepared, is not a person who has a formation, and education. . . . It happens sometimes with people who have education, that have formation, but in those cases, it is part of their nature, because that person was raised with discrimination in this way and does what he learned. (Armando)

Another interviewee considers the surprise with which new clients react at their first meeting and considers this a manifestation of racial discrimination, even though tolerable. He emphasizes that all the time their expectation is to encounter a white accountant, given that he was referred by a white colleague.

The intolerable one, I have not experienced yet. I think that it can happen at any time, but it has not happened yet. The tolerable one happens all the time, you perceive it clearly. . . . I will have a meeting on Monday with an entrepreneur whom I already know, but I am certain that he will refer me to another customer. It is very unlikely that he will make a comment saying, "Look, I am referring you to an accountant. He is black, but he does a good job." . . . Now, I am absolutely certain, about 90 percent certain, that the friend to whom he will recommend me is white. (Joseval)

The distrust with which they are observed when they are driving their cars is also a never-ending experience, even if the topic is not racism.

I find that the people . . . I don't know, I don't mind. I let it pass without paying attention. It is in the head of everyone, but the important thing is what is in my own conscience; I let it pass without paying attention, when I drive in the car, with a new car, and somebody looks at me. . . . My car is an L-200, the other day I had a BMW, I don't really care . . . if somebody points at me, I turn my face and look to the other side. (Armando)

The hegemonic position in academic circles concerning the prevalence of class prejudice over racial prejudice in Brazilian racial relations is also present in the statements of some of those interviewed. Sometimes the informants offer an interpretation that demonstrates that they believe that, in Brazil, prejudice is still class-based, or that the problem of differential treatment of blacks is caused by a lack of financial resources. Nevertheless, when inquiring more about this, an interviewee answers:

Interviewee: The question of race exists, because in Brazil, if you are rich and black everything goes, if you are poor and black nothing goes; if you are poor and white nothing goes.

Interviewer: Is it the same to be rich and white as being rich and black?

Interviewee: No, it is not as equal compared to the rich and white, because the people want to know why we are there. An example is when I participated in some social circles, I was socializing with rich people, and people wanted to know how I was there; they were very curious. I went into a five-star hotel, the people expected me to speak English, but when I started to speak with a Bahian accent . . . I stepped off an airplane, catching a connection, in the middle of all these whites and everybody was thinking that we were American or African, whenever I was with some colleague of my social level. . . . We entered the same hotel; for example, in Formula 1 trips, trips to automobile shows, people were asking why we were there; they didn't want to come and ask us, but they were always curious. (Derivaldo)

The statement of this interviewee demonstrates the curiosity and the distrust with which he is observed in social spaces frequented by members of the middle and upper class. Although he was never asked "Who are you?" or "Why are you here?" he seems to anticipate these questions. It is intriguing to notice that the interviewee analyzes the expectations of those he encounters: "I went into a five-star hotel, the people expected me to speak English, but when I started to speak with a Bahian accent . . ." It is as if the fact of being black and to frequent spaces associated with the upper classes could only be justified by not being Brazilian. After all, the representation of black spaces in Brazilian society never would allow for a different association between color and class.

From various examples, I realize that, even when they recognize that they are victims of racial prejudice, they do not seem to react. When discrimination is practiced by a customer, not reacting can be a strategy, since, after all, the business needs to sell in order to make profits; but why do they react the same way when discrimination is practiced by other people, away from the workplace?

Confronted with this question, I tried to understand how, when, and why people react with gestures, physical and verbal aggression, or appeal to legal action against discriminatory attitudes. Then I reformulated the question: "What would it take for you to take a position against a discriminatory attitude?"

From this question, I obtained several answers. In a few cases, the interviewees said they would not appeal to the judiciary power due to the dysfunction of Brazilian justice; other interviewees said that they would not like to be involved in public scandals. One interviewee mentioned that he would only take action if the offender had the same level as he, by which he meant socioeconomic level; the great majority stated that, frequently, those that discriminate were employees and not owners, thus making it inappropriate to take action, because, after all, "the poor thing could lose his/her job." Reacting against discrimination can also be related to third parties, as I learned from one interviewee, who affirmed that he would take action if the discrimination occurred against people whom he considers unable to defend themselves, for example children and some family members. The probability of him taking action on his own behalf is smaller than if the problem had occurred with someone whom he considers weak and fragile, effectively incapable of taking action.

In this sense, it is important to understand how and under what circumstances the topic of racism is dealt with at home. Different from their own educational experience in public schools, all the interviewed had their children enrolled in good private schools in Salvador, mainly attended by whites. We also know that spaces of sociability are not reduced to the classroom. Their children's contact with white children created in the parents the necessity to protect them from some type of racist prank, joke, or exclusion. They do not want their children to be humiliated; therefore, they feel it is necessary to dialogue with them about a topic until recently considered taboo: racial prejudice. Nevertheless, they were unanimous in their answers concerning how to react to discriminatory acts, and in some cases silence is advised. It is preferable not to react, that is, if it is common to address the topic of discrimination and racial prejudice when children are the victims, the same is not true for the answers offered in this situation. Making reference to racial discrimination affecting children, one interviewee commented:

Interviewee: I talk a lot with my children, because they study in a Diplomatic school that is 99 percent white. And I always say this, to remain indifferent, that if somebody discriminates it is because he is bothered; just act as if you have not seen it.

Interviewer: But do they make any comments about what happens at school?

Interviewee: They do, but I always tell them to let it go, not to give answers, not to argue; not to discuss it; not to get offended. I tell them to go to the director and tell them so they take can action. (Amando)

Another interviewee said:

Interviewee: I talk, and I do not induce any racist acts. But I say that they must protect themselves and not to let it happen; that they have to impose themselves; that outside of school, in real life, the opportunities are rare, so they have to go for it early on and not waste any time. I say that to my son every day and someday he will understand.

Interviewer: Did your father tell you these things when you were young?

Interviewee: He did not speak about it, but he showed me. He did not speak the way I am talking to you, but he was always someone who worked very hard, and he was always a person dedicated strongly to his family. So I try to do the same thing. (Eraldo)

We cannot forget the difference between differing social contexts under which parents and children grow up. Topics that until recently were treated only within the academy and black-power movements are now in the media and shown on prime-time television. As I demonstrated, all the interviewees mention existing racism in Brazilian society; however, this does not mean they all react to discriminatory acts. There is still a large gap between the recognition of racial discrimination and taking action when confronting discriminatory acts.

The majority of the interviewees of this research have a trajectory presenting that they were children born into poor families, and, depending on their social and economic upbringing, their stories are shorter or longer. Those that migrated from the countryside to the capital tell the story of a large family and of different strategies used to survive in the city—a job as a domestic servant among the women and informal commerce among men were the most quoted. After this first moment, they talked about what they considered their first job and all the other jobs they had before becoming entrepreneurs. Strangely, skin color only appears in these narratives in the adult phase and, frequently, through a third person, who referred to them as being black in an offensive, almost accusatory tone. Only one of the interviewees told the story that she was discriminated against during elementary school, and in fact her understanding of race and color has been different ever since childhood.

My interpretation follows some studies that have demonstrated the existence of an intrinsic relation between modernity and negritude. Based on the life stories of the interviewees—typically the first, and oftentimes the only, members of the family to experience mobility—I argue that the experience of being a member of the middle class seems extremely important for the recognition of difference between "us" in ethnic or racial terms and "others," thus restricting the possibilities of a late identification. In other words, while they occupied the base of the socioeconomic stratification, living in slums, these individuals did not feel out of place, and they were not seen as such. The opposite occurred when they started to assume positions of power, to occupy positions of prominence in the labor market, to live in middle-class neighborhoods (which, in Salvador, are predominantly white), to go to social spaces frequented by the middle class, such as bars, stores, and restaurants, and when they enrolled their children in good private schools.

The same way that identities seem to reconfigure themselves in late modernity, for the interviewed of this research, black identity definitively resists the use of identity in a collective political sense, going more in the direction of an identity that serves individual needs, most of all to gain access to full citizenship; that is, the emphasis falls back onto the individual right and not onto collective strategies of mobilizing ethnic resources. Even if they are ill-informed and not worried about racial questions, the belief in the inferiority and incapacity of blacks prompts them to problematize and reflect on the Brazilian model of race relations.

Notes

1. A preliminary version of this chapter was published in *Cadernos Pagu* (23), 2004: 199–228.

2. The research presented in the text was conducted with black businesspeople in the beginning of 2000 in Salvador.

3. I define *middle class* with objective criteria, such as education, occupation, and income. In previous research, I problematize the use of the notion of middle class when applied to blacks and the expression *the black middle class*. See Figueiredo 2002.

4. The information presented in this chapter was gained through research conducted for the dissertation "The Black Middle Class Does Not Go to Paradise: Trajectories, Profiles, and Identity Among Black Entrepreneurs."

5. In my master's thesis, I dedicated a chapter to explaining social whitening utilized by various authors. I observed various examples of racial discrimination cited by those interviewed. Guimarães attests that people with more schooling and those who live in large cities are more likely to denounce being the victims of racism (Figuredo 2003; Guimarães 1997: 51–78).

6. Considering the limits of a chapter, I utilize a number of examples of discrimination and racial prejudice, including those that are not considered as such by those interviewed. This allows the reader to have a better understanding of the subject. The identities of those interviewed are kept anonymous.

7. I refer to the major vulnerability of the symbolic point of view that differentiates physical violence suffered by poor blacks.

5

The Political Shock of the Year: The Press and the Election of a Black Mayor in São Paulo

Cloves Luiz Pereira Oliveira

Since the beginning of the 1980s, there has been an emergence of black candidates winning electoral races at the municipal and state levels in Brazil. The election of Alceu Collares of the Democratic Labor Party–Rio Grande do Sul (PDT-RS) for mayor of the city of Porto Alegre in the municipal election of 1985 marked the beginning of the phenomenon of black candidacies in major Brazilian capitals.[1] In the state elections of 1990, Collares, who was a political heir of Leonel Brizola, won the office of governor in Rio Grande do Sul, while the black businessman Albuino Azeredo, PDT-Espíritu Santo (ES), was elected in Espírito Santo. Six years later, in the municipal elections of 1996, São Paulo economist Celso Pitta, originally from Rio de Janeiro, became "the political shock of the year," according to the national press, when he was elected mayor of São Paulo (Barros and Morris 1996). Obviously, the significance of Pitta's election, which was extensively covered in magazines, newspapers, and television news, was due to the fact that the fifty-year-old man from Rio de Janeiro, who had never run for political office before, happened to become the first black person elected in the largest city in Brazil. Considering the importance of Pitta's victory, given that it is still rare for black politicians to win mayoral or gubernatorial seats in large cities, it is understandable that his election was an important journalistic event (Felinto 1997; Kachani 1996).

The victories of black candidates are not only provoking, but also impact Brazilian political-electoral dynamics. Electoral disputes involving black politicians, even when they do not win, have in past years greatly influenced local and national politics. Such elections bring discussions of issues that are usually absent in political debates, such as problems of racial inequality, social exclusion, and ethnic and racial voting. The campaigns of Edvaldo Brito, Brazilian Workers Party (PTB), of Salvador, Bahia, in 1985 and of Benedita da Silva, Workers Party (PT), of Rio de Janeiro in 1992, resulted in political debates that addressed such issues (Oliveira 2002).

The emergence of black candidates to legislative and executive positions since the late 1980s, their low rate of electoral success, the increase in the use of marketing technologies to construct candidate and party images in campaigns, and the influence of media in electoral processes raise the main question with which I am concerned: What is the influence of color and racial identities of black politicians on their campaigns? Considering that white male elites have monopolized political offices in Brazil, an additional question that should be addressed now is, What happens when a "black horse" enters the race with a real chance to win?[2]

If we place this question in terms of recent studies of the media, politics, and electoral campaigns, the following additional questions are raised: What influence does the color or racial identity of candidates have on defining discursive strategies of black politicians and their adversaries in campaigns? What are the dynamics of debates between candidates and public opinion during electoral campaigns involving black candidates? What are the electoral strategies used by black politicians to adjust their candidacies to the electorate's expectations, considering that images of blacks are marked by stereotypes that disqualify them to exercise power in Brazil? One notices that these questions mention aspects such as the dynamic of debates between candidates, the relationship of candidates and the electorate, and the issue of candidates and public opinion during campaigns. These are especially interesting questions when black politicians appear as strong contenders in electoral runs in major Brazilian capitals.

Until the 1996 election, only white politicians were real contenders for positions in São Paulo's city hall. Historically, rich white men affiliated with conservative political parties occupied the position of mayor or councilperson. For this reason, the emergence of the economist, Pitta, as the first black person with a real possibility of being elected in the largest city in the country was a landmark in the history of Brazilian politics. What was most intriguing in Pitta's run for mayor was the way Pitta, his adversaries, the media, and civil society organizations treated race and color. Elections are a microcosm of society, and as such they reflect the social, economic, cultural, and political dynamics of society in material and symbolic ways. As Mancini and Swanson (1996) have pointed out, we can suppose that the existence of prejudice against blacks in Brazil—which represents them as individuals who lack beauty, intelligence, and the capacity to lead and as unqualified to exercise power when compared to whites—means that the racial variable can be an important factor for defining the terms of participation of blacks as candidates in elections.[3]

The media played a prominent role in the mayoral campaign as it relayed politicians' speeches during the election period. The political propaganda and debates among candidates, parties, civil society organizations, and the media gained significant space in television, radio, and the news press. The press, in particular, carried extensive campaign coverage, producing a special section for it. In this context, political variables, such as political platform, experience in politics, and candidates' and voters' ideological positions, were in tension with what Downs (1957) calls "non-political variables," such as race, gender, and religion, which also influenced the development of campaign debates.

According to Figueiredo (2000), since 1980, newspapers have played a role in electoral and political processes at the national and regional levels, although they have competed with other media, political parties, and unions. Therefore, Dias (1995) explains that some factors demand that political analysts observe the nature of press coverage during elections because of the fact that the press influences the production of the political agenda, the construction of politicians' images, and the extent to which agendas and images constructed at the beginning of the electoral race remain until the end of the race. Oliveira's (2004) research demonstrates the importance of analyzing the press's treatment of biracial elections in Brazil. At a time that studies on the emergence of North American black mayors point to their electoral success, it must in part be due to the visibility that the media grants to covering their campaigns. As Oliveira observes (2004: 110), this visibility leads to positive and negative consequences, for example, the racialization of such elections.

> On one hand, candidates were granted free advertising space to quickly project their campaigns in the electoral race, thus to quickly start the process of spreading their images. On the other hand, a lot of visibility contributed to the generation of hostility and fear among white voters as much as it did to the advances and consequences of the election of a black mayor. . . . The headings, calls, and framing of the news were wrought with ethnic and racial undertones as, for example, "candidate Harvey is trying to become the first black mayor of the city," "Lee is a defender of affirmative action," and "candidate disagrees with affirmative action" to racialized elections.

Political factors such as partisanship have always been considered in studies of electoral campaigns in Brazil. Nevertheless, race, gender, and the style of press coverage are also important factors that have been overlooked by Brazilian social scientists. I consider these factors in studying election dynamics. This chapter analyzes the role of the press in the 1996 São Paulo elections, which ultimately resulted in the victory of its first black mayor.

Journalistic Coverage

My study is based on analysis of press coverage by two leading São Paulo newspapers, which were both important sources of electoral coverage: the *Folha de São Paulo* (*FSP*) and the *Estado de São Paulo* (*ESP*). The *FSP* provided their own analysis of press coverage. I rely on this coverage in my analysis. This is because it was a leader in daily reporting, producing useful charts and tables in a highly segmented and competitive market; its ability to penetrate different segments of society; and its considerable importance as an agent of influencing public opinion of a highly educated and politicized public of *Paulista* society, such as professionals, teachers, and university students.[4] In addition, the *FSP* dedicated more space to electoral coverage than its competitors. The *ESP* competes with the *FSP* in the *Paulistano* market (Chaia et al. 2002). Because of the lack of time and resources, my research is only dedicated to a systematic analysis of election coverage of the 1996 mayoral elections of São Paulo carried out by the *FSP* using quantitative and qualitative methods. The analysis of the *ESP* was based on quantitative data research carried out by the Datafolha Institute, which compared electoral coverage of the *FSP* and the *ESP*.[5] Thus, the present chapter is based on quantitative data from this research and qualitative data from content of the *FSP*.

As previously stated, the *FSP* granted more space to covering the municipal elections than any other newspaper. According to the *FSP*, its periodical dedicated 208.5 pages to the election from August 2, 1996, to November 15, 1996. This period corresponds to the eve of the beginning of the Free Schedule of Electoral Propaganda (HGPE) and to the second round of the elections. This space is almost two times more than the *ESP*'s coverage.

The space granted by the *FSP* for some candidates corresponded to their positions in opinion research. The newspaper considered surveys carried out by Datafolha throughout the electoral period as one of its main instruments for planning coverage. Considering this, the style of framing electoral coverage in the format of a *horse race* guided journalists' narratives by defining the number and order of appearances of candidates.

In the 1996 elections, twelve candidates ran for city hall of São Paulo: two women and ten men. Among them, at least three could be classified as Afro-descendants. These candidates represented twenty-seven parties in the largest municipal electoral college of the country, made up of 6.8 million voters. Like other elections during the 1980s, this election was made up of a number of different ideological beliefs (Chaia et al. 2002). They formed seven coalitions and five independent parties, which represented an array of political-ideological trends from left to right. Only five of these candidates appeared as real competitors for city hall, since all other candidates together reached only 2 percent of the valid votes. One must agree with Chaia et al. (2002: 19) when they highlight that "São Paulo's political market is small and is self-regulated by the main parties."

Surprisingly, Mayor Paulo Maluf supported the Afro-Brazilian Pitta, a black economist, as a representative of his party, the Brazilian Progressive Party (PPB), to compete against experienced contenders of local and state elections. Pitta's main political experience was limited to the time he was secretary of finance of Maluf's cabinet. Former mayor of São Paulo Luiza Erundina, who was Maluf's predecessor from 1989 to 1991, successfully secured approval to represent the Workers Party (PT). The untiring senator José Serra once more was nominated to represent the Brazilian Social Democracy Party (PSDB). Former mayor of Osasco Francisco Rossi was the candidate of the Democratic Labor Party (PDT), while Doctor Jose Pinotti carried the flag of the Party of the Brazilian Democratic Movement (PMDB).

With the blessing of Mayor Maluf, Pitta was at the forefront of the coalition of the rightist parties, the Partido Popular Progressista (PPP) and the Liberal Front Party (PFL), known for their slogan "São Paulo does not stop." Its slogan was undoubtedly intended to appeal to the continuity of the administration's policies. Luiza Erundina led the alliance "YES for São Paulo," made up of leftist parties such as the PT, Brazilian Communist Party (PCB), Party of National Mobilization (PMN), Brazilian Socialist Party (PSB), and the Brazilian Communist Party (PC do B). Its greatest challenge was to change the idea about the PT, which was seen as a party that was not willing to negotiate. At the beginning of Erundina's campaign, 42 percent of voters rejected the idea of voting for the coalition. Among other things, one reason was that the PT would be a party of radicals that were always against any proposals of other politicians. The strategy of the campaign was to use the word "YES" on party political advertisements to represent a new proactive position and as a sign of negotiation of the candidate and her party in politics. Serra, in turn, led the center-left coalition, SP São Paulo, made up of the PSDB, the Green Party (PV), Popular Socialist Party (PPS), and the Liberal Social Party (PSL). Their slogan was meant to mobilize a feeling of *Paulistano* pride. Jose A. Pinotti was affiliated with the coalition "Viva São Paulo," which represented major parties, but was a fragile alliance. Campos Machado was with the coalition, "São Paulo Hope," made up of the Brazilian Workers Party (PTB), the National Party of the Retired (PAN), and the Party of Social Democracy (PSD). In its discourse it had an appeal to the sentiment of love for the hometown of São Paulo in its initial campaign. At the front of the Democratic Labor Party (PDT), Partido Trabalhista Social (PTS), and the Liberal Party (PL), the former mayor of the city of Osasco, Francisco Rossi, had a personal character to his campaign in the coalition properly named "Rossi for São Paulo." Dorival M. de Abreu was the candidate of a weak coalition, "São Paulo Flag," composed of three parties that did not have much political weight: the National Labor Party (PTN), General Party of Workers (PGT), and Partido Comunista do Brasil (PC do B).

Admirably, with less than fifteen days of candidate advertising using the HGPE, as shown by research carried out on August 14, Pitta had already won 28.6 percent of intended votes, just a few steps behind former mayor Erundina and former mayor Rossi. Erundina and Rossi both were at the front of the race, each one with almost one-third of intended votes. Neither of these candidates achieved the intended votes they expected in the first round of the elections on October 5. Erundina remained in second place, falling from 33.7 percent to 24.4 percent. Rossi followed behind the PT candidate, falling from his optimistic mark of 31.5 percent to a mere 16.9 percent. His performance granted Erundina the opportunity to run against Pitta in the second round.

In the first round of the election, Pitta, PPB, had 40.3 percent of the total electoral coverage including text, graphs, and photos. Serra, PSDB, occupied 26.2 percent; Erundina, PT, 22.2 percent; and Rossi, PDT, 9.3 percent (see Table 5.1). It is notable that the candidates from small parties had been almost invisible in the pages of newspapers during this period (2.2 percent). We see that the *malufista* candidate (Pitta) did not have the same coverage in the *ESP* as in the *FSP*, although he continued to be cited more than others. The *ESP* cited Pitta more than Erundina, and both more than Rossi.

It is odd that Serra obtained more visibility than Erundina, despite that he was always behind her in opinion polls. It is probable that Serra's campaign attacks against his adversaries generated sufficient controversy to the point that it stimulated a greater number of name citations than former mayor Erundina. Following Figueiredo et al. (2002), we can assume that the PSDB (*peesidebista*) candidate added to his image and campaign more powerful elements of visibility. In this way, he was successful at breaking the criterion of proportionality set by opinion polls. Nevertheless, we cannot dismiss the hypothesis that the prevalence of a certain affection for the PSDB (*tucano*) party aided in his success. He obtained more space to divulge his candidacy. In turn, since he was a leader in the race, Pitta was guaranteed 58.7 percent of space in election coverage. Erundina, in turn, had restricted appearances of 41.3 percent, and this coverage guided the *ESP*.

Analyzing beyond the space granted to each candidate for news articles, graphs, and photos published by newspapers regarding these politicians, we can make an evaluation in qualitative terms about the treatment the news media gave to the image of each candidate. I now look at not only the visibility of candidacy coverage, but at the valence or how candidates were treated. The media research of the *FSP* provided by Datafolha identified newspaper references to candidates as positive, negative, or neutral in their coverage of candidates. It is from the analysis of the effect of visibility and valence that I infer the orientation of some means of communication in the electoral process (Aldé 2004). Emphasizing that analysis of valence is a main key to examining newspaper bias in their treatment of candidates, Aldé (2004: 110) states:

> In a democratic model in which the occupation of public media space is the main political capital, we consider that, from the point of view of candidates, neutral news counts as in favor, that is . . . to indicate the candidates' effectiveness in occupying their spaces in means of communication. Negative material, on the contrary, goes against their interests. It is appropriate to

Table 5.1 Appearance of Candidates in Electoral Coverage of the *Folha de São Paulo* and the *Estado de São Paulo* Newspapers from August 8 to November 11, 1996 (%)

Candidates	First Round		Second Round	
	Folha de São Paulo	*Estado de São Paulo*	*Folha de São Paulo*	*Estado de São Paulo*
Celso Pitta, PPB	40.3	34.2	58.7	57.5
Luiza Erundina, PT	22.0	21.4	41.3	42.4
José Serra, PSDB	26.2	26.8	—	—
Francisco Rossi, PDT	9.3	14.2	—	—
Other candidates	2.2	3.4		
Total	100	100	100	100

Source: Datafolha, November 1996.

emphasize that the simple account can be negative or positive according to the proper content of the event.

To this proposition, Aldé (2004: 110–111) clarifies:

> To classify material as favorable or harmful to candidates and their campaigns, without apparent intention on the part of news, allows us to go beyond the self-proclaimed neutrality of the press, at a time that it tries to be objective in the regulation of news. Their decision to be positive or neutral already represents a political choice. Therefore, the selection and frequency of material that favors or harms candidates should be attributed to editorial decisions that either obey marketing decisions, appeal to sensationalism, or political criteria. In this way, different political facts and events, that candidates want to be promoted and want to have an impact in electoral dynamics, can gain valence in newspapers. Some points are common and inevitable, others indicate the editorial tendencies, more or less explicitly to its political preferences.

Table 5.2 shows the percentage of the valence of news material in relation to the candidacies of Pitta, Erundina, Serra, and Rossi in the *FSP* and the *ESP* for the time period August 8, 1996, to November 11, 1996. These data suggest that, generally, coverage of the *FSP* was more harmful to candidates' images. The *FSP* published more negative material, while the *ESP* opted to take it lightly on all the candidates and showed a propensity to publish more neutral and positive material than negative. To analyze the behavior of these newspapers, I concentrate on Pitta's and Erundina's treatment as they were finalists of the race.

Table 5.2 Valence of Electoral Coverage of the *Folha de São Paulo* and the *Estado de São Paulo*, August 8 to November 11, 1996

Candidates	Newspapers	Valence of News		
		Positive	Negative	Neutral
Celso Pitta, PPB	*FSP*	30.9	34.0	35.1
	ESP	35.0	30.2	35.2
Luiza Erundina, PT	*FSP*	36.3	25.0	38.7
	ESP	45.3	18.2	36.5
José Serra, PSDB	*FSP*	31.8	32.6	35.6
	ESP	46.3	23.7	30.0
Francisco Rossi, PDT	*FSP*	37.6	12.9	49.5
	ESP	48.0	6.2	45.8

Source: Datafolha, November 1996.

Notes: These data correspond to the texts, photos, and graphs in relation to candidates Celso Pitta and Luiza Erundina in the coverage of periodicals in the two rounds. The valence of the referring materials was computed for José Serra and Francisco Rossi only during the first round.

Celso Pitta in the News

Since the beginning of the campaign, there were more negative references to Pitta than any other candidate. The *FSP* made the relationship between Pitta and Maluf a salient issue. They emphasized his relationship to Maluf rather than his party affiliation, the PPB, in news coverage. Thus, the phrase "the candidate sponsored by Mayor Paulo Maluf" and "the godson of Maluf" constantly followed Pitta's name throughout the campaign. In journalistic accounts or in what was expressed by other candidates, Pitta was viewed as passive and always as a benefactor that was protected by the mayor. Some phrases used to refer to Pitta were "Mayor Paulo Maluf sponsors Pitta," "the shade of Maluf," "the Mayor's doll," and "the Ventriloquist doll."

When Pitta's competitors referred to him as a marketing product, this was a strategy to disqualify him as a viable candidate. Some newspapers referred to him as the "yogurt candidate" or the "soap candidate." Thus his image was attacked by accusations that he was a marketing product. Almost all of his competitors influenced readers and the electorate to view him negatively by affirming that he did not have his own ideas and that his speeches, words, and gestures were directed by marketing advisers of Maluf.

In this context, the press collaborated with political advertisers in the São Paulo electoral process and amplified debates between various actors involved in the campaign. A similar phenomenon was observed by other researchers in their studies (Ansolabehere and Shanto 1994; Dias 1995; Figueiredo et al. 1997). Beyond debates, the main São Paulo newspaper acted in a paternalistic way toward voters by guiding them on what they should observe and know about candidates and their campaigns. In the words of the ombudsman of the *FSP* regarding the positioning of his company in the first round of the election, "the denunciations and the details published in the press, in the *Folha,* contributed to undo television mystifications" that were occurring during the campaign (*FSP* September 29, 1996). The press's electoral coverage was characterized as disclosing political propaganda of candidates from television, guided by a concern to disclose the structure of campaigns and the strategies used to persuade voters.

I draw attention to the press because it not only takes on the role of the "art critic," but tries to explain to the greater public the logic of the production of campaigns, as identified by Jamieson (1992). What we see is that the main reporters and contributors to the *FSP* acted as guides to voters by instructing them on how to understand the complex mechanisms of politics in case they had not received proper instruction. The mechanism that the press so much feared was the extensive use of political advertisement to persuade the noncritical voter, who takes for granted anything that appears on television.

Opinions from critics published in the press and Pitta's competitors insisted on the idea that his success was due to the strength of support from a political leader, support of a partisan machine, and the use of marketing resources, and that if he won the election, he would not know how to walk, speak, or think. In the press, the success of Pitta's candidacy was described as a result of the artifices of Mayor Maluf and his gurus; the advertising executive, Duda Mendonça; the political propaganda propagated in the HGPE; and commercial intervals of television. It is interesting to note that the most recurrent words used to mention his success during the campaign (as well as the election) were to emphasize the idea of surprise: admiration, astonishment, shock, and enragement. For the newspaper, Pitta's political inexperience, his lack of formal political participation, and partisanship made him appear as "new, a virgin, whose final shape could be crafted and polished by the electoral campaign with its marketing tools, transforming him into a 'competent' product, with an education from abroad, 'participation in private initiatives' and 'the right hand' of a city administration whose accomplishments, correct or not, are scandalously visible" (*FSP* August 18, 1996: 10).

The concern of the *FSP* to inform people about Pitta's campaign backstage contributed to the propagation of the idea that Maluf's candidate was a marketing product and this damaged his image. Using newspapers as a campaign vehicle, his adversaries constantly criticized Pitta's use of marketing tools. In the press, they insisted that Pitta was a marketing product whose good performance in the HGPE could be credited, almost exclusively, to training by his assessors. Some newspaper and magazine editorials insisted on making analogies between Pitta as a candidate and products such as hamburgers, yogurt, and soap. The goal was to attack the candidate's image and insist that his projects were shaped by propaganda. This is illustrated by three articles published by the *FSP.*

In the first one, the newspaper investigated Pitta's educational background. They inquired about his school grades and performance in school from former colleagues and teachers. The news article pointed out that "the real" Pitta "was not outstanding," and was not "an excellent student," but was certainly a hard worker and a reserved person. In the second one, the São Paulo newspaper reporter interviewed three plastic surgeons to consult them on what should be done to the faces of each of the four main candidates to improve their image: Pitta, Erundina, Serra, and Rossi. This article was entitled "Doctors make over the faces of candidates," which discussed plastic surgeons' opinions about correcting small natural imperfections or results of aging of the candidates and how they could improve their physical appearance to fit their personalities. Examples are softening Erundina's brave look and alleviating the "serious expression" of Pitta's face. These were some of the problems pointed out regarding Erundina's and Pitta's faces (*FSP* June 23, 1996).

Putting together the opinions of plastic surgeons with marketing coordinators of each candidate, this example stands out because it explains the role of advertising executives as producers of the best image of their customers, emphasizing the similarity that existed between them and plastic surgeons. Among the four main candidates, doctors recommended that Pitta was the one with a better appearance; however, it was recommended he "narrow his nose and [have] surgery to cut some muscles from his forehead to brighten up his serious look." Former mayor Erundina, according to specialists, would need to invest more resources to improve her image. According to the article, "the [Worker's Party, PT] *petista* candidate, Luiza Erundina should get lipo-sculpture in her face . . . , surgery in the tip of her nose . . . a peeling or lifting . . . , and the lifting of her eyelids . . . to improve her appearance" (*FSP* July 23, 1996). This investment would cost R$10,800.

The third example is a news article published in the *FSP,* August 25, 1996, a few days after the first debate promoted by the Bandeirantes Television Network. This news article revealed the theatrical component of electoral races and showed Pitta's strategies to face his adversaries in the debate.[6] Pitta's campaign used a qualitative research technique using focus groups. Reporters informed readers that during the debate, he had his performance monitored by marketing assessors of his campaign, who used information from a group of voters regarding their impressions of the candidates. He used this information to inform his speech and performance. According to the article, "Each gesture or word of Pitta was evaluated and the evaluation transmitted immediately to the advertising executive, who directed the candidate during intervals."

These three examples above showed newspaper readers some curiosities of the elections, which focused on discursive strategies of each candidate and the nature of the personas each one incarnated. What is particularly notable is the extreme critical position that the *FSP* assumed in relation to Pitta. In light of the fact that Pitta's campaign really did use the image of Mayor Maluf to endorse his candidacy, in the same way, Erundina's marketing coordinators were not shown as having any concern to publicly incarnate her as a candidate with "gurus of propaganda." This makes it impossible to endorse reports of the *FSP* that affirm that their newspaper coverage was impartial.

What is remarkable in the debate between the press and Pitta's consultants is that those that tried to paint an image of Pitta as subservient to the commands of a *godfather* politician could also be viewed as a guarantee that promises would be fulfilled. Using media as an outlet to publicize his candidate, it was with no constraint that the advertising executive Mendonça declared to journalists that "anyone who has a godfather like Maluf must take advantage of it" (*FSP* July 28, 1996: 10). What led Mendonça's claim was the fact that the mayor enjoyed an excellent approval rating of 50 percent. Pitta's campaign staff believed that the same attacks that said that Pitta was Maluf's doll, in a certain way, contributed to strengthening his campaign slogan. It emphasized that because Maluf supported Pitta's candidacy, this would ensure the administration's continuity.

In its report of media coverage, the *FSP* supported the notion that Pitta's media treatment was "sufficiently balanced." Pitta's coverage in the *FSP* was

30.9 percent positive, 34 percent negative, and 35.1 percent neutral. The *ESP* could use the same argument. In the *ESP*, 35 percent of his coverage was positive, 35 percent neutral, and 30 percent negative. The ratio of negative material reflects that the *FSP* as well as the *ESP* served as a site of dialogue and confrontation between candidates. Most of Pitta's attacks were directed at him because he was a candidate at the forefront of the election and because of his association with the existing government.

Luiza Erundina in the News

The press's treatment of Luiza Erundina was less harsh than that given to Pitta, but no less damaging to her candidacy. The former mayor had few negative news articles, photos, and graphs. Totaling treatment in both the *ESP* and *FSP*, only 25 percent of the coverage about her was negative. She was dealt with positively in 36.3 percent of published material and neutrally in 38.7 percent. In the *ESP*, she received more favorable treatment than Pitta. Her name was in 18.2 percent of negative material, 45.3 percent of positive material, and 36.5 percent of neutral material.

The *FSP* shows that beyond having faced the attacks of a variety of adversaries throughout her campaign, Erundina also struggled with the need to overcome the internal problems of her party. A great part of the negative material concerning her involved the conflicts between her and the leadership of the PT. These conflicts were precipitated by disagreement with her political propaganda in the media. The first disagreement occurred because of Erundina's resistance to her television time on the HGPE being divided with other candidates who were running for election in cities of the metropolitan region of São Paulo. A more serious conflict was the first week of the *Petista* television propaganda, at the beginning of August. The majority of the PT did not agree with the concept and strategy of Erundina's campaign. The *Petista* leaders did not like the idea of Erundina trying to avoid negative images by asking the party to support messages that, according to them, compromised the identity of the party.

As for the first incident, Erundina tried to refute the lines of direction of the party, but accepted the requirements of the state director, so she yielded part of her time on television for the campaigns of other candidates of the ABC region.[7] Expressing dissatisfaction, she argued that her program time being shared with other candidates threatened her message because they would defend a platform different from hers (*FSP* July 18, 1996: 10). The outcome of the problem was complicated, and once again she had to yield to pressures of the party and change her campaign's projection. It is interesting to note that all this controversy, extensively debated in newspapers during almost all the month of August, appeared because of the slogan "The PT Says YES."

Erundina had the highest rejection rate among the four strongest candidates—42 percent, about 12 percent above the second most rejected candidate by local voters. She had to change her image and the image of her party (see Figure 5.1). The principal objective of her campaign was to change the image of the PT as a radical and sectarian party, unwilling to negotiate with those from other political parties, regardless of the political party's agenda. The word "YES" was chosen to show that the PT was willing to negotiate with others; Erundina's slogan stressed, "Erundina Says YES." She represented the coalition "Yes to São Paulo," which, as aforementioned, was made up of the PT, PSB, PC do B, PCB, and PMN. The word "YES" was the principal mark of the campaign and was stamped on t-shirts, printed in pamphlets, mentioned in jingles, and included in vignettes.

In accordance with Erundina's advertising executives, the strategy to use YES as part of the campaign aimed to give a direction of plebiscite to the election. The intention was to make the 1996 election an opportunity for *Paulistano* voters to reveal their opinion of her previous experiences as mayor from 1989 to 1992 (*FSP* July 15, 1996: 9). In an effort to reconstruct her image and the image of her party, she met politicians from different parties who had difficulty dialoguing with PT politicians, as, for example, the São Paulo entrepreneurs and the labor union Syndical Force. Erundina's marketing struggle to redefine the image of the party guaranteed strong criticism from the party, which led Erundina's advertising executive, Celso Luducca, to quit.

According to Luducca, the "light version" is that a lack of the PT's ideological discourse provoked dissatisfaction in radical segments of the party,

Figure 5.1 Rate of Rejection of Candidates for Mayor of São Paulo, 1996 (as percentage of all voters)

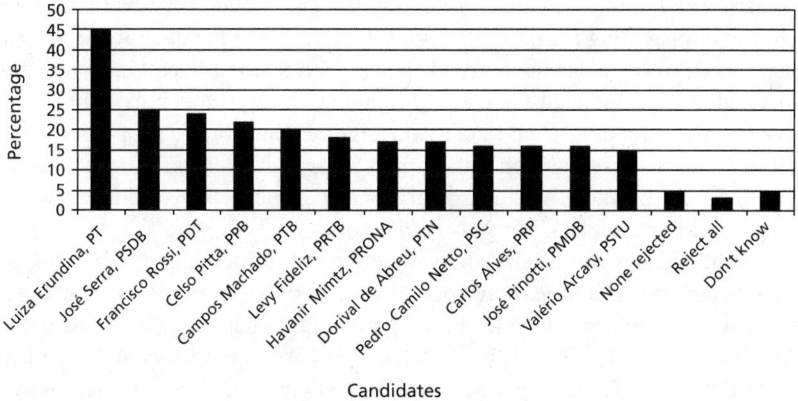

Candidates

Source: Datafolha, August 24, 1996.

which were to be used in television ads. Differences about the most appropriate concept generated fights within the PT and some became public. Some of this criticism was because some members of the party rejected the concept of the campaign that said YES.

The *Petista* leaders insisted that such a slogan displayed the attacks of adversaries. Their reasoning was that if someone approves of the PT that says YES, it suggests that another PT that existed said NO. Such a message contributed to strengthening arguments of critics that declared that the PT was an organization that only knew how to critique others and did not have the maturity to negotiate. One of the first voices to disagree with the strategy of the campaign was Aloísio Mercadante. Mercadante is an economist and was a candidate for vice-mayor for Erundina. According to Luducca, Mercadante's criticism of the concept of the campaign was an expression of his resentment for not being chosen as the PT's mayoral nominee in São Paulo.

Beyond Mercadante, then president of the PT, Luiz Inácio (Lula) da Silva was also critical of Erundina's discursive strategy. Even supporting his party nominee on a political ad that aired on television, Lula did not hide his dissatisfaction with the routes Erundina's campaign had taken. According to the *FSP* (August 15, 1996: 4), "For Lula, the slogan fixed the idea that Erundina's PT was the only one that said YES. The PT of him and other leaders would be the one that says No. He feared the use of this slogan against the party in the future." The exposure of these divergences about the central idea of Erundina's campaign contributed to strengthening the idea that the PT was a divided party, which had difficulty defining their line of action.

According to the *FSP* (August 15, 1996), the ascent of Pitta and the fall of Erundina in intended votes sounded an alarm signal that stimulated criticism of the *Petista* campaign's discursive strategy. Mercadante insisted that the campaign had to be more offensive and had to have more attacks against Maluf's administration. The critics of Mercadante contributed to the fall of the slogan "The PT that says YES" with only fifteen days left for advertising. The change in marketing for the campaign caused a loss in the quantity of graphic materials (posters and handouts) and, in part, electronic ads (spots and vignettes) that had to be abandoned to give way to a new concept. It is important to note that much of Erundina's and Pitta's campaigns counted on the support of an extensive and expensive support staff of marketing professionals. To carry out television ads for Erundina's campaign, the advertising executive, Luducca, would receive R$1 million (*FSP* August 15, 1996).

Reading the commentary on the controversy surrounding the PT's slogan, we can understand a little more about the scene of the race. It is notable to see the divergence of opinion on the most appropriate strategy for the PT campaign, which unleashed a crisis in the party and provoked an open confrontation of its leaders, such as that between Erundina and her candidate to be vice-mayor and the removal of her marketing coordinator. As if there were not enough internal cracks in the PT, the *Paulistano* voter was also informed that Erundina was suffering a boycott from the party's director, who refused to embrace her campaign and stated that the party did not have enough money to continue in the race.[8] Obviously, such news contributed to the idea that Erundina's campaign would result in successive crises.

What Happens When a Black Horse Enters the Race?

To have a black candidate with real possibilities of winning the mayoral seat in the largest city of the country made this a notable election. The possibility of Pitta being the first black elected to govern the city of São Paulo contributed to an attraction of media coverage. Coverage of printed and electronic media allowed advertising executives to become quickly involved in the process of positioning the candidate to run for office. Marketing consultants had a candidate that attracted immense media attention since first launching his candidacy, and this stimulated enormous interests. The public wanted to know "who is the guy that Maluf is supporting." Advertising executives were able to more quickly focus their attention on persuading voters on the qualities of the candidate rather than just announcing his candidacy.

It is important to note that on July 28, 1996, five days before starting the HGPE, the *Paulistano* electorate already knew Pitta. His notoriety was second only to former mayor Erundina, who was known by 65 percent of people, while Pitta was known by 53 percent. Senator José Serra was a veteran in running for city hall of São Paulo; and former mayor of Osasco, Francisco Rossi, who placed second in the run for government of the state of São Paulo two years before, was known by 43 percent of those surveyed. The electorates' lack of recognition of Serra was critical to his campaign, considering that he was frequently discussed in electronic media as he was appointed as the candidate of President Fernando Henrique Cardoso, had already been minister of Planning, and until the eve of the campaign, was the minister of Health.

The public's immense curiosity to know Maluf's candidate aided Pitta's candidacy. There are many versions to explain the emergence of Pitta's candidacy. Some say that Pitta was chosen by incumbent Maluf to be his successor in the 1996 election. Another version of the selection process suggests that Pitta was picked from among Maluf's municipal secretaries three months before the campaign, because he performed the best in a series of video tests.[9] There were suggestions that the choice was more personal for Maluf, who chose Pitta despite the fact that others performed just as well in media performances. In this way, Pitta prevailed because Maluf sought someone with a clean political background who could bear the brunt of criticism of "*malufismo*," a style of administration heavily oriented to public works projects like roads, but which neglected citizen welfare demands in housing, employment, health, and other critical issues. In this regard, Maluf rebuffed his party compatriots who feared that he was taking a risk. Their fear was that *Paulistas* would never vote for a John Doe or a black candidate (*FSP* November 17, 1996).[10]

Maluf's hunch that he should support Pitta proved to be correct. Pitta won the majority of votes in the first round, beating experienced white candidates. He received 48.2 percent of the votes. In the runoff he defeated Erundina with 62.3 percent to 37.7 percent of the vote. And he did so without mobilization from a racialized constituency. It is worth mentioning that blacks represented only 28 percent of the electorate.

The number of narratives to explain how a black candidacy that was supported by the government of a rightist party, something so uncommon in major Brazilian capitals, immediately signals the peculiarity of this election. When "a horse of a different color" enters an electoral race, the public and his competitors perceive his color.

In the preelectoral period, when the candidacies for mayor were starting to crystallize, opinion polls started to investigate the weight of nonpolitical variables, that is, the influence of identities in voter choice of mayoral candidates. Given that Pitta, a black candidate, was already recognized as a representative of the party of Mayor Maluf in the race, and that ex-mayor Erundina, was a declared northeasterner in the race, it is interesting to note that the heading of the article with results of an opinion poll by the Datafolha Institute on the factors of rejection of candidates was "Race and Origin Do Not Determine Votes" (*FSP* June 14, 1996).[11]

The article claimed that the race and origin of a candidate were not factors in elections. According to Datafolha, only 4 percent of those interviewed declared they would not vote for a black candidate and 12 percent said they would not choose a candidate from the northeast. The most interesting data are that the news article called attention to the fact that 96 percent of *Paulistanos* interviewed by Datafolha affirmed that they would vote for a black candidate and that 88 percent would vote for a candidate if they knew that he were a northeasterner. The news article gave the relative influence of some ascriptive characteristics including race, gender, origin, culture, religion, and behavior (such as sexual orientation, consumption of drugs, etc.) in voting decisions for candidates.

Research data showed that *Paulistano* voters were more inclined to reject a candidate from Rio de Janeiro by nearly 23 percent and a candidate from the northeast by about 12 percent. Curiously, gender seemed to have little influence in these elections. Only 8 percent of voters declared they would not vote for a woman candidate. Religious affiliation had a strong influence on whether or not a voter rejected a candidate, especially if the candidate was evangelical. According to the survey, if voters knew that a candidate was evangelical, 20 percent of them affirmed that they would not vote for the candidate. In the 1991 census, 78 percent of *Paulistanos* declared they were Catholic; thus this finding is not particularly surprising. Voters disclosed a greater degree of prejudice against homosexual candidates. Thirty-four percent declared they would not vote for a homosexual politician, and 7 percent said perhaps they would not vote for a candidate if they knew the candidate was homosexual. Interestingly, the highest rejection occurred for a mayoral candidate who defended proposals to legalize marijuana. Seventy-five percent of voters would not vote for such a candidate.

Datafolha's research indicated that the *Paulistano* electorate in that period seemed little inclined to racial prejudice, and that a candidate's region guided their voting decisions. This explains the insistence of some candidates to declare that they were *Paulistano* (including Serra, PSDB, and Machado, PTB), while Erundina was from Paraíba, and Pitta was from Rio de Janeiro. For this reason both Erundina and Pitta had to convince voters that they loved São Paulo like those born there. In effect, if the feeling of *bairrismo* (localism) had become an important factor, and there was a rejection of politicians from other states, Pitta ran the risk of losing up to 20 percent of his voters for being from Rio de Janeiro, while Erundina could have lost nearly 12 percent from the electorate for being from the northeast.

Erundina was particularly marked because of her multiple identities as a woman, northeasterner, and a member of the PT. Among these, to be a woman was a minor setback among voters. Six percent of those interviewed said they would not vote if a candidate was a woman, while 9 percent rejected a candidate from the northeast. If one adds these percentages together, we understand why she had the largest rejection rate of all the candidates. As shown in Figure 5.1, her rejection rate reached 42 percent, while Pitta's was 27 percent and Serra and Rossi's were 24 percent each. Research indicated that the fact that Pitta was black contributed to a rejection of 5 percent of voters. These percentages were not seriously considered by his marketing consultants to be of great concern because the other candidates had similar percentages of rejection (*FSP* August 18, 1996).

Conclusion

Pitta's consultants exhibited familiarity at dealing with the challenge of choosing a name to represent the controversial mayor Maluf, emphasizing the importance of qualitative and quantitative research in defining marketing strategies of his campaign. In the same way, it appeared that they were used to conducting the campaign of an unknown black politician. Nevertheless, in fact, making this work was not an easy assignment. According to an advertising executive who was part of this team, Pitta's name as a nominee caught them by surprise, mainly because many of them did not have experience dealing with racial prejudice in elections. To disclose the state of shock of the team and, at the same time, to test the reaction of the electorate to Pitta, the first thing they did was "to launch his candidacy in the street" with handouts of a photo of Pitta beside Maluf. According to someone interviewed, who worked in the area of communication of Pitta's campaign, this generated great curiosity from the public to know "who the *black* man was that Maluf was supporting."

To give some sense of how unusual Pitta's candidacy appears to be, in the local and national media, the word "surprise" was most used to describe the results of the campaign. In fact, there were many surprises: choosing Pitta in the first place, the increase in those indicating their intention to vote for him, his possible victory in the first round, his actual victory in the first round, his leading in opinion polls, and finally his victory. It remains without a doubt that the support of Maluf aided in his success. Pitta was successful in winning the majority of votes and beating politicians already well-known in politics.

The surprise of Pitta's performance must be due to the fact that he was a newcomer to politics and relatively unknown before running for office. I believe that these were not the only reasons. I add to this the fact that Pitta was black, and I acknowledge the potential prejudices that surround people of color, which contributed to the general expectation that he would not have a successful candidacy.

Once more it is important to highlight that until the 1996 election, the city only had white mayoral contestants. Therefore, the emergence of the economist Pitta as the first black elected mayor that year represents an important political milestone in contemporary Brazilian politics.[12] Even so, what was most striking in the campaign was how the topic of race was managed: the media played an unusually heavy role in his campaign, with political propaganda and rhetorical debates between the candidates in the press and on television. At the same time, distinct political variables were accompanied by a number of non-political variables in the contest.

Much of Pitta's electoral success is attributed to his efficient marketing strategy. He had at his disposal one of the best political marketing consultants in the country. Pitta adopted rhetoric that supported administrative continuity and deracialized his image and discourse. Both strategies seemed to have guided campaign consultants' efforts to make Pitta's presence invisible on television. They gave more space in ads to the candidate's proposals and to his sponsors, especially his patron, Maluf.

Pitta's opponent in the runoff election was Erundina of the PT. She held several political offices, including city councillor, mayor of São Paulo, state deputy, and minister of Administration. She beat Maluf in 1988 for the São Paulo mayorship mainly via a grassroots campaign. She had strong support from very active militants and neighborhood movements. In the 1996 election, Erundina presented herself as a particular enemy of the *malufismo*. In the beginning of the electoral race, Erundina did not recognize Pitta as her main adversary. She focused on Maluf as illustrated in her declaration to the press that

"Paulo Maluf will be defeated again by a woman, northeasterner, petista, and socialist" (*FSP* August 25, 1996). She protested that Maluf's railways were useful only for the bourgeoisie, which did not suffer from the city's transit problems to get to work, and accused Pitta of being Maluf's strawman (*testa de ferro*) (*FSP* October 25, 1996). Erundina's proposals carried a heavy socialist flavor, strongly emphasizing that public service should be controlled by the state, and that government should directly attend to the demands of workers and poor people (*FSP* October 3, 1996).

Clearly advertising and news coverage both contributed to Pitta's electoral success by giving salience to his campaign, image, and issues. In the words of Stephen and Yyengar (1994), one could say that Pitta rode a wave of popular support for incumbency in the 1996 election. This was consistent with what happened in other major Brazilian cities where incumbents handpicked their successors. Pitta's political discourse and image were congruent both with this electoral environment and with the preexisting beliefs about race relations in Brazil.

Nevertheless, the most interesting part of Pitta's campaign is that although his strategy was to present himself as an individual, rather than as a representative of his race, it was inevitable that his color was made visible during the campaign. I observed that the electorate, political parties, and public opinion pointed out that Pitta was black and this brought about questions regarding the influence of race in the candidacies of Afro-descendant politicians (Barros and Morris 1996; Lima 1997; Pitta 2002; Raça Brazil 1997). Pitta's candidacy led to intense debate in the press, in the heart of the black movement, and parties of the left to examine whether people vote according to partisanship or racial allegiance (Barros and Morris 1996; Cardoso 1996; Novaes 1996a and 1996b).

In conclusion, the media's treatment of Pitta's campaign is telling of how the issue of race becomes a central issue in black politicians' campaigns, even when they try to avoid this. Analyses of media treatment of black politicians seeking high levels of power are especially relevant with the recent election of US president Barack Obama. In Pitta's case, my content analysis of the *FSP*'s electoral coverage shows that the newspaper denounced Pitta's marketing strategies. It also portrayed Pitta as an actor with no control over the image he wanted to portray of himself. The media showed how his political image was constructed. Maluf and the advertising executive Mendonça were the protagonists of his campaign. Throughout the campaign, Pitta's strategy was to deracialize his message, yet the racial question started to be an important issue in debates aired during the HGPE and was amplified in journalistic coverage.

During Obama's campaign, he was criticized as a candidate who portrayed himself as postracial. At the same time, during his campaign, Obama gave his "A More Perfect Union" address in Philadelphia, which explicitly addressed race. Obama spoke about his multiracial background, US racism, and inequality. Moreover, he identified as African American while recognizing his biracial parentage as the son of an African man and a white US woman. Despite the media's continuous question of whether Obama believed racism would prevent him from being elected, Obama always answered that he did not believe that race would impede his success. Comparing the two makes an interesting case, as Obama embraced his blackness but was criticized for being postracial, and Pitta sought to de-emphasize his race. While media coverage of Pitta was biased against him, the case was the opposite with Obama. US media was sometimes criticized for being biased toward him, a seeming contradiction considering race relations in both countries.

Notes

1. That was the first direct election in the post-1964 military dictatorship.

2. This expression is taken from A. C. Broh's 1987 book, *A Horse of a Different Color: Television Treatment of Jesse Jackson's 1984 Presidential Campaign.* Washington, DC: Joint Center for Political Studies.

3. Beyond Pitta, Carlos Alves de Souza was another black politician who ran for mayor in São Paulo in 1996. Souza only received 16,974 or 0.3% of the votes out of 6,000,765 valid votes.

4. See Joel Araújo. 2000. *A Negação do Brasil: O Negro na Telenovela Brasileira.* São Paulo: Editora Senac. This work gives an understanding of the role of the media in the production and reproduction of stereotypes of blacks in Brazilian society. He examines fictional narratives of *telenovelas* that have represented images of blacks and whites and the impact on the construction of national identity since the 1950s. For a more scholarly work about the image of blacks in publicity and representational reproduction about distinct expectations of social roles due to race, see V. Reiner and T. Zaharopoulos. 1995. *The Portrayal of Blacks in Television Advertising: A Comparison of Brazilian and U.S. Television.* AEJMC Archives. January 1, 1995.

5. Fortunately, in the *Folha de São Paulo*'s analysis, to prove that the journal was nonpartisan and pluralistic, they published, based on research of Datafolha, a report of electoral coverage conducted by them and by the more right-wing *Paulistano* journal *O Estado de São Paulo* that shows in a table the coverage of the media in this election (*Folha de São Paulo* November 17, 1996).

6. The Bandeirantes Television Network promoted two debates for candidates for mayor of São Paulo in 1996. The first was on August 20, 1996, three weeks after the initiation of HGPE. The second debate between Celso Pitta and Luiza Erundina did not occur because of a disagreement between the two.

7. ABC refers to names of the main cities in the São Paulo metropolitan area: Santo André, São Bernado, and São Caetano.

8. Aloizio Mercadante was already knowledgeable about internal conflicts in the PT. It was the installment of campaign accounts of Erundina that came to confirm rumors that the *petistas* did not have resources to make payments for the campaign. According to the *Folha de São Paulo* (November 11, 1996), the PT previously spent R$4.6 million on the campaign, but was only able to pay less than half of this (R$2,007,481).

9. This process of selection was coordinated by Duda Mendonça, a campaign consultant who helped Maluf to win São Paulo's city hall in 1992, after suffering defeats in electoral contests. All aspiring candidates had their performance videotaped and then presented to a focus group to qualitatively evaluate their acceptance by different seg-

ments of the constituency. It is said that even the experience of James Carville, political consultant to former US president Bill Clinton, directed some qualitative tests. It is reported that in one of these tests, the aspiring candidates were asked if they would be afraid of being labeled homosexual during the campaign and whether they were afraid of having their image associated with Paulo Maluf, "a thief." Again, Pitta was chosen (*Folha de São Paulo* November 17, 1996).

10. A complete version of this thesis can be accessed at www.iuperj.br.

11. Datafolha's survey was conducted before and during the election investigating electoral behavior and intention to vote according to sex, age, schooling, income, color, and place of residence.

12. Celso Pitta was not the first black politician to head the city of São Paulo. In 1947, for almost a year, another black politician, Paulo Lauro, also sat in the mayoral chair, but he was appointed by then-governor Ademar de Barros to this office during the period of political transition in the country (*FSP* November 16, 1996).

Part 2

Affirmative Action Contested

6

Affirmative Action and Identity

Seth Racusen

To order what cannot be ordered or to forbid what cannot be prevented is nonsensical, crazy, and illogical.
—Judge Raquel Soares Chiarelli, 2007[1]

Racial orders constitute social structures with no clear exit. The axis of domination and the technology of domination can neither be readily ignored, as *colorblind* conservatives in the United States insist, nor axiomatically redeployed to undo racial domination. For example, contemporary South Africa would not use apartheid's technology of domination (e.g., pencil tests) to assign racial identity, and it remains unclear how South Africans define their identity under postapartheid nonracialism and how they deploy their identities for the purpose of equal opportunity policies (Posel 2001). India outlawed the use of castes in its Constitution even as it created educational, economic, and political opportunity policies based upon caste membership.[2] In the United States, a movement for a multiracial census category critiqued the rigidity of US categories without fully acknowledging its position in the existing racial order as if a new paradigm could simply be declared (Hernandez 1998: 110). I contend that racial orders possess no easy exit from domination, and explore the current implementation of affirmative action in Brazil as a case study of the general problem of exiting a racial order.

Each racial order produces a fiction that contains obstacles to remedying the inequalities it produces. The Brazilian fiction of identity as appearance has constructed an atomized and ambivalent Afro-Brazilian identity that complicates the use of categories to develop equal opportunity policies (Telles 2002: 415). In Brazil, black (*preto*) and brown (*pardo*) have historically represented distinct color identities, and most of the black movement's intended constituency has identified as brown. The black movement encountered significant difficulties in 1991 in getting Brazilians to identify according to race and not color,

89

a paradigm change.[3] Despite small but significant inroads, the vast majority of the black movement's constituency still identifies according to color and not race.[4] Thus, although identity is subjective, existing structures shape reconstructions of identity. The Brazilian fiction of identity allows multiple interpretations of certain markers that complicate the distinguishing of those on the border of whiteness and brownness, the relevant divide for Brazilian affirmative action. In those instances that universities have verified individual identity claims, the evaluators have rejected as many as one-third of the applicants,[5] a phenomenon also reflected in Brazilian surveys.[6] In Brazil, unlike the United States, mixedness has not been contained within blackness but has been its own container for many identities, including a path to whiteness (Pabst 2003: 178). Thus, the Brazilian fiction of mixedness and the system of physical differentiation have complicated the identification and verification of affirmative action beneficiaries.

In her opinion quoted in the epigraph, Judge Chiarelli viewed the Brazilian fiction of mixedness as expressing fundamental axioms about Brazilian humanity. Accordingly, in a country that blended individuals from different backgrounds, human beings inherently "cannot be ordered" and therefore cannot be distinguished for the purposes of affirmative action. Chiarelli held that the differential treatment of two siblings was "absurd" and summarily dismissed the Federal University of Brasilia's (UNB) affirmative action admissions procedures. To Chiarelli, persons in a country that "blended" identities could not be ordered. This holding rests upon an expectation of identical treatment for siblings, which ignores Brazilian social reality (Telles 2004: 148–150).

The popular interpretation of the Brazilian construction of identity as primarily a matter of appearance re-creates a false dichotomy between self-identity and the perception of others (Nogueira 1985). Self-identity and appearance to others are distinct entities that have also been mutually constituted. The flexibility that some Brazilians enjoy in their identity choices is delimited by their appearance. And their subjective identities influence how others see them. Thus, identity is fully contextual and relational, and research suggests that Brazilian self-presentation responds to perceptions of how an identity claim will be received in a specific context (Blanco 1978).

Colleges that verify identity have generally relied upon applicant appearance to others in making their initial determination of identity and applicant self-identity upon appeal. In the initial admissions processing, UNB had determined that both siblings, Fernando and Fernanda, were ineligible for quota seats based upon their appearance. Chiarelli found that determination to be sensible because "simple observation of their photos . . . verified that neither the plaintiff nor her brother is phenotypically black."[7] Nevertheless, in his appeal of that classification, Fernando declared himself black in appearance and ancestry and showed official documentation of being *pardo*. In her appeal, Fernanda also showed documentation of being *pardo* but admitted that she considered herself white.[8] UNB considered Fernanda's admission of considering herself white to undermine the veracity of her application and to violate her admissions requirements.[9] In holding this differentiation to be nonsensical and demonstrative of the "incongruence" of the university's criteria, Chiarelli was relying solely on her visual impressions and ignoring the candidates' subjective claims. In the name of defending their humanity and individuality, the judge actually ignored their subjective claims.

Thus, identity claims contain and express multiple aspirations with contradictory indications that reflect the ambiguity of Brazilian identity and the strategic calculations of multiple actors to identify themselves and others. The case of Fernando and Fernanda suggests that identity claims contain and express multiple aspirations with contradictory indications. Consider that Fernando, viewed as white by the UNB committee and the judge, showed official documentation of being brown and insisted that he viewed himself as black. Consider that Fernanda, also viewed as white by the UNB committee and the judge, also showed official documentation of being brown and revealed her identity as white. Thus, documents contradicted self-identity (in Fernanda's case) and visual inspection (in both cases), and visual inspection contradicted self-identity (in Fernando's case). A judge might have remanded the case to UNB's appeals commission to sift through the contradictory evidence. Nevertheless, the university arguably erred in admitting the brother, rather than in denying the sister, during the appeal process to their admission. Under the politically charged environment, UNB admitted the sister as well.

The separation of appearance and subjective identity as sequential steps in the admissions process indicates the conceptual trouble in the current deployment of identity for the purpose of affirmative action. The dichotomization of subjectivity and appearance effectively denied applicants a voice in their process prior to the appeal and gave ammunition to the opposition to affirmative action.[10]

The opposition to affirmative action seized upon the case of Fernando and Fernanda and another case in which UNB classified identical twins differently to demonstrate the impossibility of deploying categorical identities for the purpose of affirmative action (Soares 2004). The genuine complexity of adopting affirmative action in a country with a flexible, but hierarchical, identity structure has been sensationalized by a tripartite oppositional coalition of the media, rejected affirmative action candidates, and *antiessentialist* anthropologists. Opposition from the media, dominated by Brazilian elites, is not surprising since elites view affirmative action as a threat to their children's access to public universities, which provides free education of the highest caliber. Rejected candidates for affirmative action seats assert their strategic interests in their legal challenges to the universities. These individuals differ from Bakke (the 1978 Supreme Court decision where a white male, Bakke, sued his way into college based on his grades, thus effectively ending preferential treatment of minorities in admissions) in that many claim to have black ancestry and to be part of the subject class. The oppositional anthropologists include prominent intellectuals who have contributed to the study of race in Brazil (Fry et al. 2007; Maio and Santos 2005a). These anthropologists argue that race-conscious policies force Brazilians to identify in divisive racial categories and that race, since it cannot be based on science, cannot provide a sound basis for government policy (Maio and Santos 2005b: 181–214). The alliance of anthropologists and rejected candidates lends an unusual edge to the opposition because of their combined proximity to the beneficiary class, progressive university professors, and important segments of the black movement.

Opponents claim that Brazil fused Portuguese, African, and indigenous persons into a nation of blended Brazilians, and thereby constructed mixedness as quasi-national (Fry et al. 2007: 21).[11] Nevertheless, in contrast to these fusionist claims to have produced a *new people* by blending persons and cultures, an absorptionist state produces its new people by absorbing persons and cultures into the dominant group, which sets the terms for the blending.[12] Opponents claim that the Brazilian nation will be divided through affirmative action (Maggie and Fry 2007). Nevertheless, if Brazil were truly fusionist, why would articulations of blackness threaten this national mixedness? Why couldn't a Brazilian be black and mixed? I argue that Brazil is a color hierarchy with both fusionist and absorptionist tendencies and that the ambiguous space between fusionist and absorptionist discourses provides the political space for the opposition to affirmative action.

Affirmative action proponents hold the unusual position of being on the defensive in the debate, but winning in the real policy arena with an ever-increasing number of Brazilian universities implementing affirmative action.[13] To the claim that it is impossible to identify blacks, proponents retort that the police have no difficulty in identifying who is black (Cano 1998; de Oliveira and Santos 2001).[14] Although the discretionary behavior of Brazilian police hardly represents a credible model for state discretionary policy, the moral suasion of this response suggests the hyperbole of the opposition to affirmative action. If numerous public and private actors can routinely make discretionary determinations for discriminatory purposes, how could it be impossible to make determinations for the purpose of antidiscriminatory policies?[15]

The resulting debate represents an intellectual cul-de-sac that largely does not address the identity questions posed by adopting affirmative action in Brazil (Bracey 2006: 1231–1325). Who should be the beneficiaries of affirmative action?[16] If a candidate chooses an identity simply for the purpose of university admissions, do the principles of social constructedness require that she be accepted without scrutiny? What manifestations of black or brown identity would a candidate need to show, especially in a country that historically drew distinctions based upon appearance, and how should colleges incorporate appearance and subjective identity? Can colleges verify the identity of beneficiaries without falling into the trap of policing fraud and violating the principles of social constructedness and the primacy of subjective identity?[17] I argue that the view that subjective identity cannot be verified represents a dogmatic understanding of social constructedness and subjective identity. Identity claims are contextual, relational, and negotiable, especially in Brazil.

In this chapter, I propose three policy goals to review Brazilian affirmative action: (1) to maximize the provision of opportunities to those previously excluded, (2) to maximize the political viability and political legitimacy of the program, and (3) to dismantle or at least counter the absorptionist aspects of racial democracy. I argue that both race-based and class-based affirmative action are needed in Brazil and argue for the inclusion of three groups—poor Afro-Brazilians, poor whites, and middle-class Afro-Brazilians—as best addressing these goals. The inclusion of private school blacks and browns, especially necessary to democratize participation in the upper-echelon schools, raises additional issues. Private school whites seeking admission to competitive programs have reportedly identified as brown for the purposes of affirmative action. In a country where at least 38 percent of whites possess black ancestry, such claims are not unfounded even if they are primarily strategic.[18] I defend the verification of identity to ensure that higher-echelon opportunities are provided to those previously excluded, as well as to maximize the longer-term political viability and legitimacy of affirmative action. In subsequent sections of this chapter, I examine the Brazilian structure of identity and its influence upon the designation and verification of beneficiaries to consider the possibilities and limits of the contemporary affirmative action initiatives to transform the Brazilian social structure.

The Brazilian Structure of Identity: The Grammar of Color Identity

I concede the Brazilian structure of identity to be complex, but not so complex as to make affirmative action impossible. Even if identity appeared intractable because subaltern identity was occluded, I would argue against the claim of the impossibility of affirmative action on moral grounds. A country that has produced a widely inegalitarian society on the grounds of race would have a moral obligation to provide opportunities to those excluded, even if they failed to perceive the grounds of their disadvantaged position. In that instance, it would be justifiable to explore policy alternatives that would reach Afro-Brazilians without explicitly naming them.

Although Brazilian identity is complex, it provides a basis for policy distinctions. Brazilians often differ in labeling themselves and each other in consistent categories (Blanco 1978: 78–85). Nonetheless, they use a commonly understood framework of physical characteristics to characterize themselves and each other on a hierarchical color ladder (Blanco 1978: 96). Thus, they can more surely rank themselves and each other from lighter to darker. This section examines four key characteristics of the Brazilian identity structure that interact with affirmative action: (1) the number and nature of categories, (2) the difference between self-identity and assessment by others, (3) disagreements in the assessments of others, and (4) the relationship of ancestry and identity.

Historically, Brazilian identity has been officially constructed in terms of color and not race, an emphasis on appearance over descent. By *official,* I refer both to the census question, which asked Brazilians for their color, and to researchers who also asked Brazilians for their color independent of census categories. As has been widely noted, Brazilians have claimed more than 100 identities on at least three occasions:

- 136 in the 1976 Census Household Survey (PNAD),
- 143 in the 1998 National Employment and Manufacturing Survey (PME), and
- 492 in a 1970 study by Marvin Harris.[19]

Harris argued that a country with 492 identities could not effectively discriminate, a view that some extend to affirmative action. I argue that the sheer number of categories is neither an obstacle to discriminatory behavior nor affirmative action as evidenced by the case of India and its several thousand castes.[20] It was impossible neither for Indian elites and their colonial occupiers to discriminate against *Dahlits* and other castes nor for the state to construct affirmative action policies. Instead of the number of categories being determinative, I argue that the nature of categories matters more. Categories may not be the mutually exclusive groups that clearly perceive and maintain the boundaries between them and others (Lamont and Molnar 2002: 167–195).

In Brazil, there are a handful of salient categories with many derivatives (Harris 1970: 4). Seven categories (*branco, moreno, moreno claro, pardo, preto, negro,* and *claro*) account for 95 percent of the overall population (Telles 2004: 82). Most of the other categories, cited by only a few respondents,[21] pertain to brown Brazilians articulating their positionality within mixedness (Pabst 2003), their aspirations to whiten (Schwarcz 2003; Moura 1988), and their distinctiveness from blackness on the hierarchical ladder.

More Brazilians claim the census identities *pardo* and *preto* in the open-ended question than in a close-ended question. I distinguish societal identities, those used on the street and volunteered in open-ended survey questions, and state or census identities.[22] The most popular identity for census *pardos* and census *pretos* in 1995 was *moreno,* a societal identity. Variations of *moreno,* such as *moreno claro,* represent a smaller, but still significant, identity. The popularity of *moreno* led to the claim that the census bureau "imposes" identity on Brazilians with its choice of categories, especially for those identifying as *moreno* (Harris 1994). More recent data have shown a sizeable shift toward *negro* and the two census categories (*pardo* and *preto*) and away from *moreno* (Racusen 2004: 799).

Although many Afro-Brazilians have preferred societal to state categories, surveys have shown that Brazilians can identify to a census category. For example, 99.4 percent of the respondents in the 1998 national survey claimed a state identity (Schwartzman 1999: 5). The few Brazilians unable to locate themselves in a census category generally do not have enough schooling to be eligible to enter a university.[23] Thus, these data do not support the opposition's argument that affirmative action causes tangible harm to Brazilians unable to place themselves in an affirmative action category.

Brazilian self-identity often differs from another's perception, which significantly impacts affirmative action; this is especially true for those who self-identify darker than someone else's perception. In the 1995 Zumbi survey, interviewers viewed 19 percent of self-identified *pardos* and 2 percent of self-identified *pretos* as white.[24] This impacts the definition and verification of beneficiaries. Should beneficiaries be defined according to self-identity, consistent with the primacy of self-identity, or the view of another person? If affirmative action represents a response to current discrimination, the view of others would be the best proxy for who was most likely to encounter discrimination. Whichever choice would be made would raise the second question: how might the discrepancy between self and other be addressed in the process of verification? A further complication for the discrepancy between self and other is that Brazilians do not consistently identify others. In his important studies of Brazilians in the northeast, Harris found that Brazilians disagreed about the meaning of racial labels and the application of those labels to specific persons, especially for persons viewed to be in intermediate positions between white and black (Harris 1964; Harris 1970).

Two questions in the 2002 Brazilian Social Study (PESB) survey illuminate this phenomenon. First, respondents evaluated eight photos according to census categories. They reached an overwhelming consensus (95 percent) on three photos, which they viewed as white or black, and a strong consensus on four photos, which they predominantly viewed (85 percent) as white or brown. They were sharply divided on one photo: viewed as *pardo* by a large majority (72 percent) and white by a significant minority (25 percent). Members of a verification commission using UNB procedures from 2004-2005 would likely disagree on two or more of these eight.[25] Another PESB question asked respondents to assess the identity of their interviewers. Respondents disagreed about the identity of 23 of 157 interviewers (14.6 percent). Respondents viewed one interviewer as white (nine), black (five), and brown (one): whites viewed her as black, and blacks viewed her as white; virtually all respondents differentiated her from themselves.[26] These data suggest that commissions evaluating candidates would often disagree with candidate self-assessment and among themselves.[27]

Finally, could a candidate's ancestry help resolve uncertainties about identity? A majority of all Brazilians report mixed ancestry, which poses several problems for affirmative action.[28] First, affirmative action seats could be defined for persons of Afro-Brazilian descent, akin to the 1991 census campaign by the black movement to shift identity from color (and appearance) to race (Nobles 2000). Nevertheless, that would pose a problem because many whites could also claim affirmative action seats. Second, descent could be used to verify the identity of candidates for affirmative action, especially in instances of doubt. Nevertheless, many whites could also claim Afro-Brazilian ancestry.[29] Finally, siblings from the same parents can be identified or be viewed distinctly, and their common ancestry can obscure their distinctive identity, as in the opening case of the chapter (Harris 1964, 1970; Telles 2004).

Thus, the complexity of Brazilian identity, including differences in self-identity and the view of others and differences among others about someone's identity, complicate the field for affirmative action. The constitution of appearance and descent make the designation Afro-Brazilian problematic, which paradoxically leaves identity in the realm of appearance and subjective identity. The Brazilian structure of identity contains significant ambiguities, complicating the definition and verification of beneficiaries. Given these data and the dearth of opportunity in Brazil, I hypothesize that identity would be strategically deployed for the purposes of affirmative action. Despite this nuanced societal identity, Brazilians are able to place themselves in census categories, which is consistent with the *grammar* hypothesis that context influences the presentation of identity. The next section examines the influence of identity upon the categorical policies of Brazilian universities.

The Influence of the Grammar of Color on Categorical Policy of Brazilian Colleges

Brazilian racial identity has developed within a complex identity structure that melds race, color, and class as overlapping components of identity. The predominant claim for affirmative action has been to treat *pardos* and *pretos* as a unified beneficiary class, supported by empirical data that have shown a negligible difference in the life outcomes for *pardos* and *pretos* (Silva and Hasenbalg 1992; Hasenbalg and Silva 1998). The other predominant claim has been to create opportunities on the basis of class: targeting either public school students or the poor. Class-based affirmative action has represented either a pragmatic construction of the beneficiary class[30] or an alternative conception of the truly needy. Some have advocated affirmative action for darker Afro-Brazilians; a claim for a beneficiary class based upon color.[31] Studies show that *pretos* are more than twice as likely as *pardos* to report discriminatory experiences.[32] Those data, combined with the hiring preference for lighter over darker browns, could justify a greater preference for *pretos,* if affirmative action is viewed as compensatory for present or past discrimination.

How have Brazilian universities mediated among the competing claims for affirmative action on the basis of race, color, and class and addressed Brazilian racial ambiguity? The early claim that affirmative action could not be implemented because no one would be willing to identify as black has proven false. The other early claim that everyone would wish to be black for the purposes of affirmative action has proven closer to the mark. How have colleges responded to the new subjectivity of higher-education candidates? In a country in which at least 38 percent of whites also have black ancestors, some whites have declared themselves brown for the purpose of university admission (Telles 2004: 92–93). Must verification of candidates violate the principles of social constructedness and the primacy of subjective identity, as some claim? I argue that such a view represents a dogmatic understanding of social constructedness, and that the cost to program legitimacy in not verifying outweighs the cost to verification. I argue that verification does not have to violate the principles of social constructedness and that it can be conducted in a way that maximizes program legitimacy.

Whereas the national debate has demonstrated the political cost of verifying beneficiary identity, I argue that there is also a cost to not verifying identity. Verification curbs the potential awarding of seats to those not intended and also provides needed parameters to candidates about their identity claims. Thus, the legitimacy of the program can be undermined without some verification process.

In this chapter, I propose three principles to animate Brazilian affirmative action policy: (1) to maximize the provision of opportunities to those previously excluded, (2) to maximize the political viability and political legitimacy of the program, and (3) to counter the absorptionist aspects of racial democracy. I argue that maximizing opportunities to those previously excluded is morally just in a country with rampant inequality and will also provide stronger ongoing political support for affirmative action. The broadest conception of the beneficiary class includes three constituencies: (1) Afro-Brazilian public school students, (2) white public school students, and (3) Afro-Brazilian private school students. The inclusion of Afro-Brazilian public school students should be relatively noncontroversial. The inclusion of white public school students is justifiable on several grounds. First, white public school students also deserve opportunities in a highly egalitarian country and their inclusion also increases the political viability of affirmative action. Second, the poor are most likely to self-lighten so that some self-identified poorer whites might be socially viewed as brown (Telles 2004: 96–97). Third, the inclusion of this group minimizes the need for verification of racial identity because an error would result in a white public school student gaining a university seat. Finally, Afro-Brazilian private school students, having faced persistent discrimination, deserve inclusion. Their inclusion would also provide the strongest demand to viably diversify the higher-echelon universities.

Maximizing the political legitimacy of affirmative action entails strategic considerations, such as maximizing potential supporters, minimizing potential opposition, and ensuring that affirmative action be viewed as fair by others. Providing opportunities for the broadest constituency as discussed above will maximize supporters and minimize opposition. The expansion of real opportunities, part of the federal government's current plan, can also maximize supporters and minimize opposition. Rejected university candidates who oppose affirmative action would be affected by the expansion of real opportunities and represent the most crucial sector of the tripartite opposition by providing the ammunition for the greater opposition. University verification of identity can also be conducted in ways to maximize the legitimacy of the program in the eyes of the broader public.

Affirmative action on the basis of race directly counters the absorptionist aspects of racial democracy by providing the first material incentive to identify as black or brown. In so doing, affirmative action also communicates that racial identity can positively affect life chances. I argue that this ideological aspect of affirmative action is critical in the sense that the right to have rights precedes the actual use of any right. Surely affirmative action students need self-esteem to fully engage in a university historically catering to the elite. The succeeding sections examine university practices in designating and verifying the beneficiaries of affirmative action.

Designation of Beneficiaries

The adoption of affirmative action by Brazilian universities has had a historic impact in a country that had denied having racial discrimination until 1996 (Maio and Santos 2005: 181–214). During the ensuing decade, racial discrimination became part of the public discourse, and fifty-one public universities adopted affirmative action.[33] Most of these universities (61 percent) constructed beneficiary classes with multiple constituencies (Machado 2007: 139–160). The universities that targeted a sole constituency were most likely to designate public school students (nine) and indigenous students (five). None of the universities with only one beneficiary group targets Afro-Brazilian students (Machado 2007: 139–160). These data surely indicate the relative political weight of the different beneficiary groups.

Of the multiple claims for affirmative action beneficiaries, I consider the three most relevant for this chapter:[34] (1) race—all browns and blacks, (2) color—the darkest blacks and browns (who are unmistakably black or brown), and (3) class—public school students and the poor. The criterion of color has the dubious virtue of being the politically least viable criterion but potentially offering the greatest challenge to the absorptionist aspect of racial democracy. The use of color narrows the beneficiary class to darker Afro-Brazilians who are more likely to report discrimination and therefore constitute a worthy beneficiary class. Of the three criteria described above, the color criterion would seem to offer the greatest challenge to the absorptionist aspect of racial democracy and the most effective corrective to the whitening bias of the labor market. Nevertheless, the use of color as a criterion for beneficiaries has encountered the most vehement political objections. Prominent black-movement activists were highly critical of the selection process at Universidade Estadual de Mato Grosso do Sul (UEMS) for countering subjective identity.[35]

The criterion of race for the designation of blacks and browns as a unitary beneficiary class enjoys greater political support than the criterion of color. The criterion of race creates real opportunities for Afro-Brazilians, but does not create opportunities for poor whites or differentiate among Afro-Brazilians. It would challenge racial democracy by providing the first material incentive for someone to identify as Afro-Brazilian, but not offer a corrective to the general white or light hiring preference. Also, its opportunities would be more accessible to Afro-Brazilians of greater means.

The criterion of class enjoys the greatest political support in Brazil and provides opportunities to those excluded in the past. Nevertheless, it has three fundamental problems. First, it does not necessarily offer a proportionate share of seats to Afro-Brazilian public school students. Empirical research has suggested that class-based policies cannot remedy Brazilian inequality (Arias, Yamada, and Tejerina 2004: 355–374; Martins 2003). Second, it does not provide opportunities for Afro-Brazilian private school students. Third, this approach does not challenge racial democracy.

The conception of the beneficiary class is strengthened by the use of multiple criteria, the practice at most universities. Race and class have been combined within the beneficiary class in at least four different approaches in Brazil. The first three approaches use separate lists, while the fourth approach awards specific points for racial and class identity, akin to the "Harvard Plan of Action" of 2007, which upholds having a diverse student body as one admission criterion within a unitary process. In Brazil, university admission generally is based upon entrance examinations. Students take a qualifying examination that establishes their overall skill attainment. Those that pass take a second examination that ranks students according to specified skills for their major. Students are admitted to specific departments based upon these examinations. Under the provision of affirmative action, separate lists and examinations generally have been utilized for beneficiary classes, and candidates decide whether to seek admission through the universal system or the affirmative action program. Each of the four approaches treats the three target constituencies distinctly: Afro-Brazilian public school students, white public school students, and Afro-Brazilian private school students.

- *Race and class:* This approach, used by six colleges, combines race and class to provide opportunities to Afro-Brazilian public school students.[36] This approach does not offer opportunities to Afro-Brazilian private school students or white public school students. This approach represents the narrowest conception of the beneficiary class and provides fewer social opportunities to those previously excluded. It will probably not be able to generate much long-term political support. It does have the virtue of identifying a beneficiary class that could be viewed as doubly worthy, thereby reducing the need to verify beneficiaries.

- *Race inside of class:* The current federal proposal for affirmative action sets aside one-half of the seats in the federal universities for public school students. Within the seats for public school students, colleges make proportionate shares available to Afro-Brazilian and indigenous students, reflecting the census demographic data for each state.[37] This approach, the most widely used (fifteen colleges),[38] includes white public school students and represents class-based affirmative action that also offers proportionate representation for Afro-Brazilians. The approach is probably the most political efficacious because it provides opportunities to white public school students while reducing the imperative to verify beneficiary racial identity. Nevertheless, this approach omits Afro-Brazilian private school students. See Figure 6.1 for a graphic display of race-class construction for beneficiaries.

- *Race or class:* This approach, used by seven colleges, creates opportunities for candidates on the basis of their racial or class identity.[39] This approach represents the broadest conception of the beneficiary class, admitting Afro-Brazilian private school students and white public school students, as well as the Afro-Brazilian public school students. Pending its implementation, Afro-Brazilian public school students might have to choose between beneficiary groups or might be able to apply through multiple lists. Nevertheless, this approach has not prioritized opportunities among beneficiaries, and, arguably, Afro-Brazilian public school students deserve priority over other public school students and Afro-Brazilian private school students.

- *Race and class as bonus points:* Finally, race and class can be viewed as supplementary factors. Three Brazilian universities use a Harvard-like system that awards points for race and class that are added to the examination score.[40] The early data from one of these universities, Universidade Estadual de Campinas (UNICAMP), which awards ten points for race and thirty points for class, show that the program has increased Afro-Brazilian and public school presence, but not at a rate that has kept up with the increase in demand.[41] This approach could theoretically provide the most sophisticated approach to the construction of the beneficiary class, by including all three constituencies and by prioritizing

Figure 6.1 Constructing the Beneficiary Class

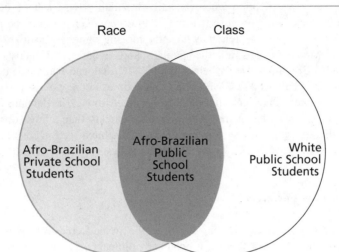

Race   Class

Afro-Brazilian
Private School
Students

Afro-Brazilian
Public
School
Students

White
Public School
Students

Source: Datafolha, August 24, 1996.

Afro-Brazilian public school students over other public school students
and over Afro-Brazilian private school students.

Notwithstanding the public rancor over race-based affirmative action,
class-based affirmative action has been implemented by single-beneficiary
and multiple-beneficiary programs (Machado 2007: 148). This surely reflects
the historical salience of social class in Brazil, the tremendous need of the
poor, as well as the current political balance of forces, including the vociferous opposition to race-based affirmative action.

The construction of the beneficiary class has implications for the imperative to verify identity. The first two approaches combine race and class simultaneously and reduce the imperative to verify identity. Indeed, only one of
twenty-three universities (4 percent) using these approaches verifies identity.[42]
The last two approaches treat race and class separately, which could engender
a greater need to verify identity. Indeed, five of the seven universities (71 percent) that use the broader race or class approach verify identity.[43] For the
higher-demand programs in the public universities, Afro-Brazilian private
school students must be eligible for the affirmative action seats to viably diversify those programs, which creates a mandate for verification. Limiting candidates to Afro-Brazilian public school students will not generate enough demand
for openings at higher-echelon universities.

In addition to supporting the designation of the broadest beneficiary class and the use of verification wherever Afro-Brazilian private school students need to be included, I propose that the various beneficiary groups be prioritized. The bonus-point system may have the ranking right by prioritizing public school Afro-Brazilians first, then public school students, and finally private school Afro-Brazilians. Nevertheless, both UNICAMP and Faculdade de Tecnologia–São Paulo (FATEC-SP) grant three times more points for public school attendance than for racial identity. As noted above, the demand for the Afro-Brazilian seats has increased much more quickly than admissions, suggesting that the weighting system be evaluated. The next section considers the verification of beneficiaries by selected universities.

Verifying Beneficiaries

Verification of racial identity has generated the greatest controversy for affirmative action.[44] Clearly, there are social and political costs for verifying identity and also for not verifying identity. I argue that verification is necessary for the longer-term viability of affirmative action, to maximize the opportunities available to those excluded, and to reduce the absorptionist aspect of racial democracy.

The verification problem is more pronounced at the more competitive universities. A strategic candidate will consider how to improve her chances for admission to a competitive program and whether or not to apply for affirmative action seats. This strategic use of identity was highly evident in the first year of affirmative action at the Universidade do Estado do Rio de Janeiro (UERJ). Apparently, more than a quarter of UERJ applicants changed their identity during the two entrance examinations. Some candidates darkened themselves, changing from white to brown or black, and some lightened themselves, changing from brown or black to white.[45] The group who darkened themselves presumably sought to increase their chances to gain admission to the university. The group who lightened themselves may have decided that they did not wish to, did not need to, or could not justify claiming to be black or brown for the purposes of university admission.[46] For example, one applicant for medical school, Gabriella Fracescutti, considered darkening herself for the purpose of admission, but did not:

> I have friends who are whiter than me and didn't study or do well on the exam, but they wrote down they were [black] on their application and they got in. My grandmother is black. I could have written down that I am black, but I didn't feel right about that. In a country like Brazil, everyone's blood is mixed together.[47]

Such calculations have also been evident at UNB. Karinny, a blond candidate for nutrition studies, decided to seek an affirmative action seat, reasoning that "if others are benefiting, why shouldn't I?"[48] I suggest that what's at stake are not Gabriella and Karinny's decisions, but the overall legitimacy of affirmative action because candidates are highly aware of their competitors' decisions.

The perceived fairness of Brazilian affirmative action is not simply how affirmative action affects the overall provision of opportunities, but also whether affirmative action can be administered fairly. Apparently, many of the admitted affirmative action students were whites who had been counseled by university professors to darken themselves for the purpose of admission.[49] The perception that others are using identity opportunity to gain university admittance destabilizes and delegitimates affirmative action. With the knowledge that other candidates are darkening themselves, other whites will also be tempted to darken themselves. Thus, I argue that a highly competitive admissions process without verification procedures will increase uncertainty and serve to delegitimize affirmative action.

Does social constructedness require the automatic acceptance of subjective identity? If a candidate chose a subjective identity simply for the purpose of university admissions, do the principles of social constructedness require that that be accepted without scrutiny? I argue that such a view represents a dogmatic understanding of social constructedness and does not acknowledge the strategic use of identity or contemporary understandings of the complexity of identity. Although I defend the importance of verification, I recognize that verification of racial identity is a delicate matter that must be conducted based upon the principles of social constructedness and in a way that maximizes program legitimacy in the eyes of ordinary Brazilians.

Any method of verification can yield an assessment that differs from subjective claims. As discussed previously, survey data suggest that the verification will differ from the individual's self-identity in approximately 15 percent to 20 percent of the cases. Data from four universities that have verified identity show differences in self- and other assessment in between 5 percent and 35 percent of the instances (see Table 6.1). Surely, university candidates have more incentive than survey respondents to shape their identity for the purposes of university admission, which would predict these higher rates. This divergence between self and other poses challenges as to whether the rate of disagreement can be minimized and whether the process and the actual assessment can withstand review.

From the comparative arena, colleges verifying identity could employ some of the following methods to verify a candidate's identity: (1) official documents that testify to a candidate's identity; (2) visual examination of the candidate; (3) interviews with candidates about their self-perception, their behavior, their treatment by others, or their prior discriminatory experiences; and (4) the testimony of others, including a candidate's family, neighbors, coworkers, or members of various reference groups about the individual's self-perception, reputation in the community, self-presentation, behavior, discriminatory experiences, and physical appearance.[50]

Table 6.1 Evaluation of Candidates by Four Universities

University	Year	Candidates Evaluated	Candidates Rejected	Percentage Rejected
UEMS	2003	520	76	14
	2004	1,053	191	18
	2005	908	319	35
UNB	2004	4,385	212	4
UFPR	2004	573	127	22
UFMA	2008	1,987	343	17

Sources: UEMS (Universidade Estadual de Mato Grosso do Sul): Maria Jose de Jesus Alves Cordeiro, "Tres anos de efetiva presença de negros e indigenas cotistas nas salas de aula da UEMS: Primeiras analises," in Andre Augusto Brandão (org.), *Cotas Raciais no Brasil: A primeira avaliaçã* (Coleção Políticas da Cor, 2007). UNB (Universidade de Brasília): "Para a UnB, 21 rejeitados agora são negros," *Folha de São Paulo Online,* June 23, 2004, http://www.universiabrasil.net/portada/actualidad/noticia_actualidad.jsp?noticia=70782. UFPR (Universidade de Brasília): Ciméa Barbato Bevilaqua, A implantação do "Plano de Metas de Inclusão Racial e Social" (na Universidade Federal do Paraná, Curitiba, December 2005). UFMA (Universidade Federal do Maranhão): "Coluna Bastidores," *O Imparcial,* February 1, 2008.

In practice, Brazilian colleges have employed a combination of the first three methods, including the evaluation of candidate photos, interviews with the candidates, and the presentation of identity documents. At least two colleges also conducted internal appeals in which rejected candidates generally prevailed. In making their initial determinations, the colleges have emphasized the physical appearance of candidates. In the appeals, colleges have also considered the experiences and perceptions of candidates, their racial consciousness, and their ancestry, among other considerations.

Only six of the fifty-one Brazilian colleges with affirmative action programs verify candidate identity.[51] Currently, four colleges primarily use interviews, one primarily uses photos, and one primarily uses documents to verify identity.[52] Most colleges have adopted other measures to tighten identity in lieu of actual verification, and require other criteria that can be more readily verified (such as public school attendance or family income).[53] This section briefly surveys five of the Brazilian colleges that have verified identity by the type of verification they use.

Photos

Of the three universities that have used photos to verify identity, only one still does: UEMS. The other two, UNB and Maranhão (UFMA), have shifted to interviews to verify identity. At UEMS in 2003, political leaders, university officials, and black-movement activists sought to avoid the trouble with self-identification that had occurred at UERJ. State Representative Pedro Kemp (PT) sponsored the new affirmative action law and argued that the process of implementing affirmative action would be "fragile and susceptible to fraud" if applicants declared their own identity, and black-movement activists advocated for social control.[54] Subsequently, the UEMS vice-chancellor, Leocadia Petry Leme, announced that *pardos* would not be considered *negros* under this law and would not be eligible for the affirmative action openings. She also announced the formation of a commission composed of black students, black professors, and black-movement activists to verify applicant identity.[55] Although the commission considered holding interviews with candidates, it decided instead to require candidates to present a photo. As shown in Table 6.1, the commission rejected 76 (14 percent) of 530 applicants in its first year who did not possess the necessary phenotype. According to a member of the commission who was also the president of the State Council for the Defense of Negro Rights (CEDINE), Naercio Ferreira Fernandes de Souza, the seventy-six lacked the necessary facial characteristics of a negro: "thick lips, flat nose, and frizzy hair."[56] The commission eliminated some lighter Afro-descendent applicants, which de Souza defended, because "society discriminates against the color of the negro. It is not a matter of genes or blood, but physical traces."[57] Dr. Edna Roland, coordinator of the UNESCO program against racial discrimination in Brazil, sharply criticized the UEMS approach for (1) differentiating between negros and Afro-descendents, (2) presuming that all negros had particular physical traces, and (3) excluding lighter Afro-descendents.[58] In subsequent years, the UEMS commission rejected considerably more candidates: 191 (18.1 percent) in 2004 and 319 (35.1 percent) in 2005 (Cordeiro 2007).

UNB was the second college that decided to verify the identity of its affirmative action applicants. Two anthropology professors, Jose Jorge de Carvalho and Rita Laura Segato, proposed that the university adopt affirmative action in response to the discriminatory treatment of Arivaldo Lima Alves, the first black doctoral student in the anthropology department in 1999 (Carvalho 2005: 239–240). Influenced by the UERJ experience and allegations of fraud for admission to the affirmative action program for entrance in the diplomat corps, officials at UNB worried about the problem of fraud.[59] Although UNB considered conducting candidate interviews, the implementation commission decided in favor of photos because of concerns for the efficient handling of student applications.[60] This concern with fraud led UNB to diverge from the original proposal for affirmative action by the two professors, who had recommended that "social consequentialism" could properly constrain candidates.[61] Reflecting the concern with fraud, UNB decided to modify the UEMS system by requiring that UNB take candidate photos (against standardized backgrounds) to prevent the altering of photos.[62]

UNB set a very high standard for rejecting candidates and therefore a very low standard for admitting candidates. If any of the six members of the UNB commission thought a candidate was brown or black, that candidate was admitted. In other words, the UNB commission had to reach unanimity not to admit a candidate. This high standard for rejecting candidates had several consequences. First, this probably contributed to the very low rejection rate at UNB compared to other colleges (see Table 6.2). Second, the commission effectively set the admission bar very close to whiteness, and apparently some whites managed to gain admission to UNB.[63] Third, UNB claimed that the actual impact of the photo requirement significantly exceeded the 4.8 percent rejection rate by deterring others from applying.[64] Fourth, the media closely scrutinized every rejection. The UNB commission classified at least two sets of twins differently, and at least two additional brother-sister combinations differently, each of which became a cause célèbre for the media and the opposition to affirmative action.

UNB permitted rejected candidates to appeal the college's assessment. As indicated by Table 6.2, few (16 percent) of the UNB candidates appealed their rejections. These much lower rejection and appeal rates conform to the view that the low bar for admission resulted in the admission of whites, and that many of the rejected candidates perceived themselves as white.

UFMA was the third university to adopt the use of photos to verify candidate identity, although it would do so for only one year. In 2007, its first year of implementing affirmative action, UFMA established a Validation Commission of three members to review photos. The commission reviewed the photos of all candidates, and invited candidates about whom it had doubts for interviews. In all, the commission validated the identity of about 80 percent of the 925 applicants. According to Fernanda Pinheiro, a member of the commission, the rejected candidates did not show "any trace [of blackness] or any circumstances of disadvantage,"[65] which could represent a standard closer to UNB's.

Table 6.2 Appeals by Rejected Candidates at Two Universities

University	Year	Candidates Rejected	Appeals	Appeals as % of Rejected Candidates	Successful Appeals	Successful Appeals as % of Appeals
UNB	2004	212	334	16.0	21	61.8
UFPR	2004	127	103	81.1	70	68.0

Sources: UNB (Universidade de Brasília): "Para a UnB, 21 rejeitados agora são negros," *Folha de São Paulo Online*, June 23, 2004, http://www.universiabrasil.net/portada/actualidad/noticia_actualidad .jsp?noticia=70782. UFBR (Universidade Federal do Paraná): Ciméa Barbato Bevilaqua, A implantação do "Plano de Metas de Inclusão Racial e Social" na Universidade Federal do Paraná, Curitiba, December 2005.

Documents

One university, the Universidade Estadual de Goiás (UEG), verifies candidate identity by presentation of official documents. The affirmative action program at UEG, initiated in 2004, included seats for Afro-Brazilians, public school students, and indigenous or disabled students, and permitted candidates to apply for one of the quota systems and the universal system simultaneously. All quota candidates are required to provide official documentation: indigenous students must provide a letter from the federal agency for indigenous affairs, the National Foundation of the Indian (FUNAI); public school students need to prove their matriculation through middle school; and Afro-Brazilians need to show "an official public document that confirms the candidate's black identity, such as a birth or marriage certificate."[66] Lacking that, candidates for the Afro-Brazilian seats can submit a declaration of blackness officially registered by a public notary, which apparently cost approximately R$75 in 2006.[67] This last method of documentation appears the most expensive and also the least rigorous.[68]

Interviews

Three universities use interviews to verify candidate identity. The first, the Universidade Federal do Paraná (UFPR), strongly influenced by the UNB plan, developed its affirmative action program in 2004. Nevertheless, instead of requiring that candidates be photographed, the university would conduct a short interview when candidates submitted their applications. To gain admissions through affirmative action, candidates had to be unanimously approved by the commission, a much higher standard than at UNB. Consequently, the UFPR commission questioned the identity of 22 percent of the candidates for the quota seats. Of the 127 rejected candidates, 81 percent appealed, and most of these prevailed. Most of the candidates who appealed viewed themselves as *pardo* and either showed an official document or a photo of their family. Many alleged having a black parent, and some alleged a black grandparent.[69]

In its first year of affirmative action, UFPR enjoyed a significant growth in black candidates and admissions. In subsequent years, the demand for black candidates declined but still remained above the pre–affirmative action level. Marcilene Garcia de Souza, a member of the commission, and Carlos Moreira, Jr., the president of UFPR, both thought that this decline in demand was a response to the commission's rigorous verification process.[70] Thus, the differences in methods—requiring unanimity to admit rather than to reject—and the actual standards moved the line for candidates further toward *pardo* at UFPR than at UNB. The higher rejection and higher appeals rates also suggest that the standard at UFPR was further toward *pardo*.

In 2008, UFMA modified its affirmative action admissions process to call all quota candidates—not just those in doubt—for an interview. Of 3,041 eligible candidates, approximately one thousand did not appear for the interview.[71] Of the 1,987 interviewed, the twenty-five-person Commission of Validation did not accept 343 (17.3 percent), who subsequently competed in the universal system.[72] The 1,644 approved candidates represented just over one-half (54.1 percent) of the qualified candidates.[73] The commission had made its determinations based upon a short interview and classified twins individually, as had UNB. The rejected twin, Ana Caroline, claimed her interview had lasted less than five minutes and consisted of three questions: (1) Why do you want to study Communication? (2) Did you study in public school? (3) Do you understand the [purpose of the] quota system?[74] During the several-month controversy, the university never located its records from her interview.[75] According to the director of the commission, Professor Carlos Benedito Rodrigues da Silva, the purpose of the interview was to evaluate the candidate's perception of her blackness in daily life,[76] including how she views herself socially and how she presents herself to her family, as well as her reasons for choosing the quota option.[77] Ana Caroline was ultimately admitted to UFMA through political pressure.

UNB revised its affirmative action admission policy to verify candidate identity based upon interviews as of January 2008 in response to the ongoing controversies.[78] Candidates viewed the new system as fairer and more difficult to scam. Nevertheless, even under the new system, some candidates reported a "grand mixture of color" among their competitors. Apparently, one candidate was "so white that everyone laughed" when he entered the waiting room, and this candidate was reportedly accepted by the commission. The interviews at UNB were also short and also consisted of three questions: (1) What is your name? (2) Why do you consider yourself black? and (3) Why are you seeking a quota seat?

Discussion

I claim that the interview represents the best verification method to maximize the political and societal legitimacy of affirmative action, maximize the opportunities available to Afro-Brazilians, and diminish the absorptionist aspects of racial democracy. To maximize political and social legitimacy, the verification method needs to recognize the primacy of subjective identity and also the social reality of identity, which entails mediating between self-perception and the perception of others. Thus, candidates must be able to speak during the process of verification, which the use of photos or documents fails to grant. Until 2008, UNB candidates did not get to speak until their appeal, which recognized neither their due process rights nor the primacy of self-identity. Nor does the use of documents recognize the reality of Brazilian identity and past practice in which official documents have been issued without regard for the potential consequences for scarce public goods.[79] Documents and photos best constitute supporting, and not primary, evidence.

On what underlying assumptions about identity might interviews draw? Should interviewers seek to uncover the identity of applicants, on the theory that identity is *waiting* to be found, or seek to explore the identity of applicants in a more open-ended fashion (Saukko 2002)? If the latter, might interviews simulate travel, in the sense that new experiences, at a university or another country, enabled some Afro-Brazilians to see their Brazilian experiences through new eyes? What subjectivity might the colleges seek from affirmative action candidates? I propose that committees develop a short interview that would suffice in the vast majority of cases and a *dialogic* interview available for the more complicated cases.[80]

For the short interview, suitable for the vast majority of candidates, I propose a plural approach that emphasizes subjective color identity, the recognition of societal position, and the perception of others without any element functioning as the litmus test for identity.[81] If someone presented herself as *parda* in her daily life or was clearly perceived as *parda* by others, I claim that would be sufficient. I question an expectation that someone had already come to identify with the black movement[82] or possessed black consciousness, either of which would certainly constitute evidence of her identity, but lacking either should not constitute grounds for elimination.[83] Scholars have proposed tests of "suffering,"[84] "functional" experience,[85] or "consequentialism"[86] that emphasize different conceptions of subaltern societal position. Piper's suffering test (1992) was a litmus test of whether she was "black enough," experiences that lighter Brazilian *pardos* also face. Yang's functional test (2006), an effort to move away from a conception of policing fraud, emphasizes the recognition of discrimination.

Requiring such recognition in Brazil would represent a narrow construction of the beneficiary class since the majority of Afro-Brazilians do not report discriminatory experiences.[87] Tanya Hernandez proposes a consequentialist approach that asks an individual to recognize how her appearance and self-presentation affect her treatment: "When first interacting with others, in what ways does your appearance affect the interaction?" (Hernandez 1998: 168–169). Hernandez's consequentialism overlaps Piper's suffering test in a more open-ended fashion and elicits a broader recognition of racialized experiences than those generally conceived as discriminatory. While all three notions are relevant for Brazil, I suggest that Hernandez's consequentialism would be most pertinent in a country with coded behaviors most aptly described as racial and color etiquette.[88] I argue that this consequentialism would need to be incorporated in an exploratory, rather than accusatory, style to grant primacy to the candidate's subjective identity.

Several questions could elicit subjective color identity and recognition of subaltern positionality. First, how does the candidate identify on a daily basis?

Presumably, she would offer or be asked to provide concrete instances, such as friends, associates, or community members who could validate her identity. UNB has asked several questions that reflect Hernandez's concern with the mutual constitution of identity and experience: (1) Why do you consider yourself black?[89] and (2) How is your life as a black?[90] Second, how do others view (and treat) the candidate on a daily basis? Again, either the candidate would offer, or be asked for, concrete instances. A variation might be "Does anyone outside of your family view you to be _____ [identity given above]?" These questions bring community perception and daily experience into the assessment. Although ancestry is not determinative, I claim that having a black or brown parent matters in Brazil and would propose a third question to elicit parental identity.[91]

Consider how those three questions—daily self-presentation, community perception, and parental racial identity—would play out in the toughest case: *novos pardos* (first-time browns), stimulated by the benefit of access to higher education to identify for the first time as brown. How might a university distinguish between *novos pardos,* who deployed identity simply to maximize their life chances, and those who had actually come to rethink their identity because of the opportunity?[92] The three proposed questions would not seem helpful to make this determination. *Novos pardos* could not viably claim to have presented themselves or to have been perceived as brown. Nor would parental ancestry necessarily differentiate a light brown from a white, although having a black parent has been sufficient in practice to gain admission. Thus, a broader, dialogic approach to identity that draws upon Hernandez's notion of consequentialism seems especially relevant for such cases.

What might this broader dialogic approach to the identity of *novos pardos* entail? A committee would presumably focus on two elements: (1) the nature of the change in identity involving exploring the candidate's considerations triggered by the new opportunity, and (2) the candidate's deeper recognition of the consequences of her appearance in daily life. UNB asks candidates, "Before signing up for the UNB entrance examination, had you ever thought of yourself as *negro*?"[93] That question would not establish whether someone whose new identity was triggered by the possibility of affirmative action had come to genuinely rethink her identity, which I argue is the central question. Interviewers might ask whether she had previously wondered about her identity, and if so, talk about that in an open-ended fashion. Interviewers would seek to elicit the elements of that wondering: her multiple personal and social influences. She might have a sibling who identified as white, another who identified as brown, a darker parent, a lighter parent, and distinct relations with the extended families of both parents, while most likely privileging the extended family of the white parent. She undoubtedly had the experience of being treated as white sometimes and as brown sometimes in social settings, and may have learned to avoid the settings in which she would be treated as brown. Interviewers would seek to draw out her recognition and experience of these diverse influences, opportunities, and treatment by others. Hernandez's consequentialism would be extremely relevant to inquire about her recognition of how her "appearance affected the interaction."[94] The intent would be to locate the substance of her claim to be brown and her recognition of the consequences of her brownness, rather than simply authenticating her Afro-Brazilianness. In addition to eliciting innermost thought, interviewers would explore whether she communicated those thoughts to others. Admittedly, this broader dialogic verification would tread on soft ground, but I argue that to be a necessary space for individual *novos pardos* and to understand the nature of the identity shift from affirmative action, necessary for a new paradigm of identity.

Because of the complexity of individual verification, colleges also seek to impact the macrolevel, the larger market of applicants. Thus, one college with a lower rate of rejecting candidates (UNB) claimed to have deterred other applicants from applying and to have had a greater impact on the macrolevel.[95] At UFMA, the number of candidates who failed to show for interviews tripled the actual rejection rate, suggesting that no-show candidates feared the interviews. The higher initial rejection rate at UFPR, compared to UEMS or UNB, was thought to lower applications in subsequent years, also suggesting a relationship between verification and macrolevel demand.[96] These data suggest that colleges need to be aware that too much deterrence could yield a drop in demand and perhaps also create a backlash among rejected candidates.

The nature of the interview will impact the ability of the verification commissions to make determinations in the difficult cases. Currently, the interviews conducted at UFPR, UNB, and UFMA are short and governed by efficiency, a significant consideration given the large demand for public universities. At UEG, a notary public can issue an official statement of identity for a sizeable fee. Perhaps the process of confirming identity is best conducted outside of the university admissions office so as not to overburden the various universities, provided that the outside entity designated is appropriate for the task. Designated black-movement nongovernmental agencies (NGOs) or an official agency could confirm candidate identity, similar to the certification of candidate eligibility for indigenous affirmative action seats in Brazil. A longer interview conducted separately from the moment of the university entrance examination could allow for a calm, probing interview that could maximize the legitimacy and stability of the process. Based upon the UNB experience, I suggest that the fuller interviews would be necessary for no more than 10 percent of the applicants. These interviews could illuminate a rethinking of Afro-Brazilian identity in Brazil and lead toward a new racial paradigm. That, as I explore in the closing, seems to be the heart of the controversy: can Brazil remain Brazil under a new racial paradigm?

Conclusion

When Brazil's former president Cardoso initially opened the public discussion about affirmative action in 1996, he conceded the existence of racial discrimination, a statement of historical significance, while also insisting that Brazilians would need to find Brazilian solutions to racial discrimination (Maio and Santos 2005: 185). During the ensuing decade, a growing debate emerged about those Brazilian solutions in which opponents continually asserted the impossibility of implementing affirmative action in Brazil because of the nature of Brazilian identity. Initially, they argued that no one would wish to claim to be black, given deep-seated historical stigma, even to gain an opportunity. That argument has proven wrong, and many whites have been willing to claim to be black or brown for the purposes of gaining university admission. The other prominent argument about the impossibility of affirmative action was the converse: that everyone would want an affirmative action seat, and that it would be impossible to determine who was really black. Although that argument has also proven not to be true, it landed closer to the mark.

The first five years of affirmative action have shown that the considerable ambiguities of the Brazilian structure of identity have provided sufficient opportunities for strategic action, and that Brazilians have deployed their identity strategically. Although the opposition has overstated the consequences of the complexities of identity, important questions about identity and public policy warrant further consideration. The black movement's initial effort through the 1991 census campaign to encourage Brazilians to identify on the basis of race and not color has developed a following. Nevertheless, I argue against requiring such racial consciousness on the part of candidates for the university and that black or brown color identity should be sufficient.

Affirmative action surely represents a paradigm shift in Brazil. Affirmative action represents the first material incentive in Brazil to identify as black or brown, an important counterweight to *racial democracy.* Affirmative action is increasing the educational opportunities for blacks, browns, and the poor, which also will create identity shifts. University-educated Afro-Brazilians will most likely be more inclined to self-identify as black.

Further, the nature of the identity shift by *novos pardos,* another consequence of affirmative action, will signal the nature of the paradigm shift. Has the strategic opportunity of entering universities led *novos pardos* to reconsider their identity or to seek personal gain?

I contend that the current moment can only be understood as a collision between past and present identity structures and the discursive ambiguity between fusionist and absorptionist fictions. The provision of targeted opportunities for the historically oppressed, those who were to be absorbed, represents a historically significant counterweight to the societal pressure to be absorbed. These opportunity policies also provide an incentive for anyone in the country

to identify within the dominated group. Consequently, others also seek benefits intended for dominated persons, which contributes to the collision between
past and present identity structures. Winant characterizes this dynamic, the ex-
haustion of an old paradigm prior to the development of a new paradigm of
identity, as a worldwide phenomenon (Winant 2006: 987–988).

How might affirmative action affect Brazil and its structure of identity?
From my thesis about the grammar of identity in Brazil, one could imagine
several possibilities. The first, the specter raised by the opposition and Thomas
Sowell, is that state identity will trump societal identity and that Brazil will become bipolar (Sowell 2004). In a sense, that fear parallels the black movement's hope that affirmative action will yield a new paradigm for identity
based upon an overarching African ancestry.[97] Certainly identities change over
time, but I argue that such change occurs through societal mobilization rather
than a single declaration for a public benefit. State identity would have to matter beyond university admissions for such a change to be plausible. A second
possibility would be that the *grammar of identity* would be able to adapt to the
new circumstance. In that view, Brazilians would continue to treat state identity as something to be declared in specific contexts, such as university admissions. I think that that view would underestimate the nature of the change. I
hypothesize instead that there would be a new synthesis of state and societal
identities, to be shaped from many factors yet to emerge.

New knowledge and methodologies about racial identity will be needed
to perceive this new synthesis of identity. The understanding of race in Brazil
that the opposition has defended so staunchly was developed through an orientalist paradigm that has presumed US race relations as the norm.[98] Seminal
studies showed that Brazil did not have US-style racial dynamics, which said
little analytically about Brazilian dynamics.[99] Perhaps the much-maligned
racial commissions may contribute to a new understanding about identity and
to the production of a new subjectivity: new ways of moving beyond the color
paradigm.[100] Thus far, the majority of the black movement recoils from the
category *moreno* because of its association with whitening. The battle in the
twentieth century centered over the construction of the middle of the color
spectrum, declared *moreno* by Freyre. Might the black movement find a new
way to contest that construction by inventing a new category connoting mixedness and blackness? Could an absorptionist dynamic be transformed into a dynamic that was genuinely fusionist based upon the power of renaming?

One policy goal I posed initially was whether affirmative action policy
counters the absorptionist aspects of racial democracy. Consider that the historical preference for whiter or lighter employees can be expected to continue.
Thus, employers hiring through affirmative action would be expected to hire
the lightest browns available. Ultimately, does opportunity policy in a color
hierarchy need to offer layered benefits, privileging those at the bottom over
those at the middle over those at the top? Would employers need to be expected

to hire the darkest of the equally qualified candidates? Those questions, not yet considered, may be pertinent for Brazil to seek an exit from its racial order.

Notes

The author conducted research for this chapter on a summer research grant from Anna Maria College. The author wishes to thank Jan French and Joyce McNickles for their comments and support with this chapter, and especially Tanya Hernandez, Anani Dzidzienyo, Bernd Reiter, and Yolanda Paschal for their extremely thorough review of a draft of the chapter.

1. Processo N. 2004.34.00.022174-8. 2007. "Fernanda Souza Lopes de Oliveira v. Fundação Universidade de Brasília." 21ª Vara Federal do Distrito Federal, *Revista Consultor Jurídico.* May 31. http://conjur.estadão.com.br.

2. India carefully prescribed the circumstances under which the government might use "forbidden criteria." See Galanter 1984: 215.

3. For a discussion of the role of the census bureaus in the definition of categories see Nobles 2000: 15–17.

4. After a century of declining *pardo* and *preto* identity, small but significant increases in these identities and the emergence of *negro* identity have developed in the past decade. See Racusen 2004: 797.

5. Six universities currently verify the identity of applicants: the Federal University of Brasilia (UNB), the State University of Mato Grosso do Sul (UEMS), the Federal University of Parana (UFPR), the Federal University of Maranhão (UFMA), the State University of Goiás (UEG), and the State University of Ponta Grossa (UEPG).

6. In Brazilian surveys, there is a much higher discordance between respondent- and interviewer-attributed identity than in the United States. On Brazil, see Telles 2004: 89; on the United States, see Smith 1997.

7. Ultima Instancia. 2007. "Irmãos tem mesmo direito de concorrem as cotas para Negros, diz Justica." May 31. http:/ultimainstancia.uol.com.br.

8. Ação Declaratoria com Pedido de Antecipação de Tutela. 2004. Fernanda Souza Lopes de Oliveira v. Fundação Universidade de Brasilia. *Vara de Direito da Circunscrição Especial Judicaria de Brasilia.* July.

9. Although the judge raised questions about the admissions criterion, the admissions requirements clearly stipulated that candidates declare their identity in either the census category of brown or black, declare their belonging to the black race, and have a picture taken that will be evaluated by a UNB commission. In this instance, Fernanda's application was rejected on the second criterion.

10. UNB's recent revision of its admissions procedures to use interviews instead of photos will likely increase the role of subjectivity in the process. See Montegenro 2007.

11. Yvonne Maggie. 2006. "Does Mário de Andrade Live On? Debating the Brazilian Modernist Ideological Repertory." Unpublished paper. *Observa* 22. http://www.observa.ifcs.ufrj.br/bibliografia/artigos_periodicos/MaggieYvonne_macunaima_eng.pdf.

12. On state strategies to manage political minorities, see Horowitz 1985; Young 1994; Thornberry 1991.

13. As of January 2008, fifty-one Brazilian universities had adopted affirmative action admissions policies, according to the monitoring project at the Laboratory of Public Policies (LPP) at the State University of Rio de Janeiro (UERJ). See Antônio

Gois. 2008. "51% das universidades estaduais adotam ações afirmativas." *Folha de São Paulo.* January 8. http://www1.folha.uol.com/br/folha/educção/ult305u361070 .shtml. For the most detailed report, see Machado 2007.

14. Frei David Raimundo dos Santos, among others, has offered this response. See Viviane Barreto. 2003. See also Santos 2006: 7–8.

15. Consider here also the actions of countless building doormen, employment recruiters, realtors, and others. See Schwarcz 2003: 44.

16. Fry and Maggie argue that affirmative action represents the death of *pardos, cabloclos,* and *morenos.* See Fry and Maggie 2007: 279–280. Nancy Leong argues that the use of discrete categories constrains multiracial identity. See Leong (Fall 2006/ Spring 2007): 17.

17. Laura Jenkins and Tseming Yang both warn about fraud doctrine. See Jenkins 2004; Yang 2006.

18. See Telles 2004: 92–93. The work of Pena and Bortolini (2004) suggests a much higher figure—in excess of 50 percent and in excess of 75 percent for three of Brazil's regions.

19. The 1976 PNAD has been extensively discussed by Nelson do Valle Silva and Clovis Moura, among others; see Moura 1988. The 1998 PME study is discussed by Simon Schwartzman; see Schwartzman 1999: 83–96. Harris identified 246 racial terms, which he doubled because of the different possible meanings for each gender in Portuguese; see Harris 1970: 2.

20. Galanter reported between 2,000 and 3,000 castes. See Galanter 1984: 8.

21. Petruccelli notes that 77 of the 143 categories of the PME had only one claimant. See Petruccelli 2006: 6.

22. Scholars have identified numerous systems of deploying identity within Brazil. Sheriff distinguishes three discourses or registers of identity: (1) a descriptive discourse used to describe, rather than classify, others; (2) a pragmatic discourse used to treat others in daily life; and (3) a bipolar discourse on race that distinguishes white and black and anchors the three discourses. See Sheriff 2001. Although Sheriff acknowledges the role of relationality and positionality within the labeling processes, her account does not theorize how relationality and positionality inform the use of the three registers. D'Adesky describes five systems of racial classification, which include the popular (the 136 color identities), the myth of the three founding races (*branco, negro, indio*), the bipolar systems employed by the black movement and allied researchers, and the IBGE. D'Adesky's model is primarily heuristic. See Jacques D'Adesky. "A Ideologia da democracia Racial no Limiar do Anti-Racismo Universalista." *Semiosfera UFRJ.* Ano 5, N.8. http://www.eco.ufrj.br/semiosfra/conteudo_nt_06Dadesky.htm. Telles distinguishes three systems: the popular system, the IBGE, and the black-movement system. See Telles 2004.

23. My secondary analysis of a national survey, the Brazilian Social Study (PESB) of 2002, showed that 98 percent of the fifty-two respondents who could not place themselves in a census category possessed less than high school education. The PESB of 2002 (N = 2365) was conducted by DataUFF, a research center at the Federal University of Fluminese (UFF). Race was one of its four major themes, along with the Brazilian *"jeitinho"* or personalist culture, violence and criminality, and sexuality and reproductive health. See "O Que é o PESB." *DataUFF, UFF.* http://www.uff.br/datauff/Crdssr/ pesb_mod_sexualidade.htm and "Brazil Sample Design." *Stigma in Global Context: Mental Health Study.* Indiana University. http://ww.indiana.edu/_sgcmhs/study%20 design/brazil.htm. Nelson do Valle Silva kindly shared this dataset.

24. Datafolha Instituto de Pesquisa. 1995. 300 Anos de Zumbi. *Os Brasileiros e o Preconceito de Cor, Report,* p. 164.

25. At UNB, under cautious procedures, anyone was admitted under affirmative action if one evaluator of the group of three viewed the person as brown or black. All three evaluators would have to view the person as white for that person not to be admitted. All candidates not admitted were then viewed by the entire group of six evaluators. Anyone viewed as black or brown would be admitted. The rejected candidates were those still unanimously viewed as white.

26. Secondary analysis of the PESB 2002 conducted by the author.

27. The commissions have generally sought to reproduce the *eyes of society* rather than the perspective of trained experts. These survey data about respondent views reflect the eyes of society. There is an important distinction between respondent views of the interviewer (second-person assessment) and of photos (third-person assessment of someone not present).

28. A majority of whites (52 percent) claim African or indigenous descent. Much larger majorities of blacks (75 percent) and browns (80 percent) claim European or indigenous descent. See Telles 2004: 93.

29. It is important to note that this complexity in distinguishing browns from whites does not seemingly apply to distinguishing indigenous persons from whites. Twenty-nine percent of whites and much larger proportions of browns (48 percent) and blacks (44 percent) claim indigenous ancestry. See Telles 2004: 93. Distinguishing indigenous from nonindigenous Brazilians could be analogous to distinguishing white from brown. Nevertheless, indigenous identity is authoritatively established by a document issued by the National Foundation of the Indian (FUNAI) based upon a letter from a tribe. The lack of controversy over this process contrasts markedly with the heated rancor over the so-called racial tribunals.

30. Helio Santos and Antonio Carlos Arruda da Silva, important Brazilian activists, advanced a proposal in the early 1990s for affirmative action for public school students as the most viable and pragmatic way of reaching blacks. Peter Eccles also suggested this approach. See Peter Eccles. 1985. "Blacks, the Law, and Human Rights in Brazil." Unpublished article (Cambridge: Harvard Law School), p. 53. See also Rochetti 2004.

31. This preference has been expressed in several instances: at UEMS and for public sector hiring in the Ministry of Agriculture, see Nascimento, Solano, and Beatriz Velloso 2001. *A Semana,* EPOCA. December 16.

32. I have conducted an unpublished secondary analysis of the 1995 Datafolha Zumbi survey that demonstrates this effect. See Turra et al. 1995; Telles 2004.

33. See Antônio Gois. 2008. "51% das universidades estaduais adtoam ações afirmativas." *Folha de São Paulo.* January 8. http://www1.folha.uol.com/br/folha/educção/ult305u361070.shtml.

34. Claims have also been advanced for indigenous Brazilians and those physically different.

35. See letter from Edna Roland. 2003. *Folha de São Paulo,* Decenber 24.

36. Six colleges use the joint criterion of race and class. For the Universidade do Estado da Bahia (UNEB), the Universidade Federal de Alagoas (UFAL), the Universidade do Estado de Mato Grosso (UNEMAT), and the Universidade Federal de São Paulo (UNIFESP), see Renato Ferreira. Universidade do Estado do Rio de Janeiro, Laboratório de Políticas Públicas, Programa Políticas da Cor na Educação Brasileira Mapa das Ações Afirmativas no Ensino Superior. http://152.92.152.60/web/CDREUNIÃO/SerieDadosDebate/index.htm. For the Universidade Federal da Bahia (UFBA) and the Universidade Federal do Recôncavo da Bahia (UFRB), see Manual do Candidato. http://www.vestibular.ufba.br/manual/Inform_Gerais2008.htm.

37. See article 2 of the Projeto de Lei 3.627/2004. Brazilian Congress. http://www2.camara.gov.br/proposições.

38. Fifteen colleges place the criterion of race within the criterion of class. For the Universidade Estadual de Feira de Santana (UEFS), the Universidade Federal do ABC (UFABC), the Universidade Federal de Juiz de Fora (UFJF), the Universidade Federal do Pará (UFPA), and the Universidade Estadual de Londrina (UEFL), see Machado 2007: 139–160. For the Universidade do Norte-Fluminense (UENF), the Universidade do Estado do Rio de Janeiro (UERJ), the Fundação de Apoio à Escola Técnica do Rio de Janeiro (FAETEC-RJ), the Universidade Estadual de Minas Gerais (UEMG), the Universidade Estadual de Montes Claros (UNIMONTES), the Universidade Federal de Santa Catarina (UFSC), and the Universidade Federal de São Carlos (UFSCar), see Renato Ferreira. Universidade do Estado do Rio de Janeiro, Laboratório de Políticas Públicas, Programa Políticas da Cor na Educação Brasileira Mapa das Ações Afirmativas no Ensino Superior. http://152.92.152.60/web/CDREUNIÃO/SerieDadosDebate/index.htm. See also Centro Federal de Educação Tecnológica da Bahia (CEFET-BA). Edital de Abertura de Inscrição. http://sistemas.cefetba.br/scripts/seleção/2008.2/edital .pdf; Universidade Estadual de Ponta Grossa (UEPG), Comissão Permanente de Seleção Processo Seletivo Seriado 2007. http://www.uepg.br/cps/; and Universidade Federal do Rio Grande do Sul (UFRGS). Manual do Candidato. Vestibular 2008. http://www.vestibular.ufrgs.br/cv2008/manual_cv2008.pdf.

39. Seven colleges use the criterion of race or class: Universidade Estadual de Mato Grosso do Sul (UEMS), Universidade Federal do Maranhão (UFMA), Universidade Federal do Paraná (UFPR), Universidade de Brasília (UNB), Universidade Federal de Santa Maria (UFSM), Centro Universitário de Franca (FACEF), Universidade Estadual de Goiás (UEG). See Renato Ferreira. Universidade do Estado do Rio de Janeiro, Laboratório de Políticas Públicas, Programa Políticas da Cor na Educação Brasileira Mapa das Ações Afirmativas no Ensino Superior. http://152.92.152.60/web/CDREUNIÃO/SerieDadosDebate/index.htm.

40. Three colleges augment a candidate's score with points or a percentage: the Universidade Estadual de Campinas (UNICAMP), the Faculdade de Medicina S.J. do Rio Preto (FAMERP), and the Faculdade de Tecnologia—São Paulo (FATEC-SP). See Renato Ferreira. Universidade do Estado do Rio de Janeiro, Laboratório de Políticas Públicas, Programa Políticas da Cor na Educação Brasileira Mapa das Ações Afirmativas no Ensino Superior. http://152.92.152.60/web/CDREUNIÃO/SerieDadosDebate/index.htm.

41. Kleinke shows that Afro-Brazilian and public school admittances increased during the first two years of affirmative action. Maurício U. Kleinke. "O Vestibular Unicamp e a Inclusão Social: Experiências e Perspectivas." Working paper. http://www .convest.unicamp.br/paais/artigo6.pdf. 10. Nevertheless, university data reveal that the increased demand by Afro-Brazilians and public school students exceeded these increased admissions and that the ratio of candidates to admission became higher for Afro-Brazilians than any other group after affirmative action was implemented. See the "Perfil Socioeconômico dos Candidatos e Ingressantes Vestibular Unicamp." 2003–2007, http://www.convest.unicamp.br/estatisticas/perfil.

42. The State University of Ponta Grossa (UEPG) verifies the identity of its candidates for the Afro-Brazilian public school student seats.

43. Five universities currently verify applicant identity for seats under the broad race or class approach: the Federal University of Brasilia (UNB), the State University of Mato Grosso do Sul (UEMS), the Federal University of Parana (UFPR), the Federal University of Maranhão (UFMA), and the State University of Goiás (UEG).

44. This controversy has not been about verification per se but verification of racial identity. Neither the verification of public school participation, income, nor indigenous status has produced controversy about verification, even though there are equivalent problems. Verification of household income in an economy with a sizeable informal

labor force is virtually impossible. To my knowledge, no one has argued that because of the impossibility of verifying income in Brazil, affirmative action cannot be implemented on the grounds of social class. Nor has anyone denounced indigenous tribes as *racial tribunals* for their procedures in determining whether or not to issue a letter.

45. See "Mais pobres ficam com meno vagas das cotas." *O GLOBO,* August 15, 2003. 27. http://www2.uerj.br/clipping/cotas/cotas_pagina/cotas_pagina_mais_pobres_ oglobo.htm.

46. The strategic use of identity undoubtedly emerged in the first round as well. Thus, some candidates who darkened themselves for the second round may have lightened themselves initially. Further research would be needed to understand the strategic use of identity in Brazil.

47. See Jon Jeter. 2003. "Affirmative Action Debate Forces Brazil to Take Look in the Mirror." *Washington Post,* June 16.

48. "Brazil in Black and White." PBS Wide Angle. Film Transcript. http://www-tc .pbs.org/wnet/wideangle/previous_seasons/shows/brazil2/Brazil_Transcript.pdf, p. 4.

49. A prominent activist, Frei David Raimundo dos Santos, charged that 35 percent of the admitted blacks and browns were actually whites who had darkened themselves for the purpose of admission, and that many were counseled to do so by university professors. "Sistema de cotas apresenta mudancas em relação a 2003." *Folha Dirigida,* October 14, 2003. http://www2.uerj.br/ clipping/cotas.

50. See Ford 1994: 1233. This is also what the Mato Grosso Commission did. Tanya Hernandez (1998) proposes a consequentialist approach that would ask someone to reflect on how her appearance impacted her treatment, and if she shared her ancestry, how that information would affect her treatment. See also comments of David Santos in Barreto 2003; Galanter 1984: 290–297.

51. See Antônio Gois. 2008. "51% das universidades estaduais adotam ações afirmativas," *Folha de São Paulo.* January 8. http://www1.folha.uol.com/br/folha/educção/ ult305u361070.shtml.

52. The four colleges primarily relying on interviews to verify racial identity include Universidade Federal do Paraná (UFPR), Universidade Federal do Maranhão (UFMA), Universidade de Brasília (UNB), and Universidade Estadual de Ponta Grossa (UEPG). To verify the racial identity of candidates, Universidade Estadual de Mato Grosso do Sul (UEMS) and Universidade Estadual de Goiás (UEG) rely primarily on photos and documents, respectively.

53. Universities worry about ambiguity of the *pardo* category (Larissa Meira. 2004. "Rejeitados por unanimidade." Interview with Mauro Rabelo. *Correio Braziliense,* June 1) and include questions to strengthen the likelihood that a *pardo* applicant belongs to the intended beneficiary class. For example, many universities ask candidates whether they pertain to something larger than a census category. UFSM asks whether applicants identify as Afro-Brazilian (*Afro-Brasileiro*), with the explanation that that refers to the IBGE identities of *pardo* and *preto* (Universidade Federal de Santa Maria. *Manual do Candidato, Vestibular 2008,* p. 63. http://w3.ufsm.br/coperves/edital.php?id_ edital=29). UNEMAT asks candidates whether they consider themselves *negro* (of the black race), also linked to IBGE categories, and whether they have suffered discrimination for being black (Universidade Estadual de Mato Grosso. *Manual do Candidato, Vestibular 008/2,* p. 40. http://www.unemat.br/vestibular). UFPR asks whether candidates possess "phenotypical traces characterized in society as pertaining to the black (*negro*) racial group" (UFPR–Universidade Federal do Paraná. *Processo Seletivo 2007/2008. Guia Do Candidato,* p. 20. http://www.nc.ufpr.br/concursos_institucionais/ ufpr/ps2007/center_2007.htm). Finally, some universities warn candidates to be prepared to prove their identity legally (UFSM) or to be aware of the legal consequences of fraud (UNEMAT).

54. See *Projeto de Lei N. 2.605.* January 6, 2003. http://www.pedrokemp.com/br.

55. See "Cota de 20% para negros na UEMS exclui pardos, diz Leocadia." *MS Noticias.* June 2, 2003. http://www.msnoticias.com.br.

56. Correa, Hudson. 2003. "Em MS, Foto diz quem Entra por Cotas para Negros." *Folha Online.* Dec. 15. http://www1.folha.uol.com.br/folha/educação/ult305u14591.shtml

57. Ibid.

58. See letter from Edna Roland. 2003. *Folha de São Paulo,* December 24.

59. Gustavo Moura, a UNB student active in ENEGRESER and the affirmative action planning process, discussed the trouble at the Institute Rio Branco where allegedly 40 percent of the candidates for the affirmative action seats were white. See "Cotas por cor, não por renda," *UNB Agencia,* April 29, 2004; www.unb.br/acs/acsweb/.

60. Author's interview with Timothy Mulholhand, Brasilia, August 17, 2004.

61. See the interview with Professor Jose Jorge de Carvalho, PPCOR, Boletim N. 11, March 11, 2004, www.politicasdacor.net: "Neither I nor Profa. Rita Segato supported the utilization [of photos] . . . because we thought that there are other control mechanisms, less problematic from the standpoint of political repercussion, than this." He suggested that regular meetings of the quota students would exert a "severe moral constraint" upon opportunist candidates, which he thought would be more effective and less problematic politically.

62. Author's interview with Timothy Mulholhand, Brasilia, August 17, 2004.

63. There are many reports of white admissions at UNB. See Erica Montenegro. 2008. "Cota Racial: Aprovadas mudanças na UNB." *Correio Braziliense, Jornal Irohin Clipping.* February 10.

64. Author's interview with Mauro Rabelo, Brasilia, August 17, 2004.

65. Mieko Wada. 2007. "UFMA: Divulgada disputa por vagas." *O Imparcial,* March 21. http://oimparical.site.br.com.

66. Of course, such identification, often prepared by an official who assigned someone's identity, can also violate the primacy of self-identity. See Rafael Guerreiro Osorio. 2003. "O Sistema Classificatório de 'Cor ou Raça' do IBGE." *Texto para Discussão* N. 996. Brasilia. November. For the UEG requirement, see "Processo Seletivo 2008/2." *Universidade Estadual de Goias,* p. 15. http://www.vestibular.ueg.br.

67. Regis, Heber. 2006. "Comunidades: Cotas sem afirmação." *Tribunal do Planalto.* July 22. http://www.tribunadoplanalto.com.br/index.php.

68. Presumably, a notary would be certifying that a candidate declared herself to be black or brown in his presence. Some notaries might require support beyond a verbal declaration.

69. Bevilaqua, Ciméa Barbato. 2005. A implantação do "Plano de Metas de Inclusão Racial e Social" na Universidade Federal do Paraná, Curitiba. December. pp. 17–18.

70. On Marcilene Gacia de Souza, see "Avaliação rigida e procesos diminuem inscrição de negros." *Gazeta de Pov,* September 20, 2005. www.observa.ifcs.urgr.br. On the president, Carlos Moreira, Jr., see "Cai o numero de candidatos cotistas no vestibular da Federal do Parana." *Gazeta de Pov,* September 20, 2005. www.observa.ifcs.urgr.br.

71. The figure was cited differently in two newspaper articles. The figure of 999 was given by Suzana Beckman. 2008. "UFMA não incluira candidata em cotas." *O Imparcial,* February 14. The figure of 1,054 was given by "Columa Bastidores." *O Imparcial,* February 1, 2008.

72. "Columa Bastidores." 2008. *O Imparcial,* February 1.

73. Suzana Beckman. 2008. "Differences Between Equals." *O Imparcial,* February 10.

74. Ibid.

75. Suzana Beckman. 2008 "A Familia vai a justiça, sem advogado." *O Imparcial,* February 15; Carolina Nahuz and Adalberto Junior. 2008. "UFMA reconhece error em sistema de cotas." *O Imparcial,* March 13.

76. Suzana Beckman. 2008. "Differences between equals." *O Imparcial,* February 10; "Comissão at UFMA Admits the Possibility of Human Error." *O Imparcial,* February 12, 2008.

77. "Inscritos na cota para negros são entrevistados," *UFMA Noticias,* January 23, 2008, http://nea.ufma.br/noticias/noticia.php?id=3125.

78. Rodrigo Vizeu. 2008. "Sistema de entrevistas para comprovar condição de Negro para aprovação no sistema de cotas da UnB estreia com criticas." *O Globo,* March 10.

79. Ironically, there appears to have been no controversy in the media about this university verifying identity according to existing documents.

80. For example, Saukko (2002) proposes "agonistic dialogues" that would seek to mediate between the constructions of the *self* presented by individuals, others, and their "social world." As a point of reference, the UNB verification committee was apparently stumped by approximately 10 percent of the applicants in its first year. Author's interview with Timothy Mulholhand, Brasilia, August 17, 2004.

81. UNB included several other questions to elicit life experiences. The first was a question about discrimination: "Were you ever discriminated against?" ("Ação Declaratoria com Pedido de Antecipação de Tutela." 2004. *Fernanda Souza Lopes de Oliveira v. Fundação Universidade de Brasilia; Vara de Direito da Circunscrição Especial Judicaria de Brasilia.* July). That question would seem important to include as long as a positive answer is not required. The second was a question about romantic choices: "Did you ever have a *mulata* girlfriend?" (Junior Darse. 2004. "Concorrencia maior." *Correio Braziliense,* June 23.) This latter question seems questionable especially under the presumptions of *racial democracy.*

82. UNB included several questions that consider the candidate's consciousness as a black, not simply racial identity, but collective identity: "Do you have or have you ever had a connection to the black movement? Do you have connections with the values and with black culture? Did you ever participate in the black movement?" Ney Hayashi da Cruz. 2004. "Alunos são reavaliados pela UNB para ingresso no sistema de cotas." *Folha de São Paulo.* June 6. http://www1.folha.uol.com.br.

83. Consider that many Brazilian black activists developed their racial consciousness in college, which raises strategic and moral questions about expecting that consciousness prior to enrollment.

84. Adrian Piper's lightness subjected her in the United States to a "suffering test," generally conducted by other blacks who presented their experiences of racism to test if she had really suffered enough. See Piper 1992.

85. Yang proposed a "functional test" that emphasizes one's "experience and relationship with racial discrimination" for affirmative action. See Yang 2006.

86. See Hernandez 1998: 168–169.

87. Although there are good reasons to suspect this represents underreporting, approximately 22 percent of Afro-Brazilians report discriminatory experiences. See Datafolha Report 1995.

88. Anani Dzidzienyo (1971) first discussed the significance of Brazilian racial etiquette to maintain racial domination in 1971. Blanco also discusses color etiquette in Blanco 1978.

89. Rodrigo Vizeu. 2008. "Sistema de entrevistas para comprovar condição de Negro para aprovação no sistema de cotas da UnB estreia com criticas." *O Globo,* March 10.

90. "Ação Declaratoria com Pedido de Antecipação de Tutela." Fernanda Souza Lopes de Oliveira v. Fundação Universidade de Brasilia, Vara de Direito da Circunscrição Especial Judicaria de Brasilia. July 2004.

91. Of course, some would argue that this question simply pushes the identity question back one generation, who are also needing verification.

92. This is Yang's concern in seeking a third way between acceptance of subjective identity and traditional fraud doctrine. See Yang 2006.

93. Ney Hayashi da Cruz. 2004. "Alunos são reavaliados pela UNB para ingresso no sistema de cotas." *Folha de São Paulo,* June 6. http://www1.folha.uol.com.br.

94. Committees might develop a listing of probes for discriminatory experiences to further the explorations, such as whether someone had ever been (1) followed in a store, (2) discouraged from shopping or entering a public place, (3) stopped by police while driving or passing through a middle-class neighborhood, (4) rejected summarily and prevented from applying for employment in occupations with white customers. See Racusen 2002, especially pages 174–195.

95. Author's interview with Mauro Rabelo, Brasilia, August 17, 2004.

96. See "Avaliação rigida e procesos diminuem inscrição de negros." *Gazeta de Povo,* September 20, 2005. www.observa.ifcs.urgr.br; "Cai o numero de candiatos cotistas no vestibular da Federal do Parana." *Gazeta de Povo*, September 20, 2005. www.observa.ifcs.urgr.br.

97. Jacques d'Adesky draws the same parallel; see Jacques d'Adesky. "A Ideologia da democracia Racial no Limiar do Anti-Racismo Universalista." *Semiosfera, UFRJ.* Ano 5, N.8. http://www.eco.ufrj.br/semiosfra/conteudo_nt_06Dadesky.htm.

98. Peter Wade makes this point in his treatment of the construction of race in Latin America; see Peter Wade. 1984. *Race and Ethnicity in Latin America.* London: Pluto.

99. For example, Gilberto Freyre showed that Brazil did not resemble the post–World War I United States that he observed. His work was rich descriptively, but did not advance systemic claims about Brazilian practices. (See Skidmore 2002.) Even if his claim were true that Brazil had the "most harmoniously constituted . . . race relations" in the Americas, what would that tell us about Brazil? (See Freyre 1986.) Donald Pierson and his mentor, Robert Park, highly influenced by Freyre's orientalist paradigm, discussed Brazil in paradisiacal terms (Park 1942). Marvin Harris sought to unearth an underlying logic to Brazilian identity based upon his understanding of the mapping of identity in the United States. Although Harris acknowledged Pierson's observation that the usage of terms "varies with individuals in keeping with varying personal relations" and also that the *noise* and ambiguity of Brazilian identity could be functional to the maintenance of the social structure (Harris 1964, 1970), he did not theorize those insights, treating variation as noise rather than information about the relations between persons. He concluded that there was so much noise and ambiguity about the classification of Brazilians that he could not find a general cognitive formula for identity claims. Thus, he concluded that Brazil was not like the United States. "The larger significance of the confusion about racial identity in Bahia is that it clearly precludes systematic discrimination and segregation. In order to prevent the members of a certain group from voting, enrolling in a school, or joining a club, it is absolutely indispensable that there be a reliable means of establishing the identity of those who are to be segregated and discriminated against" (Harris 1970: 28). Carl Degler viewed the "mulatto escape hatch" as the decisive difference between the United States and Brazil, which he viewed from a US perspective. Although he acknowledged ambiguities in the Brazil-US comparison, he marveled about the use of certain linguistic expressions based upon what their use might have represented in the United States without fully analyzing what their use actually meant in Brazil (Degler 1971).

100. Merida Blanco uncovered the social and relational context that had eluded Marvin Harris. From Blanco, one could hypothesize that much of Harris's *noise* from the logic of identity actually represented individual positioning, such as "I am darker than you," or "He is lighter than me," rather than precise positions. The verification commissions face a greater challenge, insofar as Blanco was trying to simply uncover the existing structure of identity, and Brazilian identity is evolving beyond that moment. See Blanco 1978.

7

Opportunities and Challenges for the Afro-Brazilian Movement

Mónica Treviño González

The mid-1990s and early 2000s saw the adoption of a wide range of affirmative action policies for Afro-Brazilians, from both the public and private sectors. These developments are largely the result of decades of Afro-Brazilian mobilization, seeming to represent the political coming of age of this social group. In particular, the establishment of admission quotas in the majority of Brazil's prestigious public universities seems to represent a major opportunity for the entry of Afro-Brazilians into the country's decisionmaking circles.

While this is no simple achievement, the focus of Afro-Brazilian organizations on this particular facet of affirmative action is not without risk. Two of these risks stand out: first, the usefulness of inclusion in higher education for the elimination of racial inequality (presumably the ultimate goal of this program) is not automatic, as the experience of the United States demonstrates. In the same vein, admission quotas do not guarantee equality of opportunity either within the universities or in the labor market.

Second, the emphasis placed on higher education is clearly problematic for the development of a large-scale mass movement, insofar as this goal is entirely out of the question for a large proportion of Afro-Brazilians, who barely have the opportunity to attain a secondary education. The problem here is two-fold: there is the appearance that this is a program mainly aimed at benefiting the already relatively privileged members of the Afro-Brazilian middle classes; more importantly, the objective of this focus for more broad-based equality does not appear to be clearly articulated.

Thus, the Afro-Brazilian movements find themselves in a situation where they need to both defend the program against white elites and their apologists and at the same time explain its purpose to those Afro-Brazilians who are unlikely to immediately benefit from it, to ensure its continuation and expansion.

The purpose of this chapter is to present the state of the debate on affirmative action for Afro-Brazilians as it is represented by the arguments surrounding university admissions quotas in Rio de Janeiro state. I will argue that the opponents of this type of program have successfully couched their resistance in terms of universalist and egalitarian considerations, while it is clear that this resistance is largely based, in fact, on the protection of white privilege. I will further argue that the black-movement organizations' difficulties in countering this discourse stem at least in part from the very strategic choices that allowed them to obtain these policies, namely the taking over by nongovernmental agencies (NGO-ization) of the movement and the privileging of policy over awareness-raising.

The Debate on Affirmative Action in Brazil

The idea of affirmative action in relation to racial inequalities is most closely associated with the civil rights movement in the United States, and it has been part of the discourse on substantive equality for all marginalized groups for at least four decades. Nevertheless, it is an idea that has remained controversial, as it challenges, prima facie, the liberal ideals of the neutrality of the state and of the absolute equality of individuals. Without revisiting in detail the long-standing debate on how to balance the potentially competing principles of equality and justice, suffice it to say that since the mid-twentieth century, the idea that some form of compensatory action to ensure an even playing field has become widely accepted. Hence, it is now relatively common practice to include provisions against the discrimination of marginalized or disadvantaged groups, such as women and disabled persons, in bills of rights, as well as preferential treatment for minorities in public and private employment and education policies. This is not to say that such measures, especially the latter, have received universal acceptance, as evidenced by recent (and successful) court challenges to admissions quotas in universities in the United States.

What Is Affirmative Action?

A brief overview of the changing general meanings of the notion of affirmative action is necessary, given its controversial entry into Brazilian race politics. Initially, affirmative action was defined as an *encouragement* on the part of the state for people in decisionmaking positions to take into consideration, in their decisions on sensitive areas such as access to education and to the labor market, factors that had historically been considered to be irrelevant, such as race, color, gender, and nationality. The purpose of this encouragement was to achieve, in real life, the ideal that educational institutions and places of work reflect the composition of society (Gomes 2003: 26–27).

The concept of affirmative action was then transformed, in the sense that it became associated with the idea of achieving equality of opportunity through the imposition of strict quotas for the access of minority members to specific areas of the labor market and to educational institutions. It was also at this time that affirmative action became linked to the idea of reaching specific statistical goals for the presence of blacks and of women in particular areas of the labor market and in particular educational institutions (Gomes 2003: 27), especially in those where they were historically underrepresented. Currently, affirmative action is defined more generally as

> mandatory and voluntary policies and procedures designed to combat discrimination in the workplace and to rectify the effects of employers' past discriminatory practices. Like antidiscrimination laws, the objective of affirmative action is to make equal opportunity a reality by leveling the playing field. Unlike antidiscrimination laws, which provide remedies to which workers can appeal after they have suffered discrimination, affirmative action policies aim to prevent discrimination from occurring. Affirmative action can prevent discrimination by replacing employment practices that are discriminatory—either by intent or default—with employment practices that safeguard against discrimination. (Reskin 1997 in Heringer 1999: 62)

Although this definition applies primarily to the labor market, a similar argument has been made for access to education, especially for higher education, which in principle provides access not only to better paying employment, but also to the higher echelons of society and decisionmaking positions in the state apparatus. The core concept that makes the introduction of affirmative action an important change in racial policy in Brazil—both for the black movement and for the state—is that it differs from antidiscrimination laws in that it is preemptive as well as remedial. Although affirmative action is intended to provide some level of redress for past discrimination and its continuing effects, it is also meant to ensure that qualified candidates are not excluded merely because of their race. It not only seeks to provide redress for past discrimination and its continuing effects, but also to create the conditions for eliminating racial discrimination in the present. Indeed, affirmative action policies generally include programs to educate society about the marginalized group's history and culture, both through the media and in schools.

In the Brazilian context, the recognition of the existence of racism and racial inequality has only recently started to take root, while the notion that specific policies to remedy that inequality should be put in place is only starting to be discussed. Affirmative action for Afro-Brazilians is generally understood as being synonymous with quotas. Quotas are notoriously problematic—blunt instruments of redress—as they are often seen to provide opportunities for unqualified candidates, with the effect of unfairly favoring members of the targeted group and reducing the general quality of education provided by institutions admitting such unqualified students. In Brazil, as elsewhere, they have caused much confusion and resentment, as will be discussed below. In particular, the recent establishment of admissions quotas in universities has become the focal point of the struggle for the equal inclusion of Afro-descendents in Brazilian society.

Whether this policy is actually the best tool for achieving this goal or not will not be the focus of this discussion. Rather, the debate about its suitability will provide insight into the dynamics of the black movement's strategy, as well as into the state's and the establishment's commitment to eliminating racial inequality in Brazil. Finally, it will allow us to evaluate the extent to which Brazilian society as a whole has been receptive to or affected by the transformation of the official discourse on race relations in Brazil.

Since the implementation of a quota system for the admission of Afro-Brazilians (however defined) to the state-run universities in the state of Rio de Janeiro in 2003, there has been a relatively low level of acceptance of the policy, even among those who actually benefit from it. For instance, in the Universidade do Estado do Rio de Janeiro (UERJ), support for this policy is significantly low. Indeed, since 2004, UERJ has included a question regarding whether such a quota is a positive or negative fact. In 2004, a full 60.6 percent of all candidates who were accepted to UERJ thought this was a negative fact.[1] This proportion increased yearly, except for a hiccup in 2006 when it decreased to 59.8 percent, so that by 2007, 63.5 percent of all newly registered students held this view. This becomes more disturbing when we compare that to the proportion of quota students who disagree with the policy. Although that proportion has decreased slightly over the years, it is still a good third: 36.3 percent in 2004, 33.2 percent in 2005, 29.5 percent in 2006, and 30.4 percent in 2007 (see Table 7.1). The important question here is how to interpret the data. In other words, why is support not overwhelmingly high?

Perhaps the clearest way to appreciate the terms of the debate is to present the objections that have been raised against affirmative action quotas, and the arguments used by the black movement to counter such objections. The objections that have been raised against the adoption of quotas in Brazilian universities in particular can be divided into a few main types, although they are often held simultaneously in various combinations: those that see quotas as a violation of the principle of equality (liberal individualist/universalist ideals); those who argue that the idea of affirmative action is *imported* from the United States and thus not applicable to Brazil, sometimes even labeling the idea as *US imperialism;* those who believe that a racial quota is racist in itself and that it would perpetuate racism; and those that argue that since the problem is essentially one of class combined with the poor quality of the public education system, the real solution is an improvement of that system, with perhaps a temporary quota for graduates of such schools, but not solely black students.

Equality Principle and Constitutionality

In this view, equality is synonymous with strictly equal treatment, not taking into consideration the baggage of unequal starting positions. It has been the

Table 7.1 Societal Perceptions (percentage of respondents)

Question: Would you say that having a quota for black candidates is positive or negative?

	Applicants for Nonquota Seats		Applicants for Quota Seats		All Applicants		
Year	Negative	Positive	Negative	Positive	Negative	Positive	Quota
2004	78	22	36.3	63.7	60.6	39.4	40% black and brown
2005	74.7	25.3	33.2	66.8	61.2	38.8	20% needy black
2006	73.9	26.1	29.5	70.5	59.8	40.2	20% needy black
2007	74.4	25.6	30.4	69.6	63.5	36.5	20% needy black

Source: Universidade do Estado do Rio de Janeiro Vestibular, sociocultural data.

object of intense debate at the theoretical or philosophical level about the meaning of justice, as to whether justice requires that the state should intervene to minimize the inequalities of opportunity caused by *morally irrelevant* factors such as gender, race, or class.[2] In Brazil, the argument is that the constitutional guarantees of the equality of individuals (Article 5) should be interpreted to mean that any difference in treatment to favor any particular group is unconstitutional. Thus, the setting aside of specific quotas for employment or university admissions would violate that principle.

The response to this objection from the black movement is similarly twofold. First, they argue that justice requires that the state compensate for the unequal starting positions among citizens. The line of reasoning is that to fulfill the ideal of equality, unequal treatment is sometimes necessary to compensate for previously existing inequalities.

Second, defenders of affirmative action and of quotas point out that the constitution also contains provisions to give preferential treatment to marginalized groups. Thus, while Article 5 of the 1988 Constitution establishes that "all persons are equal before the law, without any distinction whatsoever," the following articles establish a constitutional precedent for preferential treatment for historically underprivileged groups:

Article 3. The following are fundamental objectives of the federal Republic of Brazil: I. to build a free society based on justice and solidarity; . . . III. to eradicate poverty and marginalization and to reduce social and regional inequalities.

Article 7. The following are rights for rural and urban workers, beyond others aiming to improve their social condition: . . . XX. Protection of the labor market for women, through specific incentives to be established by law.

Article 37 VIII. The law will reserve a percentage of public jobs for disabled persons and will define the criteria of their hiring.

Article 170. The economic order, founded on the valorization of human labor and on free enterprise, is intended to ensure for all a dignified existence, according to the parameters of social justice, observable in the following principles: . . . VII. The reduction of regional and social inequalities . . . IX. Preferential treatment for small enterprises established under Brazilian law and whose headquarters are located in the country. (Gomes 2003: 38–39; my translation)

Thus, the argument in favor of racial quotas is that the principle of equality before the law is not violated, and that preferential treatment is also enshrined in the Constitution.

Furthermore, black-movement activists often argue that Brazil has had measures of positive discrimination for a long time, such as the earlier retirement age for women and the fact that 30 percent of candidates for political parties must be women, as well as quotas for disabled persons in employment and Getúlio Vargas's Law of Two-thirds.[3] None of these measures have been contested on the basis of the principle of equality. The opposition to racial quotas, these activists argue, is simply a reaction of those who benefit from the status quo: "Whites are hiding behind academic titles and claim they are defending universal values. They want to make us believe that, if this helps them to maintain their privileges, it is purely coincidental" (Santos and Medeiros 2001; my translation). More generally, giving preferential treatment to Afro-Brazilians is clearly incompatible with the tenets of racial democracy. The continued adherence of the population to this notion makes quotas for Afro-Brazilians rather more difficult to accept than quotas for women, for instance, particularly by nonelite whites, who, ironically, may feel doubly excluded on the basis of class and race.

This argument is further strengthened, in relation specifically to university admission quotas, by the response of students in reference to the other quota systems in place in the self-same state university system in Rio de Janeiro. Indeed, in addition to quotas for Afro-Brazilians, the state of Rio de Janeiro has quotas for students from the state public secondary school system, as well as for students with disabilities and indigenous students.[4] The level of acceptance for those quotas is significantly higher than for those affecting the admission of Afro-Brazilians (see Table 7.2).

Whereas the maximum level of acceptance for admission quotas for Afro-Brazilian students was a mere 40 percent in 2006, the lowest level of acceptance for quotas for disabled students was 63.9 percent in 2007, and for students from public schools was 53.9 percent in 2004. Clearly, if roughly two-thirds of the students consistently have no issue with the existence of quotas for these

Table 7.2 Students Who View Quotas as Positive (in percentage)

Year	Public School Students	Disabled or Indigenous Students	Afro-Brazilian Students
2004	53.9	74.9	39.4
2005	58.8	66.5	38.8
2006	59.3	66.2	40.2
2007	57.4	63.9	36.5

Source: Universidade do Estado do Rio de Janeiro Vestibular, sociocultural data.

two groups, at the same time as a similar proportion disagrees with quotas for Afro-Brazilians, the issue is not the principle of equal treatment, but rather the application of preferential treatment for Afro-Brazilians.

These results, however limited, do suggest strongly that the issue here is specifically related to the perception of the causes and solutions of racial inequality, both among white) elites and among the intended (Afro-Brazilian) beneficiaries of policies of redress. It becomes clear, therefore, that increasing the social acceptance of university admission quotas for Afro-Brazilians should be one of the primary aims of Afro-Brazilian organizations, regardless of how effective these policies may be in terms of the broader goal of achieving a reduction in racial inequality. This is because the Afro-Brazilian movements have focused on university admissions as the flagship of affirmative action policies. A lack of acceptance of these policies, given their high level of visibility, clearly undermines the potential for political support of affirmative action policies more broadly conceived in the longer term.

Affirmative Action as Un-Brazilian

The idea that affirmative action is somehow *un-Brazilian* is more problematic, and highlights the continued power of the myth of racial democracy. This objection can itself be divided in two different variants: first, that because the incorrect notion that affirmative action was originally implemented in the United States, its use in Brazil would be a symbol of US cultural imperialism, and thus its rejection would be a hallmark of nationalism and patriotism. This first variant is exemplified in Bourdieu and Wacquant's (2002) claim that the ideological neoliberal principles of the United States are being transformed into unproblematized facts and applied ahistorically to other societies, where they are not necessarily pertinent. They specifically discuss what they call the transposition of the US bipolar system of racial classification to Brazil:

> A historical representation, emerging from the fact that US tradition overlays, arbitrarily, a dichotomy between whites and blacks over an infinitely more complex reality, can even be imposed in countries where the legal or practical principles of the . . . division of ethnic differences are completely different and which, like Brazil, were until recently considered to be "counter-examples" to the US model. (Bourdieu and Wacquant 2002: 19)

Although the authors do not posit the rejection of these notions as an act of patriotism, their argument is often used by opponents of affirmative action as a basis for that position. The counterargument most often raised by members of the black movement is, quite simply, that the fact that a good idea is not native does not mean that it is not a good idea.

What is important about Bourdieu and Wacquant's argument is that it also reflects the second variant to this objection: that the complex color spectrum of Brazil cannot be treated in the same way as the color line of the United States. This argument is more compelling, as it, at least, has the appearance of attempting to be culturally specific and grounded in the empirical reality of Brazil's complex and fluid system of racial stratification. It is also one that recurs in the media and in surveys of public opinion. Indeed, in a survey conducted among graduate students at the University of Brasília when a racial quota for admissions was being proposed, this argument was the fifth most frequently cited among those who opposed the measure (Santos 2006: 106).[5]

This objection is clearly grounded in the myth of racial democracy, which argues that hybridity is so widespread in Brazil that it is not always clear who is white and who is of African descent. Thus, it would be impossible to know who should be the beneficiaries of quotas. In addition, given the consensus that there are no objective scientific criteria for racial classification, the preferred mode for determining the racial identity of candidates is self-classification, a system already established for the national census by the Institute of Brazilian Geography and Statistics (IBGE).[6] Nevertheless, opponents of quotas often argue that some people would cheat by identifying themselves as black solely to benefit from the admission quotas.[7]

The response of proponents of quotas is that, even though there is a wide spectrum of physical characteristics, it is still possible to know who is black, since blacks are more likely to be poor, undereducated, underemployed, and the victims of police brutality. The oft-cited quip is that, when in doubt, one should ask a police officer, since they can always tell who they should put in jail; or, indeed, "any doorman in an upscale neighborhood knows whom to allow to use the main elevator, and whom to send to the service elevator" (Petruccelli 2002). The potential for cheating in a system of self-classification, on the other hand, does not worry activists. Indeed, according to them, *blackophobia* is so deeply rooted in Brazilian society that it is unlikely that someone who does not normally self-identify as Afro-Brazilian would do so merely to have access to the quota system (*Folha de São Paulo,* November 14, 2001).

Racial Quotas as Racism

Opponents of racial quotas also argue that such measures are either racist themselves or that they are likely to make their beneficiaries the object of increased racism. One such argument is clearly represented by José Roberto Pinto de Goés, a history professor at the State University of Rio de Janeiro: "The idea of racial quotas is cruel. Choosing which poor people must be saved also means condemning the rest to the usual ignorance and helplessness. . . . How can we choose who is to be saved? The criterion of the quota system is racial, and this is simply abominable" (De Goés 2001). In other words, giving preferential treatment to some because of their race is an act of racism—regardless of the fact that this particular group has been singled out for exclusion for centuries.

The usual response given by black-movement activists in Brazil is twofold: that in Brazilian universities, there is a de facto quota of 95 to 98 percent for whites, and that, therefore, the institution of a quota for black students is simply an attempt to break that near-monopoly.[8]

Another form of the argument of quotas as being racist was made by sociologist Claudio José dos Santos: "The problem is that quotas favor blacks and they end up excluding poor whites who live in the same conditions" (cited in *A Tribuna,* Febuary 17, 2002). This version of the argument reflects the survival of the view that Afro-Brazilians are not discriminated against because of their race, but because of their social class. The black movement's response to this position is to point out that, even at equal levels of education and, perhaps more tellingly, in menial positions that require no schooling whatsoever, blacks earn on average 60 percent of the earnings of their white counterparts.[9] Thus, even among the poor, blacks are more negatively affected by poverty than whites.

The last version of this argument is that those black students who are admitted on the basis of the quota system will be more discriminated against than before, and that this will create a two-tier system of education: qualified white students sharing a classroom with unqualified black students. "By admitting that someone got a place because they are black, the existence of two worlds is consolidated: those who are admitted on merit and those who are admitted on color" (*O Estado de São Paulo,* September 11, 2001). This same view was expressed by 14.7 percent of a group of graduate students at the University of Brasília who opposed the establishment of quotas (Santos 2006: 107). Similarly, an article in Brasília's main newspaper, *Correio Braziliense,* about the federal government's proposal of establishing racial quotas in federal universities, included responses from ordinary people to the question, "Are you in favor of quotas for blacks in universities?" Among these, the answer given by a student at the University of Brasília is telling: "Such protectionism would mean that they are inferior, that they can't be admitted to university on their own" (*Correio Braziliense,* September 5, 2001; my translation).

The response to this objection is again multifaceted. Proponents of the quota system claim that the argument that this measure will further marginalize black students is disingenuous, since it appears to want to protect black students from discrimination, while it may, in fact, reflect a desire to keep them out of university. Indeed, the same interviewees who fear increased stigmatization for students admitted through quotas tend to be the ones who claim that black students are unqualified (Santos 2006: 112–113).

Activists also argue that Brazil's university admissions system measures not the candidate's academic potential but her/his ability to complete an examination, which is geared toward private school graduates.[10] More importantly, they contend that given the opportunity to enroll in university, historically disadvantaged students tend to perform as well as or better than those who do not benefit from quotas.

In particular, Frei David dos Santos, founder of Educafro,[11] frequently cites the fact that his organization has had excellent results from Afro-Brazilian students admitted to the Pontificia Universidade Catolica in Rio de Janeiro through a special program set up between Educafro and this rather prestigious private university. The majority of the students admitted under this scheme have graduated in the top 10 percent of their class. This, he argues, shows that the traditional admissions process discriminates against Afro-Brazilian students, and furthermore it demonstrates that it is not a lack of ability or merit that prevents them from entering higher education.[12]

Quotas for the Poor and Improved Public Education

One last argument that is often presented in opposition to the establishment of racial quotas, particularly in higher education, is that there are few Afro-Brazilians in universities because they are generally poor and therefore they attend the notoriously underperforming public school system. Thus, this line of reasoning goes, a better solution is to improve the system of public education, thereby improving access to universities not only for blacks, but for poor people in general, and avoiding the problems of violating the principle of equality, of determining who is black, and of perpetuating or exacerbating racism. If quotas are required, they should benefit all students who attend public school, and not merely Afro-Brazilian students.

This argument is not entirely without merit, as most activists recognize. The public school system in Brazil is indeed underfunded and of poor quality. Nevertheless, proponents of a system of racial quotas point out that universalist policies in other areas have not improved the inferior social position of Afro-Brazilians, and therefore there is no reason to believe that things would be different in this case. They also claim that a reform of the public school system would require decades to bear fruit, and that the depth of racial inequality in

Brazil is such that the country cannot afford to wait any longer; more importantly, Afro-Brazilians are not prepared to wait any longer.[13] Even back in 1969, during the military dictatorship, the Army Library edited a little-known book, *Brasil Ano 2000: Um futuro sem fantasia,*[14] which concluded that, given their severely underprivileged position in society, "blacks and mulattos might resort to violence, in the next thirty years, in order to become integrated into the industrial society that Brazil will become" (cited in Martins da Silva 2003: 61; my translation).

Finally, they also argue that replacing racial quotas with a universalist policy to benefit the poor in general would be tantamount to propping up the idea that the unequal position of blacks in Brazil is purely the result of class inequalities and not of racism, and thus it would reaffirm the myth of racial democracy.

From this debate, it becomes clear that the two sides remain separated by a deep chasm. This exemplifies the lack of consensus that still exists in Brazil on both the relevance of race as a social and political category and, even when this is reluctantly accepted, about the best way to address this inequality. This raises the question of whether initiatives of the type undertaken by both the federal government and by states like Rio de Janeiro are likely to be long-lasting, since they do not necessarily reflect a social consensus on the issue. It also raises the question of how the adoption of a quota system for university admissions actually took place. I will argue that the decision to establish quotas in the higher education system is the result, once again, of a confluence of factors emanating from the local black movement and the black community of Rio de Janeiro, and from the local state—influenced by the federal government to some extent—with a particular impetus from a transnational context influenced by the Durban conference.

Causes and Effects

I argue that this partial rejection is the result of the strategic choices made by the Afro-Brazilian movements. If we separate the lack of acceptance by elites from that of the intended beneficiaries, we can distinguish two types of problems from the perspective of maintaining affirmative action. First, there is the problem of ensuring that the need for policies of redress specifically for Afro-Brazilians be accepted by the Brazilian public at large, if not necessarily by elites themselves. This would involve a campaign to highlight the contemporary existence and effects of racial discrimination in Brazilian society, and in particular, in regard to the role that public institutions of higher education play in maintaining the marginalized status of Afro-Brazilians.

Second, there is the problem of a lack of acceptance of legitimacy of these policies on the part of the potential (and actual) beneficiaries themselves. Clearly, this is a significant problem, and it is somewhat linked to the first.

Nevertheless, part of the issue here is that it is not necessarily clear what the policy is intended to do for this group, beyond getting them into university. There is a fear that they will be perceived as *second-class* students, that they will carry a stigma for having obtained a spot that they did not *merit*. While these fears are easily set aside, it is clear that efforts in this direction have not been sufficient, given that a full 30 percent, on average, of students admitted through the quota system do not see it as a positive development (see Table 7.1).

Why Focus on Quotas?
A New Organizational Model and a New Agenda

The idea of establishing some form of compensatory public policy to counter the effects of pervasive racism in Brazil is not new in itself. What is worth noting, however, is that this is the first time that they have been put in place, and this is largely the result of a strategic choice on the part of Afro-Brazilian movements.

During the 1980s, with the process of *abertura democratica* in full swing, Brazilian activists of all stripes began to organize in a new way, through non-governmental organizations (NGOs). Indeed, the majority of the organizations that had sprung up in the 1980s and early 1990s were NGOs, professionalized institutions where militancy was a full-time job rather than a voluntary activity.

This process was in large part pioneered by the black women's movement. Indeed, through their interactions with the women's movement more widely conceived, black women's organizations had the opportunity to interact with the state on a number of advisory councils. This, according to one of Brazil's leading black women activists, Edna Roland, was a priceless experience that women were able to take back to black-movement organizations:

> [The appearance of NGOs in the black movement began] mainly in organizations created by women because we had the opportunity to learn with the feminist movement, we had the opportunity to be in the state. It was very important to have the experience of working inside of the state, and to learn things like administration, finance and this kind of stuff, to learn how to create a racial organization.[15]

While *NGO-ization* presented many advantages for the Afro-Brazilian movement, including providing the material resources necessary for full-time activism (and thus circumventing the traditional problems in terms of the demands of daily survival preventing members from participating regularly), as well as the more favorable reception to proposals from such organizations on the part of the state, many members of the movement felt that this represented a distancing from the grassroots population, who could not maintain such high levels of participation. They worried that such professional organizations might not be able to adequately represent the interests of the *povão* (the people, or the masses), since they tended to attract mainly middle-class, professional Afro-Brazilians. Other activists felt that a dependence on foreign funding institutions compromised the ideological integrity of the NGOs.[16]

Nonetheless, NGO-ization became a dominant trend in both the black women's and the Afro-Brazilian movements, both because it solved the problem of a lack of mass mobilization by replacing masses of part-timers with a small, but committed, group of full-time activists and because this new form of organization seemed to be bearing fruit, as will be discussed in more detail below. Furthermore, the NGO status of black women's organizations had allowed them to participate more fully in international networks and events, such as the preparation for the 4th World Conference on Women in Beijing in 1995 and the 2nd Meeting of the Afro-Caribbean and Afro-Latina Women's Network in Costa Rica the same year. These transnational contacts and activities, in turn, provided further space for the participation of Afro-Brazilian women, even while the movement was suffering from internal divisions at the domestic level, as Roland (2000) points out.

The black women's movement, particularly through its participation in the feminist movement, had the opportunity to work with and within the state, and to acquire the organizational know-how needed to create a successful organization.[17] They then brought these experiences back to the *movimento negro* (black movement), thus enabling the latter to create links with the state and transnational advocacy networks.

An important effect of NGO-ization of the Afro-Brazilian movement was a change in the strategy of mobilization and in the demands that were presented to the state. In the early to mid-1980s, the main demand was the inclusion of racial equality as a fundamental principle of the Brazilian Constitution, and the strict criminalization of racial discrimination. Both demands were fulfilled with the inclusion of Article 5 of the Constitution (Brazil's 1988 Constitution; Banco de Dados Políticos das Américas) and complemented by recognition of the persistence of racism in Brazil by then-president José Sarney at the Commemoration of the Centennial of Abolition in 1988. From that moment, the main impetus for the mobilization from the *movimento* was antidiscrimination, highlighting specific instances of discrimination and demanding the implementation of the law. Nevertheless, the adoption of an antidiscrimination law seemed to respond to these demands, at least on paper, and allowed the state to present itself as having fulfilled its obligations on the matter. Clearly, the prosecution of individuals who committed acts of discrimination would be a step in the right direction, but it is equally clear that the systemic discrimination of institutionalized racism would not be eliminated by this law alone.

In this context, the presence of professionalized NGOs allowed some of them "to start to think in terms of public policies, not only in terms of denouncing, marching and protesting, but we started thinking 'we need political policies, public policies, we need answers, we need solutions to the problems.'"[18] Thus, the *movimento* started to discuss the possibility of implementing affirmative action policies for Afro-Brazilians, which soon became the main goals of the movement. In addition to antidiscrimination initiatives, the movement was now demanding specific policies in terms of access to health, education, and employment aimed specifically at improving the opportunities and material conditions of Afro-Brazilians as a group, rather than merely denouncing individual instances of discrimination.

In sum, the reorganization of the movement into a network of NGOs and its participation in international events and communication with like-minded organizations allowed Brazilian activists to become familiar with the processes of articulation and negotiation involved in formulating a common national position. They also became well-versed in using the type of language that would be more favorably received by government officials, and of cultivating sympathetic contacts within the government. Finally, their participation in international events and the international contacts obtained there have contributed to increasing their awareness of the usefulness of international agreements for pressuring signatory states into fulfilling their commitments (Heringer 2003a).[19]

The change in strategy for the black movement, from antidiscrimination and consciousness-raising to affirmative action, signified an important qualitative change. Given the prevailing common sense in Brazil that discrimination was the result of personal prejudice, antidiscrimination campaigns required a generalized change in mentality to achieve their goal; they needed to eradicate racism as an attitude in the Brazilian population. Nevertheless, affirmative action requires that the structures of social policy be changed, but not that the prevailing ideology be modified prior to the change in policy, which therefore suggested a more focused campaign directed at the state, rather than at the whole population. In that sense, adopting a platform for affirmative action constituted a fundamental change by expanding the location of the movement's counterhegemonic action, from ideology to practice.

Countering Rejection

If we look back at the statistics cited at the beginning of this chapter, it is clear that the lack of acceptance of admissions quotas among the general student population primarily reflects the gap between how the public understands the problem of inequality in Brazil and the activists' agenda of decreasing the effects of racism in the distribution of this inequality.

An arguably fundamental limitation of the current model of mobilization is that its adoption has not been without cost. Indeed, although the focus on public policies has had more positive results in terms of concrete actions than more traditional social movements, the movement has remained unable to expand its social base. In fact, combined with the adoption of the NGO model, it may even have reduced the movement's appeal to the masses, who feel alienated from the middle-class image of NGOs. The movement's endorsement of the program of affirmative action, which has so far focused primarily on access to university education, may have entrenched the perception that its concerns are not those of poor, uneducated Afro-Brazilians, for whom access to universities is not a pressing priority.

This issue suggests that the lack of a wide social base remains problematic for the continued sustainability of the new policies. Indeed, the hegemonic position of the ideology of racial democracy may have been challenged, but it still remains the dominant understanding of race relations for the majority of Brazilians. This explains both the resistance that affirmative action policies have encountered among elites and the general population (Heringer 2003b) and the partial disconnect between movement leaders and the broader Afro-Brazilian community. Consequently, the movement should not neglect the task of awareness-raising among Brazilians of all races, including Afro-Brazilians, if it intends to maintain pressure on the state. At its present level, civil society activism cannot, on its own, maintain the momentum for the development and effective implementation of public policies. The continued support and leadership of state actors will be necessary for affirmative action policies to be maintained, let alone expanded.

This suggests that the connection between the movement's leadership and the rank and file, as well as the general Afro-Brazilian population, requires continued attention. For instance, the *movimento*'s emphasis on preferential access to higher education has raised the specter of elitism, since many poor and uneducated Afro-Brazilians feel that such a strategy tends to favor the interests of those Afro-Brazilians who have already achieved a relatively high standard of living and class position, and does not address their own immediate needs. As a result, the movement's potential for increased mobilization could be undermined, were this perception to become generalized, and the leadership may need to reconsider its priorities.

Notes

1. All data referring to UERJ vestibular results are taken from the sociocultural surveys in "Vestibular UERJ" (www.vestibular.uerj.br). The data in Table 7.1 are responses to the question, "In your opinion, the quota of x percent of spaces at state universities in Rio de Janeiro for students who are *negros e pardos* is . . . "

2. See, for instance, Rawls (1999).

3. This law required all businesses to have at least two-thirds Brazilian employees, as opposed to foreign nationals.

4. These two categories have been, somewhat bizarrely, subsumed in a single category since 2005.

5. The four most cited reasons were, in order, (1) that merit should be the only criterion for admission to universities; (2) that being admitted because of a quota would make those black students more likely to be discriminated against; (3) that the absence of black students in the university was due not to racism but to the lack of quality public education; and (4) that quotas were unconstitutional. The first objection can be identified with the basic liberal universalist argument discussed above. The other three will be discussed below.

6. Instituto Brasileiro de Geografia e Estatisticas (Brazilian Institute of Geography and Statistics).

7. This position is also well represented among Brazil's academic elites, notably by Peter Fry and Yvonne Maggie (see, for instance, Fry and Maggie 2004; Maggie and Fry 2004).

8. Amauri Mendes, Rosana Heringer, Carlos A. Medeiros, and Frei David dos Santos, personal communications with the author, Rio de Janeiro, February to June 2002.

9. Miriam Leitão, presentation at the General Assembly meeting of Educafro, Rio de Janeiro, June 16, 2002.

10. Students are admitted to universities by taking a competitive examination.

11. Educafro is an organization that provides special preparatory courses for university admission examinations to Afro-Brazilian and poor students. It has also played an active role in the struggle for the establishment of admissions quotas in state universities, as will be discussed below.

12. Frei David dos Santos, personal interviews with author, Rio de Janeiro, April to June 2002.

13. Amauri Mendes, Rosana Heringer, Carlos A. Medeiros, and Frei David dos Santos, personal communications with the author; Luis Fernando Martins and Ivair dos Santos, personal interviews with the author, Rio de Janeiro and Brasília, February to June 2002.

14. Brazil in the year 2000: A future without fantasy.

15. Edna Roland, personal interview with the author, Brasília, June 2003.

16. Joselina da Silva, personal interview with the author, Rio de Janeiro, June 2004; Joselina da Silva, Rosana Heringer, and Amauri Mendes, personal communications with the author, Rio de Janeiro, February to August 2003.

17. Edna Roland, personal interview with the author, Brasília, June 2003.

18. Edna Roland, personal interview with the author, Brasília, June 2003.

19. Also, Ivair dos Santos, personal interview with the author, Brasília, June 2003; Joselina da Silva, Rosana Heringer, and Amauri Mendes, personal communication with the author, Rio de Janeiro, February to June 2003 and June 2004.

Part 3

The New Politics of Black Power

8

Racialized History and Urban Politics: Black Women's Wisdom in Grassroots Struggles

Keisha-Khan Y. Perry

Late in the afternoon of August 24, 2004, residents from Gamboa de Baixo, a black coastal community in Salvador's city center, armed with whistles, banners, and a megaphone, ambushed the entrance to the state water company, EMBASA, in the Federação neighborhood. Dona Maria, a white-haired black woman in her late fifties, whom some may consider an unlikely voice of neighborhood activism, led the surprise protest. None of the EMBASA employees, including the security guards, had knowledge of the protest before it happened. No one suspected that the group comprising well-dressed, mostly women and children were on their way to a political rally. They stopped at the entrance of EMBASA, and began to shout, *"Queremos àgua!"* (We want water!) Local residents came out of their houses to see what was happening. The then-thirty-year-old activist of the Gamboa de Baixo neighborhood association, Ana Cristina, stepped up to the security guards and demanded to speak immediately with the water company's directors. Gamboa de Baixo residents wanted to discuss the lack of services in their neighborhood. *"Àgua é um direito humano* (Water is a human right!)," one protester exclaimed. Dona Maria waved her water bill in the faces of the security guards and shouted, *"É um absurdo!* (This is absurd!) Why am I receiving water bills if there are no pipes installed in my home?" The security guard informed them that the directors were not available to meet with the residents. At that moment, the Gamboa de Baixo activists, already standing in front of the gates, declared that no one would enter or leave the company's premises until they met with the directors. They were willing to wait.

The security guards immediately got on the phone with administrators who promptly agreed to meet with the leaders of the Gamboa de Baixo neighborhood association. A few minutes later, one of the directors, a white male in his mid-thirties, walked toward the crowd blocking the gate. The rally cries became louder: "*Queremos àgua!*" The director asked to speak with the president of the neighborhood association. Securing her baby on her hip, Luciene shouted back at him, "*Aqui não tem presidente. Só tem morador!*" (Here we don't have a president. We only have residents!) She demanded that he address everyone right there in front of the gates. The man turned his back and walked away claiming that he refused to speak in front of everyone. Back still turned, he shouted, "I can only speak to two people." "But why?" the protesters asked. "There are too many of you and there is no room inside my office," the man replied, now facing Gamboa de Baixo residents. They gave him a brash response: "We are willing to stand. Or we can stand here in front of the gates until tomorrow." After several minutes of exchanges, the protesters and the director finally agreed to an emergency meeting inside the offices of EMBASA that included the participation of ten Gamboa de Baixo residents. The activists also agreed to free the entrance of the company during the meeting, but their verbal exchanges with the security guards continued. One woman accused the security guards of being "*capitões de mato,*" a charged racial slur against the lighter-skinned black men. A legacy of slavery, the expression translates to mean overseers or bounty men in English. She criticized them for being on the side of the white *masters* of EMBASA. The security guards were particularly perturbed when Rita, a heavyset woman in her late twenties, belted out the provocative lyrics from Elsa Soares's hit song: "*a carne mais barata do mercado é a carne negra*" (the cheapest meat on the market is black meat). The crowd joined in and sang almost in unison. Shortly after, they received a phone call from one activist inside the meeting who informed them that the negotiations were going well. One important demand had been met: EMBASA directors signed an agreement to reduce water and sewer fees. The meeting attendees later returned to the rally participants and their cries of support in front of the gates. The directors of EMBASA had agreed to an emergency visit the following week to the Gamboa de Baixo neighborhood where they would personally examine the current conditions of water supply. They also promised to complete the installation of water pipes and sewer systems immediately.

Almost five years have passed since the black women–led organization of Gamboa de Baixo protested in front of EMBASA. Today, at least one-fourth of Gamboa de Baixo residents *still* do not have water pipes or sewer systems installed in their homes. Also, while access to water remains a basic human right that should not be debated in the twenty-first century, many black families in Salvador's *bairros populares* do not have access to clean drinking water. Brazil has some of the largest reserves of the earth's water supply; yet, there continues to exist a great disparity between citizens who lack water in these urban areas and others who have water in abundance (such as in the high-rise buildings located above the Gamboa de Baixo neighborhood that until only two years ago, emptied its waste into a sewer that passed directly through the middle of Gamboa, creating a waterfall of raw sewage that polluted the land as well as the waters of the Bay of All Saints). Gamboa de Baixo's struggle for basic citizenship and human rights such as clean running water raises concerns about the way grassroots organizations in Salvador's poorest black neighborhoods have focused on concrete changes in their material conditions. Moreover, the political experiences of Gamboa de Baixo highlight the direct relationship between urban underdevelopment and the emergence of black women's militancy at the community level in Salvador.

The EMBASA protest reveals one facet of Gamboa de Baixo's ongoing political battle for their neighborhood to be integrated socially and spatially into the rest of the city center. The grassroots movement emerged after residents witnessed the government's displacement of local black communities from the city center during the mid-1990s. As residents remember it, actual fear that they were certain to be the next Pelourinho (Salvador's Historic Center) or Preguiça (now a sculpture park) galvanized the women activists in Gamboa de Baixo to organize against expulsion. The government removed the poor black population from the Historic Center during that neighborhood's restoration process. Preguiça used to be a coastal community located in close proximity to Gamboa de Baixo along the Contorno Avenue and on the shores of the Bay of All Saints. For the purposes of constructing the Museum of Modern Art Sculpture Park on the land, all of the approximately seventy-five families of Preguiça were relocated to a neighborhood in the distant periphery of the city.

As the government advanced in their plans to expel black communities from the city center and the area along the Contorno Avenue, in Gamboa de Baixo "there were women, a dozen or so women, who began to cause alarm, to shout 'look what's happening'" (Valquiria, personal interview, August 2000). From the onset, the grassroots movement found its leadership and support base in the women of Gamboa de Baixo who pushed local resistance against slum clearance and black clearance. This chapter focuses on the competing Bahian histories and local and national identities formed around those histories during processes of urban revitalization and land expulsion. "Who writes the history of the subjugated people?" asks South Asian historian Ranajit Guha (1994: 150). In the Brazilian instance, I ask the question, "Who writes the history of blacks, women, and poor people?" Through an examination of Salvador's recent urban renewal programs, I argue that history is a mechanism of state dominance in Brazilian cities. Nonetheless, history is also a political tool used by subaltern groups, such as black women in urban communities, to fight racial and gender oppression and to claim access to resources, particularly land.

This essay reflects my broader theoretical and ethnographic concerns with why and how black women organize social movements. First, I will summarize briefly the literature on the racial politics of urban spaces and the politicization of black communities in Brazil. Second, I will outline the revitalization of history and the displacement of black communities during recent urbanization processes in Salvador. Third, I will discuss the formation of the Gamboa de Baixo neighborhood movement and its grassroots political challenges to gendered racist and class-based practices of spatial expulsion and relocation. Fourth, highlighting black women activists' narratives of collective memory and ownership, I will continue with a discussion of their proposals for more democratic and participatory urbanization practices in Salvador. Finally, I will conclude with a summary of the broader implications of Salvador's urban renewal practices as a hegemonic writing of history and black women's subaltern interpretation of history for engaging in antiracist and antisexist politics.

Theoretical Considerations: Rethinking Black Resistance in Brazil

This focus on the role of history in black identity politics and resistance in Brazil emerges in part from past studies on race and social movements against racism in this predominantly black country. Recently, a number of Brazilianist scholars (Nascimento 1989; Guimarães 1995; Hanchard 1994; Hasenbalg 1979, 1996; Sheriff 2001; Twine 1998; Winant 1992) have critiqued the canonical work of Gilberto Freyre (1933) and others who maintain that neither blackness as a social category nor racism against blacks exists in Brazil. These Brazilianist scholars have documented institutionalized racial discrimination and oppression in Brazilian society in such areas as education and employment. Their studies produced analyses that call into question the hegemonic ideology of Brazil's racial democracy, a notion central in Freyre's work.

Some scholars (Hanchard 1994; Twine 1998) have sought to understand what they consider is the paucity of effective political mobilization on the part of Afro-Brazilians against racism. France Winddance Twine (1998: 9) claims that Afro-Brazilian movements have been unsuccessful because most Afro-Brazilians tend to reject a bipolar racial model and continue to accept the ideology of racial democracy. According to Twine, commonsense notions of race and race relations among ordinary people undermine the organization of an antiblack racism movement. The racial order, she concludes, is one of absolute white supremacy in which "Afro-Brazilians are noticeably absent from all positions of power" (Twine 1998: 27). While Twine identifies multiple acts of racism in her research, she was surprised to find that Afro-Brazilians fail to recognize aesthetic, semiotic, socioeconomic, and *institutional* forms of racism. The underlying assumption of her study is that the racial "false consciousness" among Afro-Brazilians should be attributed to their "narrowly defined conceptualizations of racism" (Twine 1998: 63). Thus, Twine's central thesis that nonelite Afro-Brazilians' acceptance of the hegemonic ideology of racial democracy explains their participation in, and their lack of resistance to, white supremacist socioeconomic structures.

Diverging from Twine's thesis, Hanchard recognizes that it is not simply the case that Afro-Brazilians accept the racial democracy myth and have racial "false consciousness." Hanchard (1994) observes that black activists, because of their focus on the politics of Afro-Brazilian cultural practices, have been unable to organize a mass political movement aimed at transforming *institutionalized* forms of racial inequality. A process in black activism, culturalism is an approach to Afro-Brazilian resistance that hypervalorizes Afro-Brazilian cultural practices (for example, Candomblé, Samba, and Feijoada) as national cultural symbols, but as removed from "the cultural and political contexts from which they originated" (Hanchard 1994: 21). Black movements in Brazil are unsuccessful at dismantling racial hegemony because these culturalist political practices commodify and reproduce the very cultural tendencies that sustain the Brazilian ideology of racial democracy. Hanchard believes that whites and nonwhites alike utilize the culturalist argument—that Afro-Brazilian culture permeates the fabric of the nation—in contradictory ways that end up supporting racist claims of Brazil as a racial paradise. Folkloric aspects of black culture are suitable for public consumption at all levels of society, but actual black people are not as easily welcomed in those spaces. A national focus on black culture in political movements does not necessarily dismantle racial hegemony, or conceive of notions of citizenship that affect concrete black subjects. In addition, black activists whose political work does make some attempt to shed light on the histories and processes of consciousness that produce Afro-Brazilian culture are overlooked as contributing to the hegemonic values of Brazilian racial democracy that they fight against (Hanchard 1994: 21).

Hanchard and Twine, because they have not explored black women's activism, gender identity politics, and grassroots organizing, fail to recognize the existence and central role of community-based movements in black identity politics. Foregrounding the political identity of black women in Gamboa de Baixo illustrates the ways in which grassroots organizations have advanced the racial, gender, and class interests of entire black communities. My approach is similar to that of black Brazilian feminist activist and scholar Luiza Bairros (1996: 184), who suggests that scholars of black politics must include in their analyses social movements that have significant women and black participation (for example, domestic workers' unions and neighborhood associations). Despite the claims of other scholars (Hanchard 1994; Twine 1998), the race question is very apparent in these movements. Though the scholarship in the United States has yet to recognize the central role of black women's political participation, according to many Brazilian scholars, black women have *always* organized through these grassroots political networks, oftentimes as leaders, to address the everyday concerns of their material existence (Bento 1995, 2000; Carneiro 1999; Santos 1999; Silva 1999).

Racial consciousness in the Gamboa de Baixo community movement is the unquestionable result of the central role of black women's activism. Another black Brazilian feminist scholar and activist, Sueli Carneiro, asks: "why did black women reach the conclusion that they had to organize themselves politically in order to face the triple discrimination as women, poor people, and blacks?" (Carneiro 2000: 27). Black women in Brazilian social movements recognize the salience of not only racial and gender inequality, but also of class-based struggles over material resources in their urban communities. In partial contrast to cultural practice–oriented politics, black women activists in Gamboa de Baixo focus on issues of basic survival for black communities. As the primary basic food producers, they perceive housing and land as a vital material resource for the survival of their families. Through community networks, they expand their grassroots political organization to mobilize against the racist practices of urban renewal.

The Gendered Racialization of Urban Space

An ethnographic analysis of black women's activism against urban renewal in Salvador illustrates the racial politics of urban spaces, collective gender resistance, and racial solidarity. Scholars of urban politics in Brazil have focused primarily on class constructions of urban spaces, while silencing meanings of gendered blackness embedded in discourses around land and spatial location (Caldeira 2000; Holston 1991; Meade 1997; Rolnik 1994; Zaluar 1994). Nevertheless, as Thomas Sugrue (1996: 229) argues, urban space is "a metaphor for perceived racial difference." Urban spaces, created by local acts of slum clearance and forced segregation, are the marked spatial manifestations of racial, gender, and class marginality (Davis 2006; Lovell 1999). Urban revitalization is a racial project, which in the city center of Salvador is a prime example of the discursive and material effects of institutional racism and sexism in Brazilian society.[1] This analysis exposes the hegemonic ideology of racial democracy in Brazil, contributing to recent scholarship on race and the formation of antiracism social movements in that predominantly black country.

Moreover, traditionally, the urban cultural studies "culture of poverty" literature has represented black urban life in the United States and Brazil as masculine, socially pathological, and politically bankrupt (Amar 2003; Gregory 1998; Kelley 1997; Oliveira 1997; Wright 1997). Maxine Baca Zinn (1989), Patricia Hill Collins (1989), Mary Castro (1996), and numerous others have critiqued this social science treatment of black women as villains responsible for the growing self-perpetuating underclass and the deterioration in the African-American and Afro-Brazilian family. The culture-of-poverty approach underemphasizes systemic structural material inequality, racism, and the feminization of poverty as factors in perpetuating pervasive socioeconomic inequality in black communities (Cohen and Dawson 1993; Roberts 1997). My analysis of Gamboa de Baixo undermines this approach by providing an understanding of the gendered aspects of racial and class inequality in urban spaces, while offering insights into the development of the black public sphere and the formation of political organizations within it to combat racism in Afro-Brazilian communities.

Black women activists in Gamboa de Baixo and elsewhere, leading family and community networks, make race-based demands for greater social and economic rights, political recognition, and participation in urban spaces (Cohen, Jones, and Tronto 1997). This approach to grassroots organizing allows us to understand these women's politics as a challenge to racial and gender inequality throughout the African diaspora. Black urban struggle is not only for material survival and subsistence (Kelley 1997; Sanjek 1998); it is a form of black oppositional politics against racism and sexism and for social transformation. I contribute to and expand representations of black urban communities as units in political networks, highlighting the ways in which black women make racial claims for equal access to various institutions of power. In Gamboa de Baixo, their activism forces us to acknowledge the existence of black grassroots antiracism struggles often denied in the literature on race in Brazil. My focus on black women's leadership in community organizations also undermines the notion of men as natural leaders of political movements (Collins 1990; Sudbury 1998; Smith 2000).

Furthermore, black feminist theorists emphasize questions concerning the source of black women's politics and their central role in black liberation movements. Though few have centered their studies on black women's grassroots organizations (Hunter 1998; Ransby 2005; Sudbury 1998), many scholars affirm the idea of black feminist politics as integral to antiracism movements. Black Brazilian feminist theory produced by scholars such as Luiza Bairros (1991), Sueli Carneiro (1995, 1999), Lélia Gonzalez (1985), and Jurema Werneck (2007) draws this link between antiracism mobilization and gender liberation. This recognizes the crucial role of women's leadership in black social movements—what Kia Lilly Caldwell (2000: 6) identifies as "the gendered aspects of racial domination and the racial aspects of gender domination" in Brazilian society. My research highlights the socioeconomic impact of gendered racism in Brazil, but also provides key insights into black women's participation in antiracism grassroots movements. This ethnography contributes to the virtual invisibility of black-centered research in Latin American studies and to the lacuna of literature on the political organization of blacks, particularly black women, in the region.

Black women's leadership in urban struggles over land constitutes a crucial aspect of Afro-Brazilian mobilization against racism and for collective access to resources. James Holston's study (1991: 696) of land usurpation in São Paulo's urban periphery supports the notion of land as a tool used strategically by urban groups to promote political unity. Holston argues that land rights for the urban poor are entrenched in the historical foundations of colonialism in which economic elites have maintained legal and extralegal privilege to land acquisition. Recently, grassroots social movements against this form of "local hegemony" expand "the idea of a right to legal rights" within the Brazilian legal system (Holston 1991: 722). Though lacking a racial analysis of resistance within the public domain of rights, primarily property rights, Holston's work reminds us of the historical relationship between colonialism and racism and present-day land claims for urban blacks. Furthermore, this discussion of land disputes, political cohesion, and resistance exemplifies a fundamental strategy in the black urban communities' fight for power, justice, and greater access to material resources. Black political organization against land expulsion in Salvador tells the story of a broader historical struggle for space and place within economically and racially ordered cities.

Holston also defends the need for serious consideration of colonialism in studies on land conflicts in urban Brazil. Similar studies have explored the influence of colonialism but others have linked more centrally this historical process to systems of racial oppression and the emergence of urban struggles. George Reid Andrews (1991a) and Kim Butler (1998) identify colonialism as the core of racist ideologies and social stratification in Brazilian cities, including racial segregation and economic and racialized hierarchies. As Butler writes, urban black struggles against discrimination in Salvador and São Paulo have emerged "to dismantle discrimination against people of African descent" (Butler 1998: 18). One of Afro-Brazilians' most significant political successes has been the prevention of legalized segregation (Butler 1998: 128). Racial discrimination is historically entrenched in all aspects of urban spaces and has motivated urban blacks to mobilize. Nevertheless, their collective and individual activism is a further assertion of "their humanity and right to full and equal participation" (Butler 1998: 3) within the local and national citizenship community. Urban communities have reinvented notions of citizenship that fuel mass-based movements led by blacks. Neighborhood activists in Salvador employ the discourse of rights and claims to resources in organized responses to spatially determined racial hegemony.

The Revitalization of History in Salvador

In Bahian tourism politics, both the city center and all areas along the shore of the Baía de Todos os Santos are strategically important for the development of leisure and cultural sites. Salvador has sponsored a series of projects intended to recuperate, restore, and revitalize the environment of the urban center. Founded in 1549, the city was Brazil's first capital and still holds some of the country's most historically significant monuments and buildings. In 1984, the Brazilian government declared Salvador's Historic Center, the Pelourinho (whipping post), a part of national patrimony, and in 1985, UNESCO added the Historic Center to its list of world heritage sites. Since the 1990s, the city has spent millions of dollars on revitalization projects, such as the restoration of historic buildings, fountains, and squares in the Pelourinho. In the process, the state has relocated the so-called dangerous and criminal local black population to other neighborhoods throughout the city's periphery. It has transformed the homes they previously inhabited into museums, restaurants, hotels, performance stages, and shops to serve the flourishing tourism industry.[2]

The revitalization of Gamboa de Baixo, another poor black neighborhood in the city center, constitutes a vital aspect of subsequent stages of Salvador's urban renewal program. The public image of Gamboa de Baixo is one of danger, misery, and marginality, as illustrated by police reports and local media; yet, the locale existing below the Contorno Avenue provides the ideal site for the construction of new urban spaces in Salvador. The government of Bahia began to pay special attention to the neighborhood chiefly because this predominantly black and working-class community occupies some of the most valuable land in the center of Salvador. Nevertheless, before there was an urban revitalization program for the area, there was a Gamboa de Baixo where people have lived and worked for many generations. Formerly known as the Gamboa Port or Porto das Vacas, Gamboa is a century-old fishing colony whose residents claim it began in Salvador's early colonial history.

On the shores of Gamboa de Baixo lies the São Paulo da Gamboa Fort (built in 1722 and declared a national heritage site in 1937). Some residents of the neighborhood still live inside its ruins. The Bahian Navy used the base exclusively during the eighteenth century for military reinforcement and protection of the city (Rebouças and Filho 1985). The Navy abandoned the São Paulo Fort and the surrounding area around the end of the nineteenth century. Nevertheless, during the mid-1990s, the Bahian Navy reclaimed ownership of the fort as public land, declaring that the fort was an aspect of the city's history in need of immediate revitalization for historical preservation. As in the case of the Pelourinho, the people of Gamboa de Baixo do not fit into the government's plans for the area.

The memory of a powerful capital of Portuguese America, specifically the history of economic, military, and economic might, drives the recent restoration of the forts of Salvador. The forts of Salvador were constructed to protect one of the most important financial and cultural centers in Brazil's history and the symbol of Portuguese expansion in the Americas. For instance, the São Marcelo Fort, built more than 350 years ago in the middle of the ocean near Salvador's commercial district and Historic Center, was restored during the late 1990s. Antônio Imbassahy, the mayor of Salvador at the time of its restoration, had the following comments on this:

> What more can one say, besides our certainty of completing our duty, of our commitment that we have with our history and with our future. In a city like

Salvador, where new and old mix with such harmony, such that the races form an ethnicity and that peculiar personality of being Bahian. . . . We share with everyone, Bahians, Brazilians and citizens of the world, more happiness, to see our São Marcelo Fort restored, joining the Mercado Modelo and the Elevador Lacerda, one of our well-known postcards. (Imbassahy 2000: 4)[3]

A civic duty that shows the government's commitment to the preservation of Bahian and Brazilian history, the restoration of forts in Salvador also creates new spaces for tourists to enjoy. As Imbassahy's statement shows, this image of Bahia, living in harmony with the old and new, the colonial and the modern, stems from the idea of racial mixture and harmony in Bahia. Nevertheless, Imbassahy fails to mention the violence involved in the acquisition of the land on which the forts were built or the forced enslavement of Africans and indigenous peoples whose labor created these present-day monuments.

The restoration of the São Marcelo and São Paulo da Gamboa forts is part of a broader municipal government initiative called Via Naútica, which will be developed along the coastal zone of the city during the next few years. Beginning from the Ponta de Humaitá, the project proposes to create a maritime tour through the Baía de Todos os Santos, linking various historical sites to include the restored forts, the Museum of Modern Art, the Historic Center, and the famous former slave-marketplace, the Mercado Modelo. In each fort, including the São Marcelo and São Paulo da Gamboa forts, there will be museums that tourists can visit. In the case of Gamboa de Baixo, the infamous cannon that fired one shot during the visit of Princesa Isabel will be on display. Other restored forts in Barra and Monte Serrat already have similar museum tours. The restoration of the São Paulo da Gamboa Fort poses a problem because of the population that inhabits the area and the local community's resistance to relocation during and after the restoration process.

This situation in Salvador characterizes global urban reconstruction practices throughout almost all Brazilian cities as well as in cities such as New York and Paris. A modernist vision of the city tends to include the aesthetic revival of "ugly, dirty, and mistreated" historical sites into "clean, pure, and distinct" remnants of the past. History becomes a viable product for public consumption in modern cities (Lacarrieu 2000: ii). The underlying logic is that appropriating these urban spaces gives new *hygienic* meanings to the past, representing the city as healthier, less dangerous, and *mais gostosa* (more desirable) for those living in it (Lacarrieu 2000: iii). Revalorizing the past translates into urban nostalgic desire in the local and national imaginary; that is, reconstructing the essential *good old days* as a means to rescue the identity of the city of Salvador—the city that generated the nation of Brazil, the culture of Brazil. From this perspective, the northeastern city of Salvador is an ideal site for the revitalization of history. The municipal secretary of Planning, Science, and Technology wrote the following:

The vision of tourism for Salvador is centered on leisure tourism with the extraordinary content of culture and history, involving beaches, ecology, festivals, music, and an exceptional architectonic patrimony. . . . Having been the first capital of Brazil and center of the beginning of Portuguese colonization, with their political and economic displays, and more markedly, the sedimentation of the slave regime, Salvador develops the richest historic and cultural values *sui generis* of the country, that are preserved in the form of an exceptional physical patrimony and customs. (1996: 28)

The government of Bahia wants to recapture local and national history in Salvador to boost the tourism industry, including significant investments in sites such as the Pelourinho and the São Paulo Fort. Once considered dangerous, the Pelourinho, for example, is now one of Brazil's best examples of a revived neighborhood. More importantly it is a renewed space in the national identity. The revitalization of the center of Salvador means "rescuing the identity of the city of Salvador—the city which generated the nation of Brazil, the culture of Brazil" (Institute of Artistic and Cultural Patrimony quoted in Dunn 1994: 2).

As renowned Afro-Brazilian geographer Milton Santos (1996) posits, urban memory is compromised by the valorization of a political economy that privileges the market value of property such as old mansions formally occupied by a white colonial elite. This reinvention of colonial history displaces recent urban memory of local residents, oftentimes poor black people who inhabit and use the deteriorating old buildings. The restoration of the urban center is driven only by the *symbolic* valorization and preservation of the historical product distinct from present-day reality, *erasing* the memory of slavery and racial and gender violence (for example the violence associated with the *pelourinho* [whipping post] of the Historic Center). The modernizing project, Santos also asserts, involves the deliberate social abandonment by the city government, the subsequent deterioration of the historic buildings, followed by the forced displacement of local residents during and after renovations.[4]

Nevertheless, as Michel-Rolph Trouillot (1995: 146) states, "the value of the historical product cannot be debated without taking into account both the context of its production and the context of its consumption." Urban development around the celebration of a colonial heritage excludes descendents of enslaved Africans whose labor, traditions, and customs constitute essential elements of that colonial past. Development in Bahia represents the renewal of a colonial past for both the *colonialist visitor* and the *colonized host,* reflecting the physical and spatial forms of racial and gender oppression. For example, Olodum is one of Bahia's most celebrated Afrocentric cultural organizations that moved its central offices to the Historic Center in 1990. Organized by black artists, the group creates music, dance performances, and clothing that celebrate pride in Africa and its diaspora. Even today, black cultural artifacts, such as those of Olodum, are the primary products that merchants market to tourists who visit the Historic Center. Another example is the way black people participate in this urban economy of tourism and leisure as living artifacts or representations of the colonial past. The tourism industry sells black men's and women's bodies and sexuality, creating what some scholars have identified as a production of an "Afro-Disney" in Brazil (Nascimento 1994). Examples include preparing and serving traditional Afro-Bahian food and performing Afro-Brazilian sensual dances for white audiences, and with increasing frequency, black audiences (Pinho 2008).

The Formation of the Neighborhood Movement

In this context, the Gamboa de Baixo neighborhood association, Associação Amigos de Gegê dos Moradores da Gamboa de Baixo, was founded on October 7, 1992. This organization was a direct outcome of the previous Associação de Mulheres (Women's Association), which mobilized local women during the 1980s to demand social services such as prenatal care and milk vouchers and to plan cultural events that included Mother's and Children's Day celebrations. During the 1992 outbreak of cholera in Bahia, which caused several deaths in Gamboa de Baixo alone, a few women established the neighborhood association to institute collective governance and legal representation for the community in their demands for vital resources such as clean running water and improved sewer systems. Cholera victims included the first president's father, Gegê, after whom the organization was named. The neighborhood association in Gamboa de Baixo began around issues of life and death survival.[5] The association also struggled to deconstruct the public image of Gamboa de Baixo as a spatial container of cholera. In general, the media portrayed black urban and rural communities throughout Bahia as being the loci of the disease, which presented a health threat to the nearby affluent neighborhoods, such as Vitória and Campo Grande. During frequent visits to local newspapers and radio stations, the main goal of the neighborhood association was to improve their material conditions as well as to dispel public representations of their community as unhealthy, unsafe, and dangerous to the public. An important act of contestation was their demand for the state to test the natural water sources and the public water pipes in their neighborhood. Testing proved that the victims of cholera had died from contaminated water provided by the city and not from the neighborhood's natural water fountains.

Direct action protest has proven to be the most effective tactic of political struggle for Gamboa de Baixo community activists. At public meetings and street protests, they have engaged in confrontational politics with city officials. One important strategy for activism has been the closing of the major avenue that passes above the community, the Contorno Avenue. For example, after unsuccessful requests for the water company to complete the installation of running water and sewer systems and for the Bahian development agency to repair poorly constructed homes in the neighborhood, they blocked traffic for several hours during the morning rush hour. In other instances, they have protested in front of the agencies themselves. The Contorno Avenue as a site of public protest is significant, because it divides the Gamboa neighborhood between poor and working-class Gamboa de Baixo (Lower Gamboa) and middle-class Gamboa de Cima (Upper Gamboa).

This spatial separation has upheld and reinforced hierarchies of racial, social, and economic differences between the two neighborhoods. The construction of the Contorno Avenue in 1961 constrained the previously unrestricted movement of ideas, labor, and goods. Only in the mid-1990s, as a result of organized struggle, did the government construct a concrete staircase that provided access from Gamboa de Baixo to the rest of the city. Most residents still remember the difficulty of climbing the shaky wooden stairs to reach the Contorno Avenue. For many years, infrastructural changes within the city separated and isolated them as *those below.* As a Gamboa de Baixo neighborhood association document from 1996 states:

> This is not the first time that the government intervenes in our area, always with disastrous consequences for the local communities. In the 1970s, the construction of the Contorno Avenue brought a series of damages to our communities, standing out among them, the barring of access to the community Unhão, with the closing of the road Castelo Branco, that has its opening at the present-day Radio Bahia, in Gamboa de Cima, and that continues along the upper part of the community near the arcs. This action restricted our access to a rustic route of stone and clay that begins right after the entrance of Solar do Unhão and that, due to its precariousness, caused our relative isolation and the entrance of some *marginais* (criminals), turning the area into a poorly viewed neighborhood discriminated against by the rest of the city's inhabitants.

Former activist Elena, who has always lived *below the Avenue,* points out that some women work as domestics in Gamboa de Cima and nearby neighborhoods such as Vitória that literally look down on their homes in Gamboa de Baixo. Nearly 80 percent of females (including adults and adolescents) in Gamboa de Baixo are domestic workers. Even today, identifying Gamboa de Baixo as your place of residence might prevent you from getting a job, since, as Elena claims, some employers "still think we're all thieves" (personal communication 2001). Sentiments of inferiority and superiority have run deep since the Contorno Avenue separation of the Gamboa neighborhoods, demonstrating that the construction project had more than symbolic significance. In stark difference from the flourishing city center above the Avenue, the public relegates the community literally living *below the asphalt* to a cluster of undesirables who linger behind in both space and time.

The Gamboa de Baixo protests on the Contorno Avenue transform the ways in which we conceptualize black mobilization and resistance, particularly our understanding of black antiracism and antisexism struggles in Brazil. Getting things done for poor black women in Gamboa de Baixo has meant that, when necessary, they must collectively *get in the face* of the powerful and demystify their power and control. This political approach is unlike the culturalist tendencies that Michael Hanchard argues are the definitive characteristics of black activism in Brazil. He writes that there exists "no Afro-Brazilian versions of boycotting, sit-ins, civil disobedience, and armed struggle in its stead" (Hanchard 1994: 139). Moreover, he observes that black activists, because of their focus on the politics of Afro-Brazilian cultural practices, have been unable to organize a mass political movement aimed at transforming *institutionalized* forms of racial inequality. My research on black neighborhood struggles against state practices of land expulsion in Salvador indicates that blacks *do* identify as blacks and *do* engage in gender- and race-based political projects on a mass scale. Contrary to traditional racial formation literature in Brazil, racial inequality, racism, and white privilege exist in Brazil, though often manifested in different ways than in the United States, shaping everyday black experiences with racism and sexism in employment, housing, health care, and other vital resources. Black politics are formulated through individual and collective experiences with systems of racial and gender domination and violence, such as spatial segregation and forced displacement. Furthermore, the Gamboa de Baixo protests illustrate that black activists *do* engage in acts of civil disobedience and violent struggle for basic human rights issues such as clean water, housing, and local autonomy. Their actions confirm that social movements in Brazil are struggles for the valorization of black cultural history and identity as well as for the transformation of material conditions in black communities.

Black women's leadership in Gamboa de Baixo's political organization shows the ways in which they use race and gender to mobilize their community. What is clear is that black women's experiences with marginality and exclusion are one impetus for political mobilization. As the Women's Association and the neighborhood association show, women have always been at the leadership base of community politics in Gamboa de Baixo. They claim that this is because they, as black women, are more conscious of the short- and long-term impact that land expulsion and relocation to the periphery would have on their families. A major question for residents is "What will we do someplace else, someplace we do not know?" Displacement to a distant neighborhood diminishes their access to resources such as food (fishing), transportation, jobs, health care, and education.[6] The hospitals are located within walking distance from Gamboa de Baixo, which is essential for emergency care. As domestic workers in the nearby high-rise buildings, they can keep an eye on the happenings of the neighborhood while they work. More importantly, the beach is a central place for leisure activities such as swimming and diving, playing soccer, rowing, and just hanging out. The neighborhood's traditional proximity to the ocean is also significant for Afro-Brazilian religious ceremonies. Each year on February 2, the fishermen and -women honor Iemanjá, the goddess of the sea, placing gifts of appreciation such as flowers and perfume. A week after that celebration, a thirty-five-year-old woman, Maria José, conducts her own ceremony for Iemanjá, which also involves an elaborate procession to the oceanfront and then the delivery of the gifts to the middle of the ocean. When I asked Maria José, also a board member of the neighborhood association for several years, why she loves to live in Gamboa de Baixo, she proudly exclaimed, "Living here *é bom, bom demais* (is good, too good). Where else in the city could I have my own beach to hold these celebrations for Iemanjá?" (personal interview, August 2000).

The centrality of women's participation and their collective gender consciousness fueled the community movement for the preservation of local culture and the improvement of social conditions. Ana Cristina, a neighborhood activist, provides the following explanation:

> The women believed more, women have this thing. . . . They believed that they would remove us. And the men, I think they didn't, because the men thought, and some still think that, that no, living outside is simple. That they were going to be able to return, to come, the boat stays here, to fish, but the women had a broader vision, more clear about what it was to leave Gamboa to live in another part of Salvador. So, like that, it is as if the women were defending their territory. . . . It is not because as they say, there are men who say "meeting is a woman's little thing (*reunião é coisinha de mulher*)" but we did not see it that way. We see it like this, that women are able to reach a lot farther than the men. . . . Look, this broader preoccupation of the women was just this—preoccupation with the future. (personal interview, August 2000)

Like Ana Cristina, several of the women I spoke with in Gamboa de Baixo associate their political awareness in this situation with the recognition of their own differential knowledge as women, as key members and everyday leaders of their community. From this perspective, *this thing* that empowers black women in grassroots movements around issues of survival is their experiences, what they know about life and their position in the world. Chandra Mohanty (2003: 6) supports this understanding of experience in identity construction and recognizes the possibility of identity as a basis for progressive group solidarity and political mobilization. This argument holds true for black women's political identity produced by a complex knowledge of the depth of everyday social and economic conditions that define their existence in a poor neighborhood in the center of Salvador. For example, in Gamboa de Baixo, black women experience high rates of unemployment and police abuse, because they are racialized, gendered, and criminalized by the state as thieves, prostitutes, and drug dealers. Their specific experiences with distrustful employers and police violence illustrate the negative impact of public opinions about their neighborhood and the black people who live there. Gamboa de Baixo residents struggle to dispel racist, sexist, and classist ideas about their community and to reformulate a space-based collective identity to buttress their historical claims to territorial rights, improvement in social and economic conditions, and a safe environment.

Moreover, black women's actions in neighborhood associations illustrate the power of community building in mobilizing grassroots resistance against the appropriation of land and displacement for the purposes of tourism. As the work of Feldman, Stall, and Wright (1998: 261) informs, this form of social activism "is implicitly place-bound; that is, the networks of relationships and the activism that they support more often than not are located in and may involve conflict over places." In Gamboa de Baixo, the collective sense of community reflects women's ongoing involvement in social groups they have established with their families and neighbors in the places where they live. They play central roles in forging a sense of community through the birthday parties they organize or the support networks they create when residents need essential services such as health care assistance or babysitting. Recognizing the political aspects of maintaining households and communities allows us to understand how these networks reproduce social relations, help to "sustain the social fabric of community," and politicize place-based identities. For many generations, women in Gamboa de Baixo have nurtured and provided social services to each other. Like the previous Women's Association of the 1980s, the neighborhood association is "intimately connected to ongoing struggles for rights and control over spatial resources to house social-reproduction activities that create and sustain these communities" (Feldman, Stall, and Wright 1998: 261). Women in Gamboa de Baixo continue to be the primary organizers of social activities, providing the natural training ground for their leadership in the community-based political movement when they are under siege. The long conversations on each other's doorsteps; the sharing of vital resources such as water, gas, and food; and their mass attendance at political assemblies demonstrate how personally and politically connected female residents are.

Consequently, the centrality of black women's participation in this grassroots struggle promotes the articulation of racial knowledge, consciousness, and resistance through political uses of social memory. The political organization brings to the attention of Gamboa de Baixo the colonial legacy and racism embedded in practices of land expulsion. In addition to working with other local neighborhood associations fighting against urban removal, Gamboa de Baixo's neighborhood association finds political support from NGOs and race-based organizations such as the Unified Black Movement (MNU) and the Black Union for Racial Equality (UNEGRO). Though revitalization programs are never discussed publicly by the state in terms of being racial projects, black women confirm their racial and class claims when they link their struggle with other targeted black communities, identifying the expulsion of blackness as a pattern in modern urbanization programs. Through these citywide political networks, including the landless and homeless movements of Bahia, women acquire a broader consciousness of shared experiences with racial and economic injustice. In a community bulletin, Gamboa de Baixo activists wrote the following:

> Residents, we need to stay mobilized and alert for the violent and arbitrary actions that are being taken by the mayor and the state government. . . . When they announced the cleansing, before the elections, it was not just trash that they want to remove from the center of the city, but also the blacks, the poor people, the beggars, the street vendors, the street children and everything that they think dirties the city. We are not going to let them treat us like trash. We are working people and we have rights. (Gamboa de Baixo community bulletin 1997)

Gamboa de Baixo is an example of black Brazilians' recognition that, as blacks, women, and poor people, they bear the impact of urban revitalization. This recognition exemplifies what João Costa Vargas (2004) terms the "hyperconsciousness/negation of race dialectic" that defines social relations in Brazil. Vargas (2004: 6) asserts that, on the one hand, most Brazilians negate the importance of race in structuring institutions, shaping social relations, and determining the distribution of resources and power. On the other hand, Brazilians are "acutely aware of racial differences and utilize those to (often tacitly) justify, think about, and enforce behavior and social inequalities." This hyperconsciousness/negation dialectic is useful to understand the urbanization practices in Bahia. Bahians are simultaneously hyperconscious of the racial aspects of urbanization policies while also negating the salience of race in the new sociospatial order. Nevertheless, the black communities who are most negatively affected by forced displacement from the *better* parts of the city understand that urban renewal and gentrification shape the racial landscape of the city. Finding themselves in the path of massive "slum clearance" throughout the city center, the Gamboa de Baixo neighborhood association declared in a 1996 press release, "the dissemination of this culture of exclusion . . . principally towards the black and poor population, distances it farther and farther from the so-called 'privileged'[7] areas in our city."

From this perspective, black women in Gamboa de Baixo realize that they are capable of changing history and voice concerns against the clearance of urban land. They organize politically against the displacement of thousands of poor blacks to the periphery of Salvador, which worsens their already difficult economic situations. During these moments when even city officials said in public forums that "they didn't think that 'those black women were going to speak'" (Dona Silvia, personal interview, July 2000), the women of Gamboa de Baixo actively spoke out against slum clearance programs targeting their communities, and they continue to do so. Their participation in this social movement is an important assertion of their voice in urban space discourses that previously silenced them.

For blacks in Gamboa, contesting racial and sexual domination has meant reclaiming collective power through redefinitions of blackness. Reconstructing political identities based on their own understanding of themselves as black is a source of black women's empowerment *necessary* for political action. Nice, a member of the neighborhood association, explains,

> I thought it was really important to speak about our pride in our skin, in our color, in our race. What I liked more was to look in his (any city official) eyes, and say it like this, that "I am black, with pride (*eu sou negra com orgulho*)." We didn't go to beg them for anything. We wanted our rights. It's important for us to arrive there and say, I am black, but I am black with pride. I am proud of who I am. I didn't come here to beg from you. I want my rights. The rights are mine. (personal interview, July 2000)

To be taken seriously as poor blacks is an important task for the Gamboa de Baixo community and political organization. Women often explain that their participation in this movement transforms their previous sense of powerlessness as poor black women within the racist and sexist structures of urban governance. Nice also mentions that, "if they slammed their hands on the table, we slammed loudly too, looking at them in their faces, things I would not have done before and today I do them. . . . I learned that we can't hold our heads down because we're poor, because we're black women" (personal interview, July 2000). Despite their experiences with disrespectful treatment in their interactions with city officials and police violence, these women find power in the public assertion of their racial and gender identities. Considering black women's position at the absolute bottom of the social strata, their actions during meetings and protests mark the struggle to counter their everyday experiences with racism and sexism in the public sphere.

Collective Memory of Ownership

Asserting political power and reconstructing the image of this black community in the center of Salvador is one important aspect of the female-led social movement for permanence in the area. Gamboa de Baixo's resistance occurs primarily in the context of defending their citizenship rights to use and control of urban land. Nevertheless, Gamboa de Baixo's political organization has fought to prove their legal ownership of the land. Only a few residents have documentation of their ownership. Claiming native rights to the land, they reject official discourses that the community is merely an invasion (*invasão*), or an illegal squatter settlement, estimated by the government to be less than thirty years old. A Gamboa de Baixo activist, Ivana, contests this term *invasion* as inaccurate, considering the history of the population.

I do not see Gamboa as an [land] invasion (*invasão*). I see it as an occupation. It is an occupation that was permitted because the first families came here with authorization, no? And these people married, had children, their children grew up, had children. The truth is that Gamboa is practically three families. If you grab someone right here and go over to the other side, they are cousins. They might not be close cousins, but they are cousins. I see Gamboa as an occupation, a permitted occupation. Because when they deactivated the fort, the Navy gave authorization to a few soldiers to stay here to be able to keep an eye on things. These people started the life in Gamboa, the population in Gamboa. That is why I say permitted. They gave them permission to stay. Yes, and they had children, and their children grew up and had children. There are already six, seven generations of the same family in Gamboa. That is a lot of time to say that it was invaded, that we invaded [the land]. Logically, there were other people who came from the outside, but those are few. . . . The great majority have lived here since their grandfathers, grandmothers came here or their grandparents were born here. . . . That's why when they say it is an invasion, I fight with them. . . . Of course, there weren't this many people here, but it is not an invasion. (personal interview, July 2000)

Emphasizing an extensive history of residence on the land, activists consider families to be historically rooted to the land, a land they themselves have developed. They have fought to show that Gamboa de Baixo has its own culture and history that have developed on the coast and in the São Paulo Fort. Throughout Bahian history, blacks have formed several other fishing communities like Gamboa de Baixo along the coast of the Bay of All Saints. A previously disinterested government who abandoned the fort and the land that these residents have taken care of suddenly showed great interest when they perceived the profitability of the site's restoration. Furthermore, this is an example of the abandonment and subsequent decay that Milton Santos characterizes as a deliberate phase of reurbanization. Without sufficient resources to make repairs and abandoned by local development agencies, residents live in the decaying ruins of the São Paulo Fort without running water and sewers.

As Ivana's statement shows, using history to claim land rights is a common political strategy for urban black communities of resistance such as Gamboa de Baixo, reflecting David Scott's (1999) push for the political uses of history. Collective memory of ownership is a useful way for black Brazilians to contest racial hegemony, to use history as an interpretive tool of collective defiance, empowerment, and solidarity (Hanchard 1994: 150–153). Hanchard (1994: 151; author's emphasis) writes that "'other' memories must compete with a 'public past' that is itself the result of the ability of a dominant social group to preserve certain recollections, *deemphasize* or otherwise *exclude* others." History that has been cultivated from a position of marginality operates in opposition to singular notions of history as cultural dominance. Black women activists in Gamboa have utilized their own collective memory to question constructions of local and national memories articulated by those in power. Yet, as Hanchard argues, while these memories are necessary to critique dominant notions of the past, their power is insufficient to overrule contemporary practices of discrimination.

While I recognize some of the limitations Hanchard describes, collective memory *is* the principal means of defining Gamboa de Baixo's identity in relation to this urban space. Historical knowledge functions as an alternative mythmaking process that rearticulates the experiences of oppressed peoples. In Brazil, black women use social memory, a necessary basis of counter-hegemony, not just to further culturalist politics but as a basis for engagement in confrontational politics. Particularly, a radical revision of Bahian local and national history is an aspect of expressing their sense of social belonging during urban redevelopment. My research highlights the transformative role that history plays within social relations and the political possibility of collective memory for ideological and material social change. Ashis Nandy (1983: xiii) writes, using Fanon's terms, "but the meek inherit the earth not by meekness alone." The historical knowledge of subaltern groups provides a critique of dominance and oppression and defines racial, gender, and class boundaries necessary for group consciousness and community identity formation.

Making historical claims, Gamboa de Baixo activists demand permanent legal recognition of their individual and collective landownership. They also demand the cancellation of revitalization programs for the coastal areas that involve the removal of the local inhabitants. The community's quest for land considers urbanization a necessary part of permanence. The people of Gamboa de Baixo are as much a part of the traditional landscape as is the fort. Gamboa de Baixo activists define urbanization as the "improvement of the quality of the urban environment" with an emphasis on community participation (neighborhood association communiqué 1997). Residents redefine urbanization as "greater integration with other neighborhoods of the city" and not "slum clearance" or black land expulsion. Urbanization in Gamboa de Baixo is not about aesthetic changes for future tourism but for black residents who envision healthier futures on the land. Providing alternative proposals for urbanization, Gamboa de Baixo attempts to transform the view of how Brazilian society works in ways that positively transform poor black communities. Renewal and revitalization of global cities such as Salvador do not necessarily operate in opposition to one another, offering a solution to the problem of restoring urban centers for their traditional occupants (Espinheira 1989; Santos 1987).[8]

Conclusion

Urban renewal often has been disastrous for poor black communities. For Salvador's racial and political elite, aesthetic and economic development are intertwined in their plans to promote tourism. This depends on the expulsion of blacks from key locations in the urban center and their subsequent relocation to the city's geographical periphery. Paradoxically, the presence of blacks is not just an obstacle to urban modernization. Their presence is necessary insofar as they contribute to the reification of Brazilian national identity through commodified minstrelsy and fetishism. Nevertheless, black folkloric expressions are desired without inclusion of the bodies and communities that traditionally produce that culture. In other words, a national focus on black culture in Brazil does not necessarily conceive of notions of citizenship that affect concrete subjects. David Scott (1999: 81) states that "Caribbeans have been careless with memory," and this is one example of how Brazilians have been careless with memory in ways that exoticize black cultural artifacts while excluding actual black people.

Political movements have emerged in response to unequal socioeconomic and racial segregation in city planning. Gamboa de Baixo's political organization is just one example of a black community actively engaged in protest against the racist and sexist politics of exclusion underlying urban revitalization programs. This ethnographic analysis of the grassroots organization in Gamboa de Baixo illustrates how blacks *have* mobilized politically on the basis of black identity and in pursuit of concrete political objectives centered on their rights to land. In the Bahian urban center, permanent territorial rights constitute a local idiom for the affirmation of black consciousness and cultural insurgency. During this process, social memory is crucial for a historical critique of gendered racism in Brazilian cities, and also forms the basis of collective self-definition, empowerment, and organization of poor blacks.

Black social activism in Brazil has emerged, primarily led by women at the community level in struggles for access to material resources in urban spaces such as land and housing. Throughout this chapter, I focus on the fearless black women who wage struggle on a daily basis for the preservation of local black culture and for basic citizenship rights in Salvador. An eighty-nine-year-old woman and longtime resident of Gamboa de Baixo, Nana, stated in a newspaper article that "from here I only leave for the sky" (*Bahia Hoje* August 25, 1995). Another elderly woman, Dona Detinha, also recently assured me that "I only leave here dead." These elderly women's words resonate in the Gamboa de Baixo community hymn:

Daqui não saio	I will not leave here
Daqui ninguêm me tira	No one will take me away from here
Daqui não saio	I will not leave here
Daqui ninguêm me tira	No one will take me away from here
Onde é que eu vou morar?	Where will I live?
O Senhor tem a paciência	Does the Lord have the patience
de esperar?	to wait?
Eu sou mãe de tantos filhos	I am the mother of so many children
Onde é que eu vou morar?	Where will I live?

Black women's activism in the neighborhood association continues to be a bold statement of the community's political perseverance in a spatially and socially stratified city. Future studies on black politics in Brazil must include in their analyses social movements that have significant women and black participation and leadership, such as the neighborhood association I describe in this chapter. Grassroots activism in Gamboa de Baixo forces us to expand definitions of mass mobilization as well as to reconsider the ways in which black women's political actions draw attention to the gendered aspects of Brazilian race relations. Black women protest the historical erasure of black communities in urban revitalization policies and assert their roles as producers of knowledge on the modern city in Brazil. My approach rejects limited notions of Brazilian national identity that exclude *black* racial specification or identification, a necessary step to understanding the sexist roots of racial oppression and to developing political strategies to combat such inequalities. Black women in Gamboa de Baixo demonstrate through their thoughts and actions that it is possible to construct, as the national government advertises, *um Brasil para todos,* or rather "a Brazil for everyone."

Notes

A previous version of this chapter appeared as Perry, Keisha-Khan, "Social Memory and Black Resistance: Black Women and Neighborhood Struggles in Salvador, Bahia, Brazil," *The Latin Americanist* 49, no. 1 (Spring 2007): 7–38. Reprinted by permission.

1. Michael Omi and Howard Winant define racial formation as "the sociohistorical process by which racial categories are created, inhabited, transformed, and destroyed" (1994: 55). Linking this process to hegemonic processes, Omi and Winant (1994: 56) argue that a racial project is "an interpretation, representation, or explanation of racial dynamics, and an effort to reorganize and redistribute resources along particular racial lines." Racial projects connect discursive dimensions of racial formation with the ways in which race organizes social structures and everyday experiences.

2. Henri Lefebvre (1996) speaks about the challenges faced in French cities, particularly the disappearance of public spaces, which is a similar logic that governs state interventions in city planning in Bahia: He writes that, "for the working class, rejected from the centres towards the peripheries, dispossessed of the city, expropriated thus from the best outcomes of its activity, this right has a particular bearing and significance."

3. My translation of Mayor Imbassahy's statement from the original Portuguese: "*Que mais dizer, além da nossa certeza do dever cumprido, do compromisso que temos com a nossa história e com o nosso futuro. Numa cidade como Salvador, onde novo e antigo se misturam com tanta harmonia, tal qual as raças que formaram a etnia e a personalidade tão peculiar do baiano, que a todos sabe bem receber e repartir sua alegria. Dividimos com todos, baianos, brasileiros e cidadões do mundo, mais esta felicidade, a de ver o nosso Forte de São Marcelo restaurado, compondo com o Mercado Modelo e o Elevador Lacerda um dos nossos mais conhecidos cartões postais.*"

4. Milton Santos (1984) also cites the case of black home owners who were denied the necessary loans to restore their deteriorating homes in Harlem during the early 1980s.

5. In São Paulo, Teresa Caldeira (2000: 63) documented the rise in the numbers of neighborhood associations to "obtain better services and infrastructure." Social movements in neighborhoods stem from an awareness of the deterioration and decline of public resources in poor regions of the city.

6. Richard Batley (1982: 233) asserts that, as a consequence of expulsion, "for poorer groups, removal from central areas implied a loss of a relatively favored situation, almost certainly in terms of access to public services and employment and probably also in terms of housing standards."

7. The term *privileged* is a direct translation from the Portuguese word *privilegiado*. It appears ironic and confusing that both the government and residents refer to the neighborhood as privileged, but it is because of the cultural and geographical importance of the land that Gamboa de Baixo occupies. To be privileged in Salvador means the neighborhood's proximity to the beach and the city center, or rather the actual dollar value of beachfront properties in Salvador.

8. Both Gey Espinheira (1989) and Milton Santos (1987) write about the Pelourinho and defend the restoration of the neighborhood for the local population. Santos predicted the mass displacement of the Pelourinho population before it occurred. As an alternative to relocation, he suggested that the Bahian government follow the housing models of cities such as Barcelona, where the old population returned to live in restored historic buildings.

9

Black NGOs and "Conscious" Rap: New Agents of the Antiracism Struggle in Brazil

Sales Augusto dos Santos

There are various types of black social movements and also various types of struggles against racism in Brazilian society (Santos 2007). Thus, I will define classic black social movements as black social movements from before the 1990s, to distinguish them from new forms of black movements that emerged at the beginning of the 1990s, such as nongovernmental organizations (NGOs) with a racial focus, the artists of "conscious" rap, black parliamentarians, and the militancy of black intellectuals in universities, which are some of the forms of struggle against racism and Brazilian racial inequality.

This chapter thus includes a brief discussion of two new social agents in the antiracism struggle: (1) black NGOs, which are mostly led by women; and (2) the artists of conscious rap. These emergent antiracist institutions and agents, NGOs and rappers,[1] derive directly and indirectly from the black social movement (Santos 2007). These new social agents, like the current and former black parliamentarians,[2] have participated in the antiracism struggle by extending the struggle for racial equality in Brazil. In this way, they help to create the necessary conditions for debates and the implementation of specific public policies for blacks to be integrated into Brazilian society as common citizens, and not as second-class citizens. This chapter focuses on black NGOs and rappers of conscious rap as agents of new forms of black activism.

New Forms of Struggle Against Racism: Black NGOs

Even if there has been a slowing down of traditional black social movements during the last decade of the twentieth century, as suggested by the American historian George Andrews (1998), caused, in part, by declining wages and the implementation of neoliberal policies in the country (Santos and Silva 2006), this slowdown should not be interpreted as a retreat or a weakening of the Afro-Brazilian struggle.[3] Black social movements have not been able to conquer, on a broad scale, Afro-Brazilians of different class backgrounds with a discourse that focused on the shared experience of racial discrimination and on the struggle to achieve racial equality, nor have they been able to recruit new members for the struggle, amplify the number of militant black organizations, or even strengthen the older and traditional organizations, such as the Unified Black Movement (MNU) (which would probably have given black protest a new impulse and made them—organizations and blacks—more effective). Nevertheless, black social movements have become more professional, for example, in creating black NGOs, and they have massively broadened the reach of their discourse through conscious rap. A significant part of black militancy started expressing itself through NGOs, such as the Institute of Black Women (Geledés), the Center for the Articulation of Marginalized Populations (CEAP), the Center of Studies of Work Relations and Inequality (CEERT), Fala Preta! (an organization of black women), and Criola, among others.

To some extent, black militants became more professional in terms of their qualifications and actions, but they were no less radical than in the previous decades. In other words, there was a process of *NGO-ization* of black social movements that took shape more clearly during the end of the 1980s, as has been the case with Geledés, which was created in 1988 (Roland 2000).

One of the main points of importance in this transformative process of NGO-ization of black social movements is that it redirected the way that the antiracism struggle was expressed. NGOs were able to pay, and thus maintain, black militants, which allowed for the exclusive dedication of black activists to the cause. For example, in a traditional or classic black organization, like the MNU or the Grucon, black activists, because they were guided by an ethic of antiracism struggle, practically paid to be involved in activism. In general, they used their own resources, and oftentimes tapped into already meager family incomes, to carry out actions that in most cases involved costs. Furthermore, they could only become involved in militancy or execute antiracist activities in their spare time by going to meetings on weekends or after work.

Hence, with the emergence of black NGOs, activists started to receive remuneration or salaries to combat racism in Brazilian society. Antiracism activists continue to be guided by an ethic of conviction against racism, but activism against racism became their daily work, and they received payment for it. This made for a more intense and active antiracist struggle. Activists no longer needed to worry about employment. In traditional black antiracism activism, activists that were integrally dedicated to the struggle ran the risk of losing their day jobs. The risk was real, not only because black activists sometimes had to leave their jobs without previous warning, but also because they could suffer retaliation for this type of activism. Thus, activists generally tried to participate in activities that were compatible with their work schedule. This was not always possible, since some antiracist activities took place during work hours. This is especially true for those days that the black movement tried to transform into black history commemorative holidays. For this reason, there was always the risk of losing one's job.

By participating in black NGOs, black activists freed themselves of this risk. Beyond that, they were also able to expose and denounce racism in all spheres of public life, since they did not run the risk of losing their job by way of reprisal for exposing a matter that is taboo in Brazilian society. In this way, they stimulated the antiracism struggle by increasing the black protest against racism.

It is clear that the increase of black protest in Brazilian society is not exclusively due to a sprouting of black NGOs. There are several factors that led to this development. But we cannot deny the importance of black NGOs in the last three marches against racism that occurred in the country's capital, the city of Brasília. These occurred on November 20, 1995; November 16, 2005; and November 22, 2005. Black NGOs, classic black social movements, and other organizations of Brazilian civil society were fundamental to the articulation, organization, and achievement of these marches. Therefore, it was not by chance that the activist Edna Roland, founder and activist of the NGO Fala Preta!, an organization of black women, was chosen to serve as a spokesperson at the Third World Conference Against Racism, Racial Discrimination, Xenophobia, and Religious Intolerance, carried out between August 30 and September 7, 2001, in Durban, South Africa. As a representative from an NGO dedicated to Afro-Brazilian women's issues, Roland's participation exemplifies the influence and ability of black NGOs in the struggle for racial equality.

From the second half of the 1990s, black NGOs organized and coordinated by some black activists and former activists of traditional black social movements began a dialogue between black social movements and several organizations of Brazilian civil society, as well as with international civil organizations. In this way they extended their power and influence to several organizations of civil society: for example, union offices, union workers, political parties (mostly leftist parties), and the Brazilian state; the same state that, since the year 1995, has officially recognized that Brazil is a racist country (Sales Santos 2006). Nevertheless, this recognition is not solely due to pressures from black NGOs. The state's admission is due to long years of struggle and internal pressures from traditional black social movements as well as external international pressures (Sales Santos 2006). This does not imply a denial that black NGOs also had an important role in such pressure. Sociologist Edward Telles (2003: 73) states,

> At the end of the 1990s, several NGOs of the black movement with dimension, resources, and professional capacity were created in several Brazilian states. The organization of black movements in NGOs was mirrored in the

change of social movements in general, and those organizations would become more and more institutionally represented.

Thus, black NGOs are a demonstration that classic black social movements, intentionally or not, had also become instruments of the construction of new social agents and new forms of struggle against racism that do not necessarily have the same structure, perspective on politics, vision of the world, and forms of performance of the original movements. In this manner, new forms of expression of antiracism militancy evolved and were in favor of the promotion of racial equality. In this way, the traditional Afro-Brazilian struggle by older black social movements against racism produced other agents of activism (Santos 2007), which began to emerge mainly in the late twentieth century. Traditional black movements started to perceive and recognize new agents and forms of struggle as important to strengthen older black organizations. According to the document *March Against Racism for Citizenship and Life,* produced on November 20, 1995, by Brazilian black movements:

> The racial thematic, particularly in the 300th year of Zumbi, is distinguished in a vigorous form in the Brazilian space of public discussion. This is the result of a rise without precedent, in our history of the struggle against racism. This victory resulted because of a strengthening of Black Movement organizations as much as an increase and internalization of its entities. New forms of articulation of militancy in work, unions, popular movements, political parties, universities, parliament, religious entities, governmental bodies, etc. in recent years, increased better ways of combating racism. The emergence of Black Women movements with their own expression and national character . . . doubly fight against racial and gender oppression. (ENMZ 1996: 9)

The fact is that classic black social movements, even with their retraction, as Andrews notes (1991a), directly and indirectly disseminated a critical consciousness of Brazilian race relations and inequalities between blacks and whites. And this not only occurred on the part of Afro-Brazilians who have ascended socially, since they felt and still feel the weight of racial discrimination even more so than Afro-Brazilians who have remained in their traditional social places (Andrews 1998; Moura 1994; Hasenbalg 1979), but also among workers, unemployed people, students, youth, and musicians, among other social groups that live mainly in major Brazilian metropolises, especially those in the suburbs.

In other words, just as racism is dynamic and renews and reorganizes itself in accordance with the evolution of the society and changing historical circumstances (Munanga 1994: 178), the struggle against racism is also not static. New subjects and social agents start to struggle against racism, and new forms of black resistance emerge, helping to spread the message of antiracism and racial equality. The MNU, for example, appeared at the end of the 1970s to unify the antiracism struggle of some regional and local black entities. Nevertheless, when the MNU defined what it meant to be a black movement, at the beginning of the 1990s, after approximately thirteen years of growth, this entity began to recognize that several other social forms of organizations, languages, action policies, and antiracism agents had blossomed. An example is the group of black intellectuals and researchers, among other groups that struggle for racial equality, who resist racial discrimination or fight against racism in Brazil, and present important antiracist proposals for the democratization of race relations and Brazilian society. Then, the MNU started to define the black movement as ample and plural actions with a wider scope. The MNU acknowledged that a multiplicity of groups and black organizations were involved in the struggle to combat racism. The MNU stated:

> We understand the black movement as a set of initiatives of resistance and cultural production and explicit political action to combat racism, which manifests itself at different levels, in different languages, by means of a multiplicity of organizations spread throughout the country. The 1980s introduced new risks and components to the perspective of the militant vanguard that had emerged in the last decade, which allowed for a new envisioning of how to organize a black movement. The majority of black groups and organizations grew at the margins of the then dominant repertoires and projects characterizing the end of the 1970s and considered most advanced. Adopting guerilla characteristics, the antiracism struggle spread like wildfire among certain sectors of the black population. Musicians, actors, artists, samba schools, cultural groups, study centers, political organizations, predominantly black recreational clubs, partisan groups, black intellectuals and researchers, Candomblé houses [cult houses for the practice of Afro-Brazilian religion], afoxé groups [African religion–inspired cultural activism groups], religious groups, black writers, black youth groups, unions, black women groups, advising agencies to popular movements, the black press, black political parties, black parliamentarians, and others have followed the call uttered from the stairs of the Municipal Theater in São Paulo, on July 7, 1978.[4] (Cardoso 2002: 212–213)

All Afro-Brazilians were not involved in traditional black social movements, yet some still wanted to express their indignation about racism and racial inequality. Individuals that for various reasons did not have the chance to be black activists in entities of black social movements searched for some form of expressing their indignation and fighting against racism and racial inequality in Brazil. An example of this is provided in an interview with a former director of the Brazilian Association of Black Researchers (ABPN), conducted by Santos (2007). The respondent stated:

> My religious background, as an Evangelical Christian, created its own reality, which did not include participating in black movements, become a militant in the proper sense of the word. This does not mean that my black family did not question racism inside our church, for example, and in Brazilian society in general. We were not unaware of these issues, and we stood up against racism in a way that it was compatible with Christian doctrine. We

paid attention to all activities of the black movement: the struggle for our own aesthetic that should be respected (wearing our hair natural and not straightening it, wearing clothes in bright colors and not only beige or blue, etc.); the struggle of blacks in the United States; the MNU, etc. We knew about all of this and we followed everything. At the university I tried to be involved in the movement, but it was not easy, because of my language and way of being, including my clothes and hairstyle, even though they were not Pentecostal. They were still considered white. All of this complicated my participation in groups like the MNU. It was not easy for those who follow a certain type of behavior, aesthetic, and religion to participate in the MNU. I am talking about the end of the 1980s, mainly at the beginning of the 1990s. As it was so difficult to join the already existing groups, I ended up participating in the creation of a new group that lasted about two years. The name of the group was "Black Consciousness" and we met every Saturday afternoon to read and study . . . in the center of the city, Recife. It was very good. This was in 1992 or 1993. . . . Many people were activists, without necessarily being part of the organized black movement. . . . There is a lot of protest against racism by blacks outside of traditional black organizations. (female respondent "A" from the ABPN in Santos 2007)

This lengthy quotation gives important insight into the fact that racial struggles against discrimination go beyond black organizations. For this reason, I use the expression black social movements, in the plural, rather than the singular term, the black movement. As we can see in the previous quotation, the respondent formed a group that was concerned with racial issues and, although she was not involved in a classic black-movement organization, she should be considered a participant in Brazil's black movements. As a former director of the ABPN, she has led an organization made up of Afro-Brazilian intelligentsia, which is another form of activism, given the low number of Afro-Brazilian academics. Further, she is oriented to the black movement because of her exposure to its discourse and the group she formed that focused on Afro-Brazilian issues. Because of the multiplicity of groups and black organizations, like black NGOs, there also appeared a collective and individual multiplicity of actions against racism in some areas of Brazilian society. All of these black actions, antiracism organizations, and groups in favor of racial equality characterized and extended the debate about the racial question, making it possible to include it in the Brazilian political agenda.

Rap and Rappers: New Agents of Antiracism Discourse

Another change that was important in terms of black mobilization against racism in Brazil in the 1990s was the reutilization of music, in the form of rapping, as a way to denounce and condemn Brazilian racial oppression. Although the outcry of black organizations, such as the MNU, for true racial equality had not effectively sensitized the broader Brazilian public sphere to the necessity to include the racial question in the national agenda (Santos 2007), Afro-Brazilians, who until then did not directly participate in the struggle against racism, started to sympathize with the antiracism agenda of those traditional black social movements.

Hence, young Afro-Brazilians living in the peripheries of major urban centers, especially of São Paulo, Brasília, Belo Horizonte, and Goiânia (Amorim 1997), started to sing and tell the stories of racial and social violence to which they were exposed, through reflexive and extremely critical music, thus transforming their life stories into verse by utilizing an extraordinarily fitting poetry, namely rap.

Through involvement in NGOs, hip-hop artists give exposure to their music and message and gain a role in public space as they are formally institutionalized as an organization. Further, Pardue (2005) finds that Afro-Brazilian youth who participate in hip-hop activities embrace the notion that black marginality is not simply the result of class, but of race and class. Reiter and Mitchell (2008) find that Afro-Brazilian listeners of hip-hop support the notion of black racial group identity more than those who do not listen to it. They attribute this to the consciousness-raising efforts of hip-hop artists. Pardue's (2005, 2007) and Reiter and Mitchell's (2008) findings thus provide further support for my argument, namely that rap artists function as new agents of the antiracism struggle.

Traditional black social movements had not won many allies in the fight against racism before the 1990s. Traditional channels of pleading to state actors of the Brazilian public sphere such as political parties, labor unions, and entrepreneurs, among others, who refused to include the racial question on the national agenda, were not viable solutions to addressing racism and racial inequality. The most oppressed people who suffered from racial discrimination vocally disagreed with the state's silence toward racial issues and expressed their dissatisfaction through rap music. This is a new form of black struggle. Thus, they started to use rap as a vehicle of communication to denounce racial and class discrimination in Brazil.[5] One of the most well-known groups that explicitly addressed these issues is Racionais MCs. In the introduction of the record *Raio X do Brasil* (*X-Ray of Brazil*), Racionais affirmed that the liberty of speech, by means of music, was one of the few rights that black youth still had in Brazil.

X-Ray of Brazil, for Racionais, is a strong denunciation of oppression against the most vulnerable social groups of the country: poor people at the peripheries of major urban centers who are mainly Afro-Brazilian or black. At first sight, Racionais and many groups of conscious rap present a discourse that explains the need of the *manos* (brothers) to refuse all the daily violence that the *system* imposes on the periphery. In a way, it is also a moral discourse that condemns the use of drugs (including alcohol) and idleness, among other destructive behaviors on the periphery. As rappers themselves affirm, they seek to have "a positive message" for the *manos*. Nevertheless, there is also a constant discourse of race and class that establishes a recurrent opposition between the world of blacks and whites (Fernandes 1972), rich and poor, and the periphery and the center. If at first sight the lyrics express a message of peace, or as anthropologist Amorim (1997: 106) affirms, the rap groups "sing of unity and peace in their rhyme," we cannot forget that this message is internally pacifist for the periphery itself; but it is simultaneously aggressive and in opposition to the system.

These rap lyrics verbalize an extremely racialized discourse that expresses the racial discrimination blacks are subjected to on a daily basis. In the song "Hey Boy," Racionias claims that those in power, namely whites, believe that blacks belong in prison. Further, they believe that poor people are forced to steal, and that it is not a choice, because they do not have enough money for basic human needs. Violence is another theme addressed in these songs.[6] In "Fim de Semana no Parque" (Weekend in the Park), black children are not afforded the simple luxuries such as Christmas gifts. Rather, they live in poor communities rampant with violence. Racionais develops and disseminates a consciousness about discrimination and racial inequalities that affects those in the periphery. They succeed in being more expressive and expansive than traditional black social movements. The racialized discourse of rap is a weapon that simultaneously shoots against and challenges the myth of Brazilian racial democracy[7] as well as the silence about racial issues in the country. More than this, it is a weapon from the periphery that is aimed at the center of the system. As KlJay and Mano Brown, who belong to Racionais, affirm, "We are the most dangerous blacks of the country, and we will change a lot of things here. There was a little time ago that we had no consciousness of this." Also, "I am not an artist. Artists make art; I make weapons. I am a terrorist" (KlJay and Mano Brown, respectively, *apud* Showbizz 1998). They both take on active roles as participants in black struggle as consciousness-raising agents to poor Afro-Brazilian youth.

The change affirmed above by KlJay is the active voice, which, in fact, is the title of one of their songs ("Voz Ativa"), of rappers against racism and Brazilian racial inequalities. Furthermore, it is the breaking of the white monopoly on the representation of blacks in Brazil (Bairros 1996: 183). K1Jay, Mano Brown, and other rappers challenge this with their interpretation of the racial circumstances of blacks. This is similar to what intellectual blacks are trying to achieve in academia by means of production of active knowledge-thought (Santos 2007). There is a search for the decolonization of scientific knowledge, intellectual autonomy, the proposal of policies that promote racial equality, and the rupture of monopoly or control of studies and research on blacks from the point of view of intellectuals from the white world, as expressed by Florestan Fernandes (1972). It is something so "violently pacific" that "it sabotages reasoning" and "shakes the central nervous system" of production of Euro-centric Brazilian academic knowledge. Black self-understanding of their identities and social situations is expressed in the lyrics of music of rap groups. Examples include the songs "Voz Ativa" and "Capítulo 4, Versículo 3" (Chapter 4, Verse 3), both from the Racionais MCs. In the introduction to the song "Capítulo 4, Versículo 3," they say, "60 percent of youth in the periphery without criminal activities have already suffered police violence, three out of four people killed by police are black, in Brazilian universities only 2 percent of students are black and every four hours a black youth dies violently in São Paulo." And in the song "Voz Ativa," they say that although black people are not equal to everyone, black youth now have an active voice and they need to reconstruct their pride.

The *terror* expressed above in Mano Brown's discourse aims at the non-resignation of blacks. Further, it aims at the denial of blacks that whites wanted to create and to instill in them. This terror also corresponds to the perception that poverty has a color, and that among poor people of the periphery color and race make a difference. The discourse is similar or equal to that of classic black social movements (Santos 2007), whose objective is to eliminate the ideology of racial democracy and deconstruct academic discourse, which influences a significant portion of Brazilian intellectuals who believe that different treatment between whites and blacks is due to only social class and not race. As affirmed in Racionais's song "Racista Otário" (Racist Fool): "Sociologists prefer to be impartial and say our dilemma is financial. But if you analyze well, you discover that blacks and whites seem to be but are not equal." At last, the discourse of terror helps to confront the representation of black people by whites about black people, in daily life or in the academic world. This terror, in reality, confers self-determination to blacks.

This is the vision of only one specific group of conscious rap. But it is a vision of the world not only for this group, but a vision that became a national reference for the *manos,* who are linked to rap, and for other groups who are profoundly influenced by Racionais. This vision of the world is being widely disseminated among rappers themselves, social groups that live in the peripheries of major urban centers of the country, and some sectors of the Brazilian middle class. For example, in June 1998, Racionais sold more than 250,000 copies of its third CD, *X-Ray of Brazil,* and more than 500,000 of its fourth CD, *Surviving Hell,* without the assistance of the open or large television media and without being on major national or transnational record labels.[8]

On the other hand, not all rap groups with national prestige agree completely with Racionais's ideological position. For the GOG, a group from Brasília, the racial question is not the central subject in its *Chronicles of the Periphery,* which has as a central focus the denunciation of social oppression faced by vulnerable social groups of the periphery, and poor people in general. Nevertheless, Gog, the leader of the group, acknowledges that it is "logical that blacks in Brazil have more problems." Nevertheless, he affirms that in the periphery "a bullet in the head is to blacks as it is to whites" (Gog in *Caros Amigos,* 1998: 21).

Nevertheless, even among prestigious rap groups that differ ideologically from Racionais's position and the racialist discourse in lyrics, the discourse of race and class is inevitable and consequently recurring in other groups' rhymes. An example is GOG's song "Brasil com 'P'" (Brazil with P), which also has a racialized notion of who the poor people are and who is targeted by police officers.

> Brazil with "P"
> Published research shows
> *A preference for Blacks, the poor, and prostitutes to be arrested*
> *Stop and Think why!*
> I continue,
> In the peripheries they practice perversities,
> PMs (Military Policemen).
> Standing at their stages, politicians make promises, they promise . . .
> Nothing but lies
> Only to their own advantage.
> Beaches, programs, swimming pools, palms.
> For the periphery: panic, gunpowder, pá, pá, pá. . . .
> Without penalty, life imprisonment
> Words spoken by the brother poet.[9]

Even if the construction of racial identity is not emphasized as strongly by the rap produced in Brasília as it is by that produced in São Paulo (Amorim 1997), this motive is also very present in the repertoire of rappers from Brasília, as can be observed, for example, in the lyrics of "Sub-Raça" (Sub-Race), by now-extinct Brasília group Câmbio Negro. In it there is a strong emphasis on color.

> Sub-Race
> Now brothers I will tell the truth
> The cruelties they do to us
> Only because our skin has a different color
> We are constantly pestered by cruel racism,
> Much worse than drinking from the bitter cup is having to constantly
>   swallow
> Just because you are black—that's a fact.
> We cannot learn the value of our own color,
> In schools or colleges
> Being black never was a defect,

It will always be a privilege
It's a privilege to belong to the race
that with their own blood constructed Brazil. . . .[10]

In cities such as São Paulo and Rio de Janeiro, hip-hop and rap artists generally work with NGOs, which attract Afro-Brazilian youth. These collaborative efforts and the influence of racially oriented NGOs may be one reason the discourse of marginalization differs in various Brazilian cities. It is also likely that specific historical, political, and economic characteristics influence whether marginalization is perceived as a result of class or race. The racial identity is emphasized in some places while not emphasized in others, as Amorim demonstrates above (1997).

As we can see, the Afro-Brazilian struggle against racism by means of rap concentrates basically on denouncing racism against blacks and on the denial of racial democracy. Groups that are not organic black-movement organizations participate in their struggle. These groups are new forms of antiracist mobilization but are not structured like classic black organizations, nor do they have the same forms of action as those organizations or black NGOs. They use rap music to denounce racism against Afro-Brazilians. It is a diffuse form of struggle that does not need a group of antiracism activists formally organized by means of institutions or weekly and monthly meetings, aiming to argue and deliberate on the racial question or to establish relationships with the Brazilian state to fight against racism in the country. They do not need organic leaders who are seen and recognized as leaders and political representatives of Afro-Brazilians.

Conclusion

Considering the forms of postabolition, Afro-Brazilian struggle, we can see that they are more expansive than in the past. We can talk about Afro-Brazilian struggles in the plural. All of them have and fulfill a definitive role. None are less important than the others in the fight against racism. More than this, all forms of struggle against racism by means of traditional black social movements, black parliamentarians, black intellectuals, black NGOs, and rappers of conscious rap, as we see in this chapter, contribute to denying the discourse of Brazilian white elites that there is a racial democracy in Brazil, and attempt "to break the white monopoly about the representation of blacks in Brazil" (Bairros 1996: 183) that historically put the black struggle against racism on the margin of public space.

Black NGOs redirected how to be involved in antiracism activism when they made possible the exclusive devotion of black activists to combating racism. With the sprouting of black NGOs, activists started to receive wages to fight racism in Brazilian society. While it continued to be driven by an ethic of antiracism struggle, this militancy started to be daily work with remuneration. This made possible a more intense and active stance in the fight against racism. Activism in black NGOs gave black activists the opportunity to expose racism in every sphere where they found it operating or manifesting, because they did not run the risk of losing their jobs or suffering other types of retaliation. In this manner, they were able to increase the black protest against racism in Brazil.

On the other hand, and opposite of more traditional black social movements that had always tried to conquer a place in public space, the musicians of conscious rap do not have the same intentions. They are on the edge and speak from the margins (or the periphery) against the center of the system. It seems as though this is a new form of Afro-Brazilian struggle in terms of discourse, which does not seek the negotiation of the racial question in the public sphere. They want the end of racial oppression by the center of power, which by means of racism and other types of violence has pushed people to the edge. Consequently, they preach internal union among members of the periphery and aggression aimed at the power centralized in the system as a form of self-defense. The musicians of conscious rap contribute in a particular way to fighting against racism, even though it is not comparable to the forms of struggle described by Santos (2007).

The new social agents of antiracism, such as the black legislators connected to the antiracism agenda, antiracism NGOs, black intellectuals, and conscious rappers, among others, not only put the racial issue on the Brazilian political agenda, but they also anchored the historical quest for formal and substantive equality for the Brazilian black population firmly into that agenda.

Notes

1. We should not forget that, beyond these new antiracist social agents in the antiracist struggle that I describe and analyze in this chapter, there are also some black parliamentarians engaged in the struggle, as well as some black intellectuals, as demonstrated by Santos (2007).

2. For example, Abdias do Nascimento, Benedita da Silva, Paulo Paim, and Luiz Alberto, who were all involved in antiracism struggles of black movements in the Brazilian parliament.

3. Actually, this affirmation of Andrews (1991) about the reflection of black social movements needs to be verified by means of more research that should be more complex and sophisticated. There is at least one informational source that indicates an increase of black social movements after the 1980s. The research of Caetana Damasceno et al. conducted in 1986 and 1987 and published in the *Catalog of Black Movement Organizations in Brazil* (1988) demonstrated that there were 573 black organizations in Brazil. Professor Hélio Santos affirmed that "the data bank by the Nucleus of Interdisciplinary Studies of Brazilian Blacks (NEINB-USP) found more than 1,300 black-

movement organizations with some type of cultural, religious, and political aspect. Organizations, when they do not directly address racial inequalities, operate as cultural resistance or indirectly work together with struggle" (Hélio Santos 2000: 70).

4. "MNU. I ENEN—A Step Ahead?" *Journal do Movimento Negro Unificado,* no. 18, January–March 1991.

5. Analyzing the lyrics of Brazilian rappers, or better, those that produce conscious rap, we can perceive a discourse of race and class. Conscious rap, according to anthropologist Lara Dos Santos Amorim, "is about rap when it was differentiated from funk, which is more devoted to the contents of its lyrics that seek to denounce social exclusion and the racism" (Amorim 1997: 108). In this chapter, I emphasize the racial discourse. This does not imply a denial of class discourse, but I prioritize the strong racialist discourses of conscious rap, in the face of the racism practiced against the blacks. I do not intend to fully analyze rap lyrics. I make a few commentaries about the lyrics with the intention of letting them speak for themselves. I do not want to put words in the rap artist's mouth. Nevertheless, according to Pinho (2001), "this does not mean there is no interpretative responsibility, but leaves this ultimately to the main authority."

6. In an earlier version of this chapter, I had cited six songs from the Racionais MCs group. Unfortunately I had to remove them from the current version, because I did not obtain the authorization of this group of rap musicians to publish them in my text.

7. Following the sociologist Carlos Hasenbalg, "the notion of the myth to qualify the 'racial democracy' is here used in the sense of illusion or a mistake and to intend to show the distance between representation and reality, the existence of prejudice, discrimination and racial inequalities and their denial in discursive plans" (Hasenbalg 1996: 237). The notion that I endorse and that is utilized in this chapter is a synonym of the ideology of Brazilian racial democracy.

8. *Caros Amigos,* no. 3, September 1998. It is worth noting here not all Afro-Brazilians were involved in traditional black social movements, yet some still wanted to express their indignation about racism and racial inequality. For Racionais MCs, the televised media is a great force that sustains the system that discriminates and oppresses blacks and poor people. This is the central power. According to the magazine *Showbizz* (1998: 29), "Television doesn't think." Moments before the collective interview in December 1997, "they [some members of Racionais] kindly asked reporters of Globo and of SBT to be removed." Globo TV is the main open network of Brazil until the present date and TV SBT was the second most important.

9. Lyrics reproduced with authorization of Genival Oliveira Gonçalves, author. Translated by Bernd Reiter.

10. Lyrics reproduced with authorization of Alexandre Tadeu Silva, author, and Mel Atyistic Productions and Music Efitions, Ltda. Translated by Bernd Reiter.

10

Power and Black Organizing in Brazil

Fernando Conceição

The state of Bahia, one of the twenty-seven states that together form the union of the Federal Republic of Brazil, was the first territory occupied by the Portuguese colonization, in the beginning of the sixteenth century.[1] It is now the state with the greatest black population in Brazil. Salvador, its capital, is the largest city in the state, with approximately three million inhabitants, according to the Institute of Brazilian Geography and Statistics (IBGE). Compared to the rest of the country, this makes Salvador the third largest Brazilian city. About 80 percent of Salvador's population is Afro-descendent. Even today, in the twenty-first century, African cultural influence is very strong in Salvador and manifests itself in religion, music, food, and general habits.

This chapter seeks to explore if the demographic strength of the Afro-descendent population of Salvador, together with the hegemonic power of African cultural forms preserved among this population, is able to conquer political power at the local level, namely during mayoral elections. To illustrate my reflections, I shall discuss a case: the election for mayor of Salvador in 1985. This was the first democratic election in a Brazilian capital since the military dictatorship had taken power in 1964, which had ended direct elections in Brazil. Hence, for over twenty years, the Brazilian electorate was forbidden to choose their mayors. During that time, mayors were appointed by the governors, who, in turn, were appointed by the military. The municipal elections of 1985 were thus an important stepping-stone in the long process of Brazilian redemocratization.

In the blackest state of Brazil, two candidates dominated this election: one, the descendent of African slaves; the other, a self-declaring Jew. This chapter does not seek to emphasize the ethnic-racial differences between the candidates. Rather, this case allows for an analysis of racialized political mobilization, as both candidates frequently referred to and placed themselves in relation to the *racial vote*. The black candidate did so by highlighting his blackness, and the white candidate did so by vehemently denying the importance of color and accusing the other candidate of introducing racial hatred. Doing so, he reproduced the then-predominant doctrine that Brazil was a *racial paradise*—adopting the reading of Brazilian reality developed by Gilberto Freyre (1933).

This chapter is part of a greater effort to analyze black organizing in Brazil. The case study of the 1985 municipal election in Salvador supports one of the hypotheses in this endeavor, namely that culture is not necessarily a vehicle of political emancipation, when culture is transformed into a mere good by the cultural industry (in the sense given to this term by the Frankfurt School, whose authors early on highlighted the fact that markets can transform cultural expression, thus chipping away its critical potential). It can become an instrument of ideological alienation. The most important Afro-organizations, which emerged to disseminate a discourse of racial equality and black empowerment, were in fact seduced and later absorbed by the cultural industry. As a result, they started to use their prestige and appeal to the black population in order to negotiate and forge alliances with traditional political sectors. In this regard, a comparison of the backgrounds and political strategies of the two leading candidates of 1985 is highly revealing.

Finally, it is important to note that my reflections are those of an insider and activist of the Brazilian black-power movement who has participated in the discussions around the 1985 mayoral race as an activist and journalist.

Bahia: The Black Mecca

When comparing Bahia's market successes—mainly in tourism, music, and media markets, which represent the image of Bahian black culture—the real degree of poverty, subcitizenship, and servility that entangles the everyday lives of Afro-descendents in Bahia can be analyzed, taking into account this cultural success. Blacks are the majority in Bahia, thus how is it that this majority has not been able to express itself by winning power, which is, after all, the objective of any political struggle? Is it that cultural power, and the schemes created to administer it, can turn back and work against its original producers?

One key point in the discussion of asserting ethnic identity is the contribution that each group constituting a society has to offer to its formation as a whole. In Brazil the culture and cultural contribution of Africans and their descendents is generally viewed as the largest contribution of blacks to the formation of society. If this assertion is true, it ignores other contributions, because it hides the fact that it was through labor—not culture—that blacks performed their main function of being the foundation upon which the Brazilian state was constructed. Yet blacks are constantly denied a part in the distribution of the nation's wealth.[2]

Culture, understood not in a general broad sense as a philosophical vision of the world, but as limited culture—the playful, artistic, or religious forms of vernacular manifestations—finds greater resonance and greater communicative response from nonblack groups, as something specific and characteristic of black people. In other words, in Bahia, racial conflicts are still not publicly admitted by those in circles of power. Images of black people have been eternally archetyped and folkorized: blacks are a cultural good, and, as such, they can be positioned and arranged, mistreated, and preserved. This is one of the key aspects, in the words of Maria Brandão, to the understanding of what has been called *baianidade* (Brandão 2001). Praised and celebrated inside and beyond the borders because of their magnetic force and put in the straitjacket of culture, Bahian blacks embody the paradox. Perhaps they are the paradox.

The Historical Context

Next to Rio de Janeiro (38 percent) and Recife (13 percent), Salvador's port was among those receiving the greatest number of enslaved Africans during the centuries when slave trafficking, both legal and illegal, was practiced. About 1.3 million Africans entered Bahia between the sixteenth century and 1850, which made up 25 percent of the total number of slaves brought to Brazil (Viana Filho 1988: 156–161).

The regional and cultural origins of these enslaved Africans are already well-known. In Bahia, those of Bantu origin were the majority until the mid-seventeenth century, but after that the predominance shifted to diverse Yoruba groups (Verger 1987; Tavares 2001).

After abolition, among the many groups who were involved in black organizing were blue-collar professional unions, such as that of the dockworkers. Balduíno, the main protagonist of the novel *Jubiabá,* by Jorge Amado, is one of the black leaders who was in an occupation reserved for ex-slaves. The Bahian Worker's Center (Centro Operario), created by blacks in June of 1894, existed vigorously until the 1930s. Like the Brazilian Black Front in São Paulo, it began to wither with the establishment of the dictatorship of the new state of Getúlio Vargas. At its height, the center had a membership of 5,000 associates and was, in its time, a landmark of black organizing for the Afro-Bahian community (Leal 1994).

Nevertheless, as the twentieth century unfolded and contemporary black movements emerged in the 1970s and 1980s, it appears that in certain sectors some forms of black organizing have gained more visibility in relation to the Bahian power elite. This elite, as shown by Eul-Sound Pang (1979), is oligarchical and descends to a great extent from the old slaveholding patriarchs, or *colonels,* who are the beneficiaries of the old colonial order and even of the one dominant during the Old Republic (1889–1929).

Studies of the situation of blacks in the economic formation of Bahia, produced at least since the 1980s, confirm that the extensive labor force and African cultural production have been subjugated to the interests of powerful classes that control the political-institutional power in the state (Pedrão 1992; Castro and Sá Barreto 1992; Castro and Guimarães 1992; Agier 1992; Bairros 1987). There is a strong component of racial discrimination, inherited from slavery, that keeps Afro-Bahians at the margin. Data from the National Annual Survey of Households (PNAD) about labor market participation in Bahia demonstrate systematically that there is a disproportionate concentration of blacks and browns in labor sectors that are the least qualified and worst paid. Blacks and browns participate disproportionately in jobs with the lowest remuneration, earning on average between one-half and five times the minimum wage. Whites are concentrated in employment with high remuneration—ten or more times the minimum wage. The unemployment in the Metropolitan Region of Salvador (RMS), which since the 1980s has been constantly the highest or the second highest of the country (Recife rivals), has a strong racist component (Bairros 1988).

It must be stressed that the problem of economic inequality that affects Afro-descendents, seen through the prism of racial discrimination, does not appear to be successfully solved simply by educating those who face discrimination. Citing Salvador Sandoval (1991) ("The Mechanisms of Racial Discrimination in the Labor Market: The Case of Urban Brazil"), who studied São Paulo's labor market, and Luiza Bairros (1987), who analyzed the labor market in Salvador, Michel Agier (1992) argues that "the more one moves up on the qualification ladder, the greater the difference of salaries between whites and blacks," with blacks being disfavored.

With respect to labor market discrimination, Agier observes the following: (1) the difference in favor of whites is globally bigger in nonmanual occupations; (2) in the case of industry, civil construction presents a smaller advantage for whites than in the transformative industries; (3) there is an imbalance disfavoring blacks with regard to the relation between level of schooling and performance—with the same level of schooling, blacks earn less than whites. "With exception to the case of illiterates and among the noneducated, where the difference between whites and blacks is almost zero, the growth of imbalance in favor of whites accompanies, almost step-by-step, the growth of schooling levels."

The absence of social mobility of the ethnic group is at times denied, based on the confusion that some make by observing the successful path of specific individuals able to ascend in society. Nobody denies the possibility of black people surpassing the barrier of misery and, in so doing, being accepted in circles of power. Nevertheless, the masses of blacks remain in socially inferior positions.

"The post-slavery Bahian productive system," according to Pedrão (1992: 7), "operated always under the assumption of an unlimited labor supply of an unqualified and semiqualified workforce (with relation to the qualifications needed to participate in the industrial production process)." Research about the labor market reveals that the number of workers with regular contracts and benefits in the Salvadorean metropolitan area has remained at around 30 percent over decades, for an economically active population of about 1.5 million. This results in Bahia ranking twentieth, among the twenty-seven states of the federation and the Federal District, in its Human Development Index (HDI), according to the 2005 report of the Program of the United Nations for Human Development (PNUD). Although the criteria utilized in the data-gathering of the HDI can be criticized, we can still assert that Bahia, taking into account gross domestic product (GDP) per capita, life expectancy, and education, is almost as bad as Acre, Pernambuco, Sergipe, Paraíba, Piauí, Maranhão, and Alagoas.

The modern industrialization in Bahia has its beginnings in the 1950s, with the implementation of the Hydroelectric Company of the San Francisco and Petrobras. After that came the Industrial Center of Aratu (during the 1960s, which today is in crisis) and the petrochemical complex of Camaçari in the 1970s, each of which has fewer and fewer workers and demands a more qualified labor force. The modernization-industrialization relation established new requirements of qualification for workers. This, according to Pedrão (1992: 8), indirectly amplified the biased effects of the educational system. It caused an increase in the distance between high-ranking and low-ranking high schools, and "as a consequence, between those that can pay for an education that is technologically up-to-date and those restricted to conventional education with decreasing quality and without specialization. In this way, the difficulties to overcome the separation between those that continue in mainly manual activities and those that have access to nonmanual activities are reproduced."

In Bahia, Afro-descendents (blacks and browns) represent nearly 80 percent of the workforce. As the world of emerging industry characterizes itself "by strong selectivity, that is exercised both on the basis of ascribed characteristics (such as race, sex, and age), as from acquired characteristics (like schooling and urban experience)," to the majority of the economically active black population, what is left is employment in the informal market (Castro and Guimarães 1992: 5–6).

Politics and Local Culture

The modern market, with its demands on African cultures in Bahia, but mainly in the greater region of Salvador and the Bahian Recôncavo, has made those cultures almost a material good that is used by the black population as symbolic capital. To be sure, this is not a contemplative attitude toward the rituals of this culture, but a transformation of this culture into merchandise to be negotiated in a society of consumption. In this way, popular culture loses any subjective function and any emancipatory potential as a counterideology.

Marxists that abandoned Marxism were critical of political economy, and the culturalists that are in style today might say that this culture affirms identities, but in truth it is a product, measured by the amount of revenue it can produce, and it is exclusively the product of an ethnic group discriminated against in the labor market.

Due to the economic configuration of an industrialized Bahia and to the factors already discussed,

> we understand why the black population has been attracted, first to the educational system and urban services that do not require any assets. We also understand why they have been attracted to leisure activities—arts and sports—and why they have resorted to forms of pseudo-assertion in the cultural realm, which in fact are constituted by an eclectic assembly of different, and often disparate, cultural elements, for the reproduction of their cultural memory. The black population is thus readily recruited to become elements of an urban labor market that is by definition dependent on the external market of tourism. (Pedrão 1992: 14)

Beyond the search for the affirmation of black identity, with the advent of the tourism industry and governmental politics geared to that sector, the hyper-valorization of the aspects of culture related to African roots in Bahia appears to have transformed the black masses into prisoners. Since the 1980s, local governments sought to administer cultural manifestations and products, aiming at the tourist market—and therefore at generating capital—through the assembly of a bureaucratic machine that penetrates all cultural domains and finds expression in such culminating moments as Carnival or in the merging of two separate areas under one institutional framework, namely the state secretary of Culture and Art with the secretary of Tourism.

This tendency of imprisonment has been noticeable ever since the electoral campaign for the mayorship of Salvador in 1985, the first after the military dictatorship, which constituted a watershed for the path of the organized black movement in that state—the one with the largest black presence, which has, despite its numerical supremacy, not been able to take political-institutional power.

1985: An Electoral Case Study

In the 1985 elections—the first in the Bahian capital, where 80 percent of the electorate is black—the political relevance of a racial vote was disputed for the first time. The leadership of the black movement, which, initially, between January and June was united in advancing the candidacy of a black candidate, soon was divided between the black candidate, Edvaldo Brito, and Mário Kertèsz, a self-declaring Jew. Not that the electoral dispute was openly racial:

the entire time, Kertèsz tried to avoid this kind of debate, whereas Brito actively sought it, and Kertèsz never mentioned his ethnic origin in his electoral campaign.

The split in black leadership happened when Kertèsz offered second- and third-rate municipal jobs to all leaders who supported him. All the opinion polls taken at the beginning of the electoral campaign predicted a safe margin in favor of Kertèsz. Nevertheless, there emerged a threat of radicalization of the black movement with the positions taken by Brito.

To neutralize the possibility of a polarization of the campaign between blacks (who would support Brito) and the nonblacks (who would support Kertèsz), Duda Mendonça, who was responsible for Kertèsz's campaign gaining the support of the representative part of the organized black movement, was committed to supporting Brito until June. The president of the Afro-centric group Olodum, João Jorge Rodrigues, until then an active coordinator for support of the candidacy of Brito, was the first to jump to Kertèsz's side and appeared on radio and TV channels during electoral publicity programs repudiating Brito.

Several other black leaders followed his example, and they attacked Brito the hardest, seeking to disqualify the black candidate by branding him as unprepared and uncompromising with the cause of black empowerment. The justification for the *chameleonism* of these leaders was the claim of a supposed partisan purism, in reality nonexistent in *Tupiniquim* politics. Brito was abandoned by them in the middle of the election after he lost the convocation of his old party, Party of the Brazilian Democratic Movement (Partido do Movimento Democratico Brasileiro, PMDB), and received an offer of support from the Brazilian Workers Party (Partido Trabalhista Brasileiro, PTB), an eclectic party sheltered under the command of those allied under *Carlismo*. Kertèsz, who had started his political career under the protecting hand of senator Antonio Carlos Magalhães, gained the support of the PMDB, but not without being accused by his adversaries of having bought votes. The electoral dispute between two representatives of two historically persecuted groups sheds important light on the effects of using ethnic background for political campaigns—even in such a predominantly black city as Salvador. Whereas Brito openly campaigned as a black candidate, Kertèsz, otherwise openly Jewish, sought to avoid and downplay his religious and ethnic affiliation and throughout the campaign stressed his Bahian- and Brazilianness, thus tapping into the then-predominant myth of presenting Brazil as a *racial democracy,* where race and ethnic background are superseded by an all-embracive nationalism. Brito, on the contrary, emphasized his blackness and sought to gain support among the black population, or at least among those organized in black-power organizations.

The campaign strategy Brito chose was one of stressing his ethnic background in order to garner support among Afro-Bahians, who are the majority in this state. Doing so, Brito did what other black leaders and organizations have long been doing: using culture and shared cultural background as their way to define belonging to their group and to garner support among black Bahians.[3] Kertèsz, to whom this ethnic option would have been equally available, decided not to carry his ethnicity and cultural background into the public sphere and chose to keep it in the private realm.

Afro-Brazilians have long favored culture as a way to organize and mobilize, as the account on postabolition black activism by Kim Butler (1998) demonstrates. Focusing on culture, ethnicity, and religion as the main fields to strengthen black group consciousness, however, has had adverse results with regard to the conquering of political and economic power. It has also proven ineffective to achieve integration into Brazilian society. Instead of becoming integral to the political, social, and civic body of Brazilian society, Afro-Brazilians have remained exotic elements of an otherwise Euro-dominated society and Afro-culture has been transformed into public spectacle and a tourist commodity.

This diverging strategy was again more than obvious in the 1985 mayoral dispute in Salvador. By elevating questions of culture and ancestry into the defining element of Afro-Brazilians, they have become perpetual *others,* whose identity is the subject of university seminars and conferences. Salvador has become a life museum for curious tourists and anthropologists from abroad, but increasingly also from Brazil's predominantly white south, who are able to assert their own unproblematic whiteness by contrasting it with the problematic identity of Brazilian blacks.

On a more important note—the dispute with Brito, the descendant of African slaves, in the largest Afro-descendent city of the Americas, which some happily call the Black Rome—Kertèsz won the election with 56.4 percent of the valid votes and Brito came in second, with less than 30 percent of the votes. Most of the media explicitly supported Kertèsz. The most important newspaper, *A Tarde,* even if not openly endorsing a candidate, printed several covers and editorials criticizing the reparatory tone of the black vote, embodied in Brito's candidacy. Brito secured three minutes in the Free Schedule of Electoral Propaganda (HGPE), the daily allowance of free electoral publicity, compared to the thirty minutes to which Kertèsz was entitled, based on the party coalition that backed him. In addition, Brito did not count on the support of any large media vehicles.

The Role of Cultural Groups

Between 1975 and 1980, the cultural group Ilê Aiyê revolutionized the concept of Carnival aesthetics in Bahia. It brought the racial question to the forefront, especially of Carnival, by denouncing discrimination and prejudice

against blacks. As it gained more followers among the historically relegated social stratum, it suffered severe criticism from elites, who branded the Carnival
bloc racist and radical (even though elites did not admit blacks into their social
and entertainment clubs). What we can observe in Salvador during the 1980s
was, without a doubt, the growth of the black movement, which unquestionably
fortified the power of messages transmitted by Afro-Carnival groups (*blocos*).

Afro-*blocos* had a great ability to mobilize, contrary to the groups preferred by the middle class, which only exist during the five days of Carnival
and, generally, only to promote their stars so they can launch yet another questionable album. Ilê Aiyê, Muzenza, Ara Ketu, Puxada Axé, Olodum, Malê De-
balê, and others carried activities to the communities that are normally
confined to the periphery of Salvador, during every month of the year.

Salvador takes on a number of African cultural features. Gradually people
are becoming more and more conscientious of their roots, of their origins, and
of their slave history. They are also beginning to be more aware of the semi-
slavery system, which was hidden under the mantle of racial democracy.
Eighty percent of the prison population of Salvador is black. Of the 1.2 million slum dwellers, 80 percent are black; the same is true of the unemployed
and those conducting odd jobs in the so-called informal sector that make up
around 70 percent of the about 3 million inhabitants of the city. The extermi-
nation of black youths by the police or by the action of paramilitary groups is
one of the cancers always present in the Bahian capital. These are some of the
issues Afro-centric groups problematized.

Once elected, Kertèsz invited Gilberto Gil to direct the Cultural Foundation Gregório de Matos. The main leaders that supported Kertèsz received jobs
at the second and third echelons, mainly as aids to Gil. Up to that point, the
main Afro-Bahian cultural group that was involved directly with the government was the Afoxé Sons of Gandhy, a Carnival group that is the largest em-
blem of pacifist negritude.

In the period in which he was mayor (1986–1988), Kertèsz increased his
private patrimony. He also invested in vehicles of communication, buying the
traditional newspaper *Jornal da Bahia* and space and time on radio and television. He also considered acquiring the property of the local branch of the
Rede Bandeirantes TV station, but the business did not prosper. Additionally,
he bought his own radio station, the Radio Cidade (afterwards Metropolis
FM), taking advantage of the national communication group Jornal do Brasil's
bankruptcy.

Kertèsz built alliances and was able to elect his successor in the city hall,
influencing municipal power until January 1990, when he broke with his allies. They, in turn, abandoned him, alleging that he, during the three years that
he governed Salvador, had diverted a sum of US$200 million from public
funds, through fraudulent contracts with the attorney general of Salvador
(*Procuradoria Geral de Salvador*). Kertèsz then came back and built a pact

with one of the most powerful men of the Brazilian Republic at the end of the 1990s, the oligarch Antonio Carlos Magalhães. The trial of the *Procuradoria* against him had not finally been judged until 2005, when it was transferred to the Federal Supreme Court. On the other hand, through his radio station, Kertèsz became one of the most popular communicators of Bahia.

With Kertèsz in the city hall, managers of successful cultural groups—like Olodum—supported his administration, from which they later had difficulties gaining power. Put more accurately, they were forced out some years later, when it became clear that the Kertèsz administration was one of the most harmful administrations to the municipal treasury. The mayor became rich, until 2005 when he was indicted (though not yet convicted) for fraud and embezzlement of millions of dollars that he was accused of stealing from public funds.

After the radicalization of ethnic discourse in the 1985 campaign, Afro-Bahian cultural groups started to professionalize their relationship with these types of schemes. They discovered that there could be a payoff for supporting one candidate over another. Olodum, in particular, was able to take advantage of the opportunities that were offered to them after supporting Kertèsz. At about the same time, João Jorge, president of the group, became an Ashoka fellow—a private American organization—receiving a monthly budget to continue his black militancy. It is worth noting that in the history of the Brazilian black movement from the 1980s onward, foreign institutions, such as the Ford Foundation and the Rockefeller Foundation, among others, supported some of the most important leaders.

Since the beginning of the 1980s, Ashoka has worked in Brazil, India, and other impoverished countries, including some on the African continent. They seek to identify social and community leaders, based on race or gender, whom they deem worthy of support based on their performance and influence in the group they represent. The fellowship recipient does not have to be accountable to the community he or she represents for the money he or she receives from Ashoka. In the 1990s, a significant group of black leaders received fellowships from this institution or was part of its advisory committee (generally composed of older scholarship holders). Among those were Joel Rufino, who would later, under the presidency of Fernando Henrique Cardoso, become president of the state-led Palmares Foundation (Fundação Cultural Palmares); Ivanir dos Santos, of the Center for the Articulation of Marginalized Populations in Rio de Janeiro; Normando Batista, of the Center for Popular Education; Sueli Carneiro, of the Institute for Black Women Geledés; Jairo Santos, of the National Center for the Articulation of Afro-Religious Scholars (CENARAB); and Diva Moreira, coordinator of the Casa Dandara in Belo Horizonte.

Of all the entities of the black movement, inside or outside of Bahia, no other underwent such a metamorphosis as Olodum under the command of João Jorge. Even Ilê Aiyê, founded in 1974 and accepting, since 1981, support from the construction firm Odebrecht for some of its projects, avoided taking a headlong dive into commercial adventures. Olodum was created in 1979 by blacks such as Geraldão, who had been previously involved with other Carnival clubs. He also created Muzenza later, together with Janilson Santos Barabadá, but Olodum remained different, compared to other *blocos* such as Ilê Aiyê and Badauê—which in that year already had achieved relative success because it adopted reggae, mixed with samba, as its basic rhythm.

During three or four Carnivals, Geraldão and a group of black intellectual militants, for example the poet-professor Jônatas Conceição da Silva and the videoclubster Luís Orlando, put the minuscule Olodum in the street, starting at Pelourinho Square. Following dissidence within Ilê Aiyê, where he participated as a counselor, João Jorge Rodrigues was accepted at Olodum, and accompanied by his wife, Kátia Mello, and his sister, Cristina Rodrigues. With him, the samba master Neguinho do Samba also left Ilê Aiyê. Samba had a fundamental role in the creation of the drum rhythm that later would conquer the world: samba reggae. With this new team, Olodum restructured, its initial founders left, and the new managers started to establish diverse political alliances, some quite different, to say the least.

The electoral campaign of 1985 and its ramifications stimulated the group to recruit a team of counselors and advisers from different backgrounds and spheres of influence, ranging from government branches and cabinet leaders to journalists of a broad political-ideological spectrum, both from inside and outside of Bahia. This engineering, together with the boom of Afro-Bahian rhythms initiated with the recording of the song "Eu sou Negão" (I am a proud, big, black man) by the singer and composer Gerônimo ("Nessa cidade todo mundo é d'Oxum") (In this city, everybody belongs to Oxum),[4] followed by the success of the song "Faraó" (Pharaoh) by Luciano Santos, catapulted Olodum to a new sphere of action—one of professional business relations. This was the first Afro-*bloco* to become professional.

Although it began as an entity of the black movement, Olodum started to act with ambiguity, not entirely giving up black-movement activity, but starting to transform into a private institution geared toward the market of show business. As a consequence, it became one of the companies of the Carnival industry that achieved the most media coverage and exposure. It even launched its own Visa credit card with the Bradesco bank ("The business of Olodum," *Gazette Mercantile,* August 29, 1994: 1). In that process, its leadership did not hesitate to publicly fire the director Edvaldo Mendes Araújo, known as Zulu, in an episode that has remained unclear to this day, because of the dubious loss of money belonging to the group ("Zulu, Unmasked, is excluded from Olodum," *A Tarde,* March 31, 1994, on the police page with picture).

During the presidency of Luís Inácio Lula da Silva, Zulu became president of the Palmares Foundation—an official organ of the Department of Culture directed by singer Gilberto Gil, who, in the 1985 electoral run, supported Mário

Kertèsz. A legacy of the Brazilian Communist Party and one of the important leaders of the university student movement of the late 1970s, the architect Zulu Araújo was invited to become part of Olodum's management after his term as adviser to the cabinet of the secretary of culture of Bahian governor Waldir Pires (1986–1990). Five months after the lost money was reported, *A Tarde* published a small note, this time without any highlights, stating: "Zulu has proven, with the help of the Police, that he has not taken a check from Olodum, as he was accused of taking by the *bloco*. A lot of people now fear that he will counterattack and throw the 'talc' in the fan" (*A Tarde,* August 14, 1994).

Parallel to their business success, criticisms against Olodum's managers' actions also became more vociferous: "For the sixth consecutive year, under tourists' eyes, transvestites, gays, prostitutes, artists, salespersons, and inhabitants of Pelô . . . [led] the scam at the Castro Alves Square on Ash Wednesday. . . . On the posters produced from leftover cardboard, revelers sent their messages—many of which had long been stuck in their throats and were now let to jump into the middle of the ashes. Olodum got its share. It's confirmed! Olodum sold itself and . . . look at the amount of gringos" (*Tribuna da Bahia,* February 14, 1991). "*Bloco* changes political tone for crazy parade" (*O Estado de S. Paulo,* February 13, 1994). "Pelô in black and white" (*Isto É,* September 29, 1993). As reported in the *Folha de S. Paulo* (September 15, 1992: 1 and A11): "Participation in a 'show-event' . . . the participation of Maluf divides Bahian block Olodum." The senator Antonio Carlos Magalhães, defending himself against verbal attacks from the Pernambuco minister Gustavo Krause, declared: "I am with Olodum, and I am not with *Galo da Madrugada*" (*Isto É,* July 26, 1995).

In the three years of the Kertèsz adminstration, between January 1986 and December 31, 1989, Olodum initiated the construction of its patrimony from nothing. It received donations of property; formed partnerships with influential people from the municipal, state, and federal governments; and, arguing that it needed to adapt itself to the requirements of modernity, it adapted the rhythm of its drums and lightened up its older protest lyrics to the demands imposed by the record industry. It even hosted a weekly radio program that, for some time, was put on air by a radio station belonging to a deputy connected to the Kertèsz clique.

The culminating point for Olodum in terms of market success, when it changed from a nonprofit entity into a private, capitalist company, came when the US musician Paul Simon came to Salvador in 1989 to record a music video, for one of the songs for his new album, *Rhythm of the Saints,* using Olodum and percussionists from the group Obvious Child. That episode definitely opened the doors to the local, national, and international media for Olodum, similar to what happened with the South African group Ladysmith Black Mambazo, after they participated in the prize-winning Paul Simon *Graceland* album.

Conclusion

Between the emergence of the group Ilê Aiyê in 1974 and the explosion of the so-called *blocos* and other Afro groups in the state of Bahia, starting at the end of the twentieth century, Bahia experienced diverse transformations in the approach of political elites, intellectuals, and the media toward race relations in Bahian society. The boom of songs and rhythms of these groups—which earned a significant slice of the cake of the phonographic industry, including the programs of radio syndicates, and, consequently, considerable space in the cultural sections of major newspapers—corresponded to the transformation of race relations, which crystallized the old and immovable problems of the Afro-Bahian population.

Despite mobilizing crowds for amusement, to dance in squares and avenues, there has been no direct correlation between success in the cultural market and the political struggle to gain access to the spheres of decisionmaking power of the state. A strong indicator of this fact is provided by the depressing performance of black candidates, even those supported by organized black-power movements, in the electoral disputes over parliamentary seats. The bulk of money generated by the boom of musical rhythms does not circulate among the groups that created these new musical aesthetics, which in certain moments of the 1990s captivated Brazil; the businessmen and producers of groups and singers, mainly females, of *axé* music are the ones that most profited and keep on profiting from that industry. One can get an idea of this by looking at their names: Sangalo and Mercury.

After Brito (who ended up moving to São Paulo and began a career as an accountant and university professor and was, at one point, secretary of Legal Matters to the São Paulo mayor Celso Pitta) the black population of Salvador has never again dared to launch a black candidate to dispute the position of mayor or governor of the Black Mecca.[5] It becomes clear how much culture can actually alienate people. In Bahia, the societal place of black people has been established according to the criteria of elites in power and their allies and a culture that is stripped of any elements that can challenge their power. Because of this, the very strength of Afro-Brazilian culture became the chains that hinder them in conquering other spaces of power.

What is the result of the performance of Bahian Afro-*blocos* today? To answer this question, two separate analyses must be established. One has a purely economic character; the other is a cultural-political stance.

All critiques, be they constructive or destructive, are at the end personal. My own critique is subject to further critique and, as an opinion, is thus open to challenges. Afro-*blocos* appeared in the middle of the 1970s, consolidated during the years, and, at present, some of them have transformed into capitalist companies. It was not only Afro-*blocos,* but the entire Carnival, with all its clubs and bands, did the same with the boom of new Bahian music.

These groups are organized as businesses, but they are tax-exempt because they are nonprofit entities and, sometimes, even serve the broader, public good. All of them commercialize different goods—from clothing to stickers, CDs, and other memorabilia. They enjoy, like churches and other institutions of private education, tax exemption, but they are also widely seen as serving the greater good.

When it comes to Afro-*blocos,* however, an argument needs to be made. Clubs in Bahia were born and developed as entities of black militancy, focused on the denunciation and the struggle against racial discrimination suffered by some of the population. They presented themselves as organizations engaged in the problematic of interethnic relations in a state where black and brown people are the majority. That is why Afro-*blocos* are not the same as the *axé* group *Chiclete com Banana,* for example.

The difference is that the discourse of Afro-*blocos* is entirely rooted in affirming negritude. And negritude, at least within the Bahian context, does not lend itself to the same marketing strategies as commercial products, such as a bar of soap. What can be easily observed now is the application of a form of utilitarianism to racial issues, directed toward the petty purpose of conquering a place in show business.

Critiquing this new moment of Afro-*blocos* does not imply being opposed to them and their chances to compete in the attractive and tempting entertainment market. To the contrary, I consider the growth and consolidation of a strong, black business class that is able to compete for the ranking of being bigger and better to be positive indeed. This is, however, entirely different from any political action in the struggle against the ideology of racial prejudice.

Groups such as Olodum, Ilê Aiyê, Ara Ketu, and, on a smaller scale but no less important, the Filhos de Gandhy should remain open to scrutiny from black activists, especially when they present themselves as part of the black-power movement. This is not entirely the philosophy of the Filhos de Gandhy and of Ara Ketu, but it certainly is the way that Ilê Aiyê and Olodum present themselves.

As entities of the black-power movement, they receive a series of opportunities. At the same time, the cultural industry absorbs the discourse of negritude of Afro-Bahian *blocos*—as it did with jazz and reggae and the percussion section of the samba group Mocidade Independente—and the discourse becomes detached from its political meaning. To sing—backed by strong percussion—about the misfortunes of blacks, under the current circumstances, can mean nothing more than simply earning money.

Today not even the social work that such groups develop in the community where they are based can remain free of criticism. The sole logic of any business is the accumulation of capital, of profit, based on exploiting accumulated value. To maintain the appearance that they are assisting communities with this neophilanthropic paternalism, receiving nontaxable funds and the benevolence of public opinion, which is little informed about how business is run, does not guarantee any safeguards from criticism.

The importance of Afro-*blocos* for strengthening the discourse of Bahian black-power movements should not be downplayed. But we have the obligation to oppose the use of black-movement discourse by some, subtracting from it almost all of its political substance. In many cases, what remains of this discourse is the bare minimum, which is necessary to avoid groups' discreditation as Afro-*blocos*.

By submitting to the market, driven by commercial strategizing and negotiating the symbolic capital of black culture, which has been accumulated in centuries of struggle, such organizations are undermining the ethnic group that they claim to defend. Although some have been able to garner large profits, socioeconomic indicators (education, child mortality, housing, jobs, etc.) show that dancing to the rhythm of the groups does not change the situation of blacks.

If there really is a common adversary that unifies black militancy—that is, institutionalized racism, the fruit of ideological racism, which manifests itself in the most diverse social spheres, such as in the workplace, schools, the media, and, finally, in the power structure—then the problem is to determine if all means are justified to achieve the desired ends. In other words, is it correct, in the struggle against racism that claims as its victims the descendants of African slaves in Brazil, to reduce the discourse of black awareness to a marketing game?

The Brazilian black-power movement should not be afraid of exposing its internal contradictions. These divergences are common to all active sectors of society, political parties, unions, the church, and employers. Exposing it, I do not pretend to provide ammunition to the enemy, but offer conditions to extend the facts we can use to reflect on.

There are some irreconcilable points of conflict among different approaches adopted by black elites engaged in antiracism militancy in Brazil. Two positions stand out that illustrate the dominant postures guiding black militancy. One is positivist and reproduces a discourse of modernity, without taking into account that this modernity is directly related to the exclusion of the majority in a world with a globalized economy. For the supporters of this position, the time is one of overcoming acts of black organizations; to them this is the era of the self-made man.

For ourselves, preferring a critical posture toward modernity, this kind of vision gave rise to a black movement of results, following a line of trade unionism that gained weight over the past years. Organizations of the Brazilian black-power movement are transformed into businesses benefiting few and treating the racial question as a means to achieve private ends.

These organizations, it appears, embrace modernity by avoiding conflict, avoiding facing the urban war that rages in several urban centers of the country. Like their leaders, these movements gain from such a situation, and they do not want any alteration of the current state of affairs. In that sense, instead of being modern, the discourse of this sector of the black movement is, in fact, neoconservative.

For quite some time now, this sector has made alliances with exactly those sectors that control the spheres of political decisionmaking, from which the Brazilian black population itself has been excluded. Over the past decade, black leaders have been incorporated as advisers into state apparatuses in several parts of the country—like São Paulo, Rio de Janeiro, and Rio Grande do Sul.

Bahia is a serious case that deserves analysis. There is no doubt that one of the reasons for the perpetuation of the extreme poverty of the population of that state is the role that cultural groups that supposedly belong to the black-power movement have performed over the last decade. A certain *Peleism* took root in these entities. The ethnic cleansing that occurred in the old Historical Center of Salvador (95 percent of the residents were kicked out), conducted by the state and counting on the support of those black organizations that were offered real estate once the neighborhood was restored and transformed into a tourist attraction, provides an example of this phenomenon.

In the same way, with rare exceptions, those councils that called for the participation of the black community, created by governments all over Brazil, often serve foremost to co-opt leaders. It makes no sense that, at present, these councils—in Rio or in São Paulo, for example—although they serve the government, do not visibly voice self-criticism about the violence practiced by the police of those states against the populations of the peripheries and of the *favelas*.

Another horrific fact has been the incapacity of the black-power movement to transform its discourse into votes in favor of a project of reaching power. One of the more recent examples: the parliamentary election of 2006 points to a retreat of black and popular parliamentary representation, which shrank in the Bahian Legislative Assembly as well as in the Chamber of Representatives in Brasília. Bahian voters elected only one black representative to the House of Representatives. The current situation is that there are intense debates about affirmative action policies, quotas, and the Declaration of Racial Equality. These are important issues for discussion in the legislature. Nevertheless, these are not addressed when there is little representation of blacks in the House.

Notes

1. Bahia is one of Brazil's twenty-seven states. The country is situated in South America with a geographic size equivalent to the continental United States. It was colonized by the Portuguese until 1822. Portuguese navigators arrived in the south of the

state of Bahia in April of 1500. They were on their way to India and promptly integrated Brazil into the growing Luso Empire.

2. The Country Brief of the World Bank describes Brazil as follows: "An industrial power, ninth world GDP measured by purchasing power parity (PPP, 2006), with the largest population in Latin America and the Caribbean, in the past few years Brazil has reached important economic, social and environmental advances, including macroeconomic stability and significant reductions in poverty, income inequality and in deforestation rates in the Amazon. The country is also increasing its participation in the international community, assuming a leadership role in areas such as climate change, trade, biofuels, AIDS, biodiversity and social technology" (http://web.worldbank.org). Freyre (1933) and Viana Filho (1988) are two authors that highlighted the economic value of labor of African slaves in the construction of the Brazilian economy. As such, when the Brazilian state approved the day marking the end of slave labor, May 13, 1888, it did not determine a legal means of supporting ex-slaves and their descendents. The concrete result is that all data referring to the situation of Afro-descendents (*pretos e mestiços*) prove that they are the victims of economic, political, and social exclusion in the country. With respect to this see Paixão (2003), *Human Development and Race Relations.*

3. See, e.g., the account of Kim Butler (1998) on early black organizing in Bahia.

4. Oxum is the African goddess of rivers and sweet water, whose attributes are said to be female beauty, sweetness, and vanity. This statement implies that everybody in Salvador has a connection to Africa, African religion, and African mythology; it also implies that there are no truly white, European people in Salvador and no true separation of different "races" exists—as everybody is at least a little bit black and Afro-descendent, if not Afro-inspired.

5. In 2008, Edvaldo Brito returned to local politics as a candidate for vice-mayor of Salvador, as part of a center coalition. This coalition effectively won the elections and will govern Salvador until 2012.

11

New Social Activism: University Entry Courses for Black and Poor Students

Renato Emerson dos Santos

In Brazil, the political debate of the early twenty-first century is marked by the emergence of discussions about racial inequalities, associated with the need to implement public policies for socially excluded groups (and initiatives for all segments of society) aimed at reversing educational segregation through affirmative action. This emergence represents (1) the public dissemination and popularization of critical debates around the *myth of racial democracy*, which, until recently, was confined to the restricted circles of Brazilian black-power movements and a small fraction of the academic community directly connected to the subject; (2) the encounter of intellectual elaborations with the diffuse racial conscience of Brazilian blacks, a complex set of—though little-studied—readings and behavioral norms; and (3) a reaction to the routinization of racial conflicts in our social fabric.

The environment that was established by these discussions also brought to light Brazilian society's awareness of the historical injustices and the routine violence Afro-Brazilians have been subjected to due to racism, and the resulting need for action. Whether this action is taken by the state or by other segments of society, it has become obvious that racism, now recognized as a national problem, has triggered a debate marked by the need for intervention. Not all facts, phenomena, or social processes are perceived and formulated as problems—in this case, problems of the state.

The conditions that allow for an institutionalization of the historical demands of Afro-descendants—long requested by black-power movement activists—are still being unveiled.[1] There are multiple areas of intervention, dialogue, and controversy about what concrete actions should be taken. Indeed, the so-called affirmative actions, an ample and complex set of initiatives geared toward the social promotion of Afro-descendants, have taken shape in distinct environments, despite growing mobilization and conservative forces, especially those that control media opinions.

These efforts to enact targeted racialized policies have mobilized counter-arguments, strategies, and rhetorical arguments that almost always fit the analytical framework offered initially by Hirschmann (1992):

- *futility*—the problem in Brazil is not racial, it is social; thus promoting a black elite will not solve the problem; what is needed instead is to end poverty;
- *perversity*—poor whites will be hurt; and
- *threat*—a racial conflict will be created in a country where such conflict does not exist and there will be a drop in the quality of performance in institutions that receive individuals without the necessary qualifications, which is damaging to the broader society.

These are the pillars of reactionary and conservative rhetoric in diverse geographical and historical contexts since the French Revolution, and they are again articulated now that a critique of racial asymmetry of Brazilian society is developing. These arguments encounter, however, a growing positive evaluation on the part of the population for the need and pertinence of racialized policies, a fact that is also evidenced by various opinion polls.[2]

In the process of dismantling the myth of racial democracy within the broader society, race-conscious, university-entry preparatory courses are among the most important. They are, since the 1990s, an answer to the economic and racial elitization of Brazilian universities. In Brazil, the main way to gain access to institutions of higher education is an entrance test called the vestibular, a battery of tests of all the disciplines taught in high school. In 1998, the federal government created the National Exam of Secondary Education (ENEM), and has been encouraging universities to utilize it as an entrance exam, but the vestibular remains the most common form of regulating access to institutions of higher education. In most cases, the university conducts the vestibular, although there are also cases where it is carried out by a group of universities or by an institution that specializes in academic testing and does so through a group of universities.

The high interest of the middle and upper classes to have their children accepted to university produced since the end of the 1960s a plethora of preparatory courses for the vestibular, called prevestibular courses. These courses are normally very expensive (to the point where they are commonly referred to as a vestibular industry, which costs millions of *reais* all over Brazil every year). This reinforces the exclusion of poor students from universities. It is against this exclusion that, in the beginning of the 1990s, militants of Brazil's black-power movements and other movements initiated the creation of courses for poor, black students and inhabitants of segregated areas, in a collective initiative that established a new agenda in the national public debate, the (racial) democratization of higher education.

Free prevestibular courses for blacks became popular during the 1990s and initiated a new dimension of publicizing the agenda of the Brazilian black-power movement, even if at times anchored in weak ideology. It has become undeniable that through the routine operation of these courses a considerable number of individuals, who have always experienced (but probably never undertook any effort to question) the characteristic asymmetry of race relations of this country, are driven and pushed to discuss and politicize this asymmetry for the first time.

In this sense, this chapter discusses how antiracist ideas are disseminated, not by the state or the private sector, but by race-conscious prevestibular courses that have spread in Brazil over the last fifteen years. I begin by focusing on a social movement with a racialized component, called Prevestibular for Blacks and the Poor (PVNC, Pré-Vestibular para Negros e Carentes), an initiative for the general purpose of constructing such courses all over the country, but I will also discuss the dissemination of antiracist ideas by other courses that are not connected to this movement. The PVNC is a network of free prevestibular courses initially created in the early 1990s in Baixada Fluminense, a conglomerate of poor neighborhoods in Rio de Janeiro. This network currently represents almost ninety centers of the greater Rio de Janeiro metropolitan area.

The constitution of these courses for disadvantaged groups in Rio de Janeiro arose in the 1970s. Abdias do Nascimento (2002) started the creation of a course for blacks in 1976, organized by the Center of Brazil-Africa Studies. In the 1980s, other courses were created, for example, a course initiated by the Workers Union of the Federal University of Rio de Janeiro (UFRG), first created for associates and relatives of UFRG employees and people with low income. In 1991, the program *Mangueira Vestibulares* was created, in a *favela* (shantytown) in Rio de Janeiro named Mangueira. This course was directed at students of a school in the *favela* and other residents. Outside of Rio de Janeiro, in 1992, the Steve Biko Cultural Institute was created in Salvador, exclusively dedicated to black students. This initiative had huge repercussions within the Brazilian black movement. All of these experiences were important inspirations to the PVNC. Nevertheless, these programs did not follow the same model as the PVNC. These programs continued as independent nuclei and did not create networks or other connections. The PVNC, however, as will be discussed, created an organizational model and a form of action that resulted in a multiplication of the program through the creation of a collective social actor: a social movement.

The social movement for free prevestibular courses, which grew out of the initial effort of PVNC, at present comprises thousands of such courses all over Brazil. Other networks were created and expanded to the national level, such as Educafro (Education and Citizenship for Afro-Descendents and the Poor, which exists in the states of Rio de Janeiro, São Paulo, Minas Gerais, and Espírito Santos, with more than 200 nuclei and 10,000 students) and the Movement of People without University (MSU, Movimento dos Sem Universidade), which operates in nine states (Bahia, the Federal District, Espírito Santo, Maranhão, Minas Gerais, Paraná, São Paulo, Greater Rio de Janeiro, and Tocantins), next to thousands of nuclei that act independently all over the country.

These initiatives are direct and indirect reproductions of the work disseminated by the PVNC. PVNC is characterized by internal dynamics that, on one side, fomented intense political disputes, and on the other, in a dialectical way, found in its own members vigorous political catalyzers who functioned as stimulants of its own growth, which gave rise to the dissemination and popularization of race-conscious prevestibular courses. PVNC is, therefore, a central agent in the dissemination of these courses and of the discussion of racism in Brazil.

At the same time, free prevestibular courses challenge and question the elitization of Brazilian universities and put democratization on the agenda. They do so by linking all these issues to questions of race, thus cementing it as a fundamental and integral dimension of educational rights. In this way, the movement raises the awareness of the base in its routine work, and introduces this agenda into spheres of the state and other forums that traditionally have been insensitive to it. It therefore becomes necessary to understand how this double agenda that permits dialogue among distinct ideologies, values, and social institutions, which together cause an increase of the antiracist conscience in our social fabric, is constituted. I thus elaborate on the discussion by building on earlier research (Santos 2003a, 2003b, 2005, 2006).

A Form of Social Action

The construction of the PVNC is one of the outcomes of a number of strategies of the Brazilian black-power movement during the 1970s and 1980s, among which the following are salient: (1) the education of blacks as a process of constructing new leadership and strengthening existing leadership,[3] and (2) the spreading of militants of the antiracism struggle into different spaces of struggle and social intervention, with the aim to provide this new prevestibular movement with a culture of convergence and hybridization of values, interpretations of social reality, and action. The PVNC was therefore born out of the necessity to improve the educational levels of the social base of black movements—more specifically, it arose out of discussions that took place in the 1980s, especially within a group of black missionaries (*agentes de pastoral negra*) where the idea of intervening in the passage from secondary to higher levels of education by strengthening black admissions to universities gradually formed.[4]

These debates resulted, in 1993, in the creation of the first prevestibular nucleus in the main church of São João of Meriti, in Baixada Fluminense, an area of concentrated poverty located at the periphery of the metropolitan region of greater Rio de Janeiro. The growth of this initiative led other anti-racism militants not connected to the Catholic Church to produce ideological disputes about how to conduct this initiative and which strategies should be used to guarantee its growth and dissemination.[5] From these debates emerged not just the structure of the institution, but also a broader forum for social action with great potential to be reproduced, and thus the PVNC was born. The PVNC had, in certain moments (especially in the years 1997 and 1998) more than eighty nuclei all over the metropolitan region of Rio de Janeiro.[6] A general secretary administered each nucleus, and they met every month, forming a Council of Nuclei (in which each nucleus had two representatives with rights to speak and vote). Also, three yearly General Assemblies were held (which at times had up to 700 participants), and a series of other organized structures.

The movement grew quickly: In 1993 the first course began with ninety-eight students; with dissemination by the local media plus word of mouth, 716 candidates applied in 1994. In 1994, there were six courses. Apart from students, many others appeared to serve as teachers and coordinating volunteers. At the end of 1994, there were fifteen courses, and they started to become more militant, calling themselves "fronts" and "nuclei." The use of the term *nuclei* became so widespread that it became clear that these were no longer isolated efforts, but collective action. The new courses—fronts and nuclei—were created by ex-students, who passed the university entrance exam and wanted to give back what they had received; by groups and leadership of the Catholic Church stimulated by Frei David (the main leader of the PVNC); and by militants of other social organizations, including neighborhood associations, political parties, and youth groups, that had contact with the initiative and were motivated to reproduce and extend it.

The success of the experience of the PVNC gave rise to a movement on a national scale of free, volunteer-based prevestibular courses, with or without a racial focus, and also with other possible foci. The existence of free prevestibular courses precedes this phenomenon, but as mentioned above, with the examples of the Center for Brazil-Africa Studies, the Workers Union of UFRG, Mangeueira Vestibulares, and the Steve Biko Cultural Institute, the PVNC established new landmarks for these initiatives not only for its geographic reach and the speed with which it spread, achieving a degree of penetration into society previously not reached by other initiatives, but also because of its institutional structure. This structure worked together with its organizational form and ideology. The nationalization of this form of action was the result of political articulations of its participants on a national scale, which in turn was made possible because of the inheritances and symbolic capitals accumulated by previous action and further assisted by the parallel action of other anti-racism, religious, and partisan movements and unions.

On the other hand, the PVNC differed radically from other courses, because it operated in a network. This network was the result of a complex agglomeration of solidarities and political debates, which all contributed to the construction of the organizational structures of this social movement. In Santos (2003a, 2006), I explain the structuring of this movement at two levels that were linked and fed on each other. First, the level of collective forums (Councils of the Nuclei, general secretary, General Assembly, *Jornal Azânia,* teams of racial and pedagogical reflection, educational training seminars, and regional coordinators). All these levels were dominated by a select and restricted group with certain capital (articulations, knowledge, inheritances, institutional backgrounds) and by political interests that created challenges in relation to the hegemony and legitimacy over the leadership of the movement and led them to formulate different agendas and agencies. Second, the daily routines of the nuclei, as spaces of multiple perceptions and temporalities, were brought to life by a mass of individuals, who, moved by distinct ideals, constructed a process of socializing characterized by the broad participation of distinct social subjects and a crossing of world visions and oftentimes antagonistic arguments. They were individuals; some, for example, favored and others opposed the racial character of the courses.

The institutional structures of the PVNC are the product of debates among different visions of and political projects for the world and for the movement, representing, therefore, partial victories of different fields that disputed hegemony in its foundational period. Even if, as Giddens (1989) warns, the interventions of different agents involve rationalizations, which might avoid unintended outcomes or suppress the effects of unrecognized conditions, it is possible to identify fundamental landmarks in the institutional structures that reflect the influence of the hegemonic ideology of Franciscan Catholicism. The nuclei of the PVNC, and the majority of the free prevestibular courses, created and established themselves according to the following basic principles:

1. Self-management—Students, ex-students, and teachers make up a good part of the nuclei. This aspect confers a degree of autonomy of decision-making to the nuclei that, faced with the routine tensions and clashes between their daily routines and collective forums, create a potential rupture within the movement. On the other hand, this autonomy valorizes the routine debates of the nuclei as decisionmaking units, which has the effect of motivating, creating, and strengthening the participating subjects through a culture of participation that treats democracy not as a mere institutional format, but as a daily practice of interaction.

Even if many of the nuclei are characterized by despotic managements (after all, all animal revolutions have their pigs[7]), there are many cases of open conflict and even disposition of coordinators by students and teachers who then take over the coordination, which is highly unlikely within the formal spaces of education. This experience urges members of a prevestibular to participate and become politicized, which is an integral part of the approach of this initiative. Thus, the prevestibular gains a dimension of political education through its daily practice, which leads to a context where new values are created and reproduced. A new coordination, when it assumes responsibility of a nucleus, even if formed by subjects inexperienced in the political and civic initiatives of the PVNC, does not abandon, at least in its discourse, the political practices that have become crystallized in the movement, such as the course Culture and Citizenship, which aims at politicization through subject areas that are not necessarily part of university entrance exams.

2. Financial commitments—There is an almost complete absence of financial commitments. Normally the students contribute about 10 percent of a minimum salary, which is used for the acquisition of the necessary educational material, food (for courses functioning all day on Saturdays and Sundays), funding of transportation costs for teachers, and, if possible, financial aid for the vestibular registration fee payments, in case they are unable to get vouchers. This characteristic, which is rooted in the Franciscan tradition that dominates the PVNC, creates a resistance to the majority of prevestibulars against external funding, be it public or private. This nonacceptance of external funds makes the creation of partnerships and cooperation with the state and with the private sector impossible. It provides space for other actors more willing to cooperate with the state and private actors, such as NGOs, social movements, and a series of organizations and actors from other fields that expand and consolidate by offering paid prevestibular courses, thus allowing for each type of organization to delineate its own territory.

3. Voluntary work—Teachers and coordinators all volunteer, in a context marked by general demobilization and loss of activism in diverse social movements in Brazil. This general tendency is paradoxically contrasted by the emergence of this new form of solidarity and participation, even if it is not overtly political. This last aspect is fundamental in the structuring of the network to the extent that the prerequisite for entering the PVNC is—other than the mastery of the content of each discipline by the teachers—their own desire to enter the movement. The PVNC works with whoever volunteers, as the majority of the courses, with few exceptions, have no fixed criteria for the recruitment of new mili-

tants or collaborators, which creates a difficulty in standardizing teaching. That way, the PVNC constitutes a socializing public space, a plural (or pluri-ideological) actor, where it becomes possible, through multiple ways, to reconfigure collective identities in everyday practice, a space where democracy (essentially conflictive) is radicalized and decisions are multiple and made together as students are able to assume the responsibilities of coordinators, teachers, and other roles in the nuclei.

Ideological Pacts and
the Dissemination of the Race Discussion

As the prevestibular courses are transformed to this "hybrid subject of citizenship"—using the expression of Burity (2001)— they open up different possibilities for social inclusion and crossings between agendas for political discussion and intervention, which explains why each nucleus has a distinct relation to the foundational questions of the movement that created the prevestibular courses.[8] This situation was very important at the beginning of the construction of the PVNC, as the racial question—which became its flagship—was confronted with a more class-based approach from the Baixada Fluminense region (which was relegated to second rank, but not abandoned). The result was that racial quotas became their main objective, justified by their importance in causing poverty and by injustices in the field of education. This arrangement is articulated in each nucleus, with other arguments and forms of intervention, according to ideology established through routine discussions among members. In the routine of the nuclei, this multiplicity of discussions and interventions has two complementary and contradictory effects.

First, as the result of a political culture[9] marked by the need to aggregate individuals to guarantee the conduct of basic tasks within the prevestibular courses and by disputes for leadership of the movement, values, such as tolerance and sharing, are promoted and participation is stimulated. Hence, prevestibulars rest on weak ideological pacts, which creates a paradox. Such ideological pacts, on one hand, have great potential to be replicated, thus their power of diffusion; but, on the other hand, they are easy to break. These breaks occur both at the individual and collective level. On the individual level, they manifest themselves, for example, in a high turnover of teachers in many of the nuclei. At the collective level, the abandonment of the subject of race in the names of some courses is indicative of a whole series of resistances to the real, and not just the formal, ideological principles of the movement's founders. These resistances are constituted, especially, in the teaching of a discipline of little importance: the Culture and Citizenship course, a course that is geared toward the critical politicization of students and does not necessarily prepare them for the university entrance exam.

The example of the Culture and Citizenship course helps demonstrate how these ideological pacts, despite their weaknesses, are maintained and guarantee a minimum of necessary cohesion to the movement's structure, yet still permit the dissemination and strengthening of antiracist consciousness. Culture and Citizenship is not just another discipline in the PVNC. It is an important and distinctive sign of the alternative, popular, and critical character that is inherent to the prevestibular courses of this kind. Its origin reflects the debates around the construction of a distinctive pedagogical proposal, intrinsically linked to the political character of the courses, idealized as a way to spread political arguments during the entire time of the discipline, in such a way that the prevestibular becomes an initiative of popular education.[10] Nevertheless, the principle of self-management also translates into pedagogical autonomy, in an environment where, as mentioned above, the ideological affinity was not a criterion for the aggregation of teachers, which allowed for some individual resistance to the politicization of courses so that the initial proposal was not entirely achieved. Culture and Citizenship is thus a means of convergence among preparation for the university entrance exam, political awareness, and the search for an adequate pedagogical proposal to the reality and interests of social segments involved in the PVNC.

Not teaching Culture and Citizenship is thus perceived as reproducing the traditional political-pedagogical project, perceived and identified as an instrument of exclusion. All of the popular university entrance prep courses—not only of the PVNC, but also those inspired by it—started adopting the course, even if under different names. In the case of Educafro, offering this course is a requirement for any nucleus that affiliates itself to the network. During some years, the offering of the discipline was even controlled through the administration of a test called Citizenship Vestibular, which also allowed the nuclei to control the contents administered, according to preestablished guidelines.

In the PVNC, the resistance to Culture and Citizenship typically takes the form of camouflage strategies, where the content appears, but is not clearly identifiable. How does this happen?[11] Through a false assimilation of the agendas of both sides, that is, those related to daily practices and those of the collective forums. In a complex tacit agreement, subjects legitimize each other mutually in their positions through a noncorresponding dialogue. In the daily routines of the nuclei, strategies are created that deny the movement component of PVNC and negate its political agenda. In a typical fashion, overtly political practices of the movement are denied. This normally starts with the very discipline of Culture and Citizenship, which, in many nuclei, starts to be relegated to a position of secondary importance. An article published in the *Jornal Azânia,*[12] October 1996, reads:

I am going to cite some examples of the attitudes of those who underestimate the importance of this discipline:

- Many Pre-Vestibulars only have 1 or 2 Culture and Citizenship classes per month;
- The class is generally scheduled at difficult times for both teachers and students. Example: the first class, the last class, or the class after lunch;
- There is a "closing of eyes" regarding absence or presence of students in the class.

The boycott is attributed to . . . those that find the discipline boring, and find it more important to study Mathematics, Physics, Chemistry, and Biology, which are, in fact, the disciplines required for the tests. . . . There are courageous volunteers, who are led by philanthropic spirit, but who have not been able to take a qualitative step, in the sense of freeing themselves from naïve visions about the existing social problems in our country, and thus they end up reproducing these naïve visions within the nuclei. It is not surprising that students are not able to understand the facts, but what about the coordinators and teachers?

Hence, countering the hegemonic discourse, which is geared around the production of consciousness and based on the two pillars of the movement: (1) the politicization of action, which found its maximum expression in the discipline Culture and Citizenship, and (2) the daily routines that offer multiple strategies and tactics of denial and resistance. To maintain unity, this denial is transformed into negotiation, made feasible by the ambivalence of the hybridity that structures discourse (Bhabha 1998).

None of the nuclei entirely drop the course, but in many the efforts attributed to it are clearly weak. A paradox is thus established, which manifests itself most clearly in the treatment given to the race issue: on one hand, the hidden denial of individuals regarding the politicization of teaching racialization; on the other hand, the crystallization of a form-function that, although necessary in some instances, introduces a tension that exposes hidden racial and political dimensions. Thus, even where politics and racialization are denied, there are moments when these dimensions are evoked, and that occurs in an environment in which the political culture described above is marked by values such as tolerance and sharing and does not set in motion the systematic mechanisms of repression and silencing of antiracist manifestations. These are a fundamental part of Brazil's sophisticated racism, which is traditionally more rigorous in punishing those denouncing it than those practicing it. The racial question, when denied by the coordinators and members of the faculty of a free university entrance prep course, is contained or repressed, at most, into a latent condition, ready to emerge with all its power, stirred up by the smallest noise. Faced with the fact that the radicalization of positions mobilize differences in the form of alterities that make it impossible to be together, this situation of presence or absence of the argument about the racial question becomes the condition for the formation of ideological pacts (which are, in this case, weak), but at the same time it allows for subjects to become mobilized, for individuals to position themselves, and for a confrontation of understandings that were previously ignored.

Another set of effects of the multiplicity of agendas of discussion and intervention that are in constant dialogue during the daily routines of university entrance prep courses is the social capiliarization of antiracist discourse. A diffuse racial consciousness, as a latent potential in the social fabric that is immobilized by silencing mechanisms, finds a routine that is favorable to the establishment of questions, a routine that is, at least, permissive, even if racialization is not an expressed flagship of action. Some elements of the historical context of the 1990s contributed to the emergence of the race discussion in the routine of courses, which were not directly related to the participants of these courses. The strengthening of the intervention and of the visibility of the black-power movement in the second half of the 1990s (since the 1995 march in Brasília on the occasion of the 300th anniversary of the death of Zumbi of Palmares), with the subsequent recognition, by the federal government, of the existence of racism in society, and the production of a series of research and reports (including by official agencies) denouncing and publicizing racial inequalities and culminating in the implementation of special policies to support Afro-descendents—all of this creates a context where it becomes impossible to reproduce the social construction of free university entrance prep courses without a racial dimension. Nevertheless, beyond the Culture and Citizenship course that evokes political topics (which, many times, are taught together with the writing and composition classes), there are other strategic moments of constructing these university entrance prep courses conducive to the racial discussion.

Construction of Free Prep Courses and the Racial Question

The privileged place for the racial discussion in a free university entrance prep course is the Culture and Citizenship course. Its elevation to the position of central importance for any political content of the course, to the detriment of a presentation of other political arguments in the construction of all courses, did not exclude the politicization of some classes, but this is dependent on the teacher making use of the prerogative of pedagogical autonomy. Culture and Citizenship is, therefore, the privileged strategic moment to introduce racial discussions in all free university entrance prep courses, whether or not they are related to the PVNC.

In the specific case of the PVNC, the presence of the race discussion in Culture and Citizenship was not merely a manifestation of the political agendas that created the movement. As argued by Santos (2003a), this discipline also functioned during a period of internal disputes over the leadership of the PVNC as an instrument for strengthening the position of some participants that circulated in the nuclei giving lectures on Culture and Citizenship. Indeed, the pedagogical proposal elaborated for the course, presented in the form of a folder, which was handed out and also reproduced in the *Jornal Azânia,* proposed that it be taught, preferably, as a lecture, and this same proposal suggested some topics. In 1995 and 1996, a list of topics and persons giving lectures on Culture and Citizenship was circulated. A number of these lecturers sought leadership roles in the movement.

The movement thus consolidated the habit of inviting knowledgeable people to lecture in this course, which crystallized into one of the main legacies transmitted by the PVNC to the university entrance prep courses that multiplied nationally in the second half of the 1990s. In this way, militants of the black-power movement gained the opportunity to discuss the theme of antiracism even in courses where racial issues were not a main pillar of daily routines among coordinators and teachers. This helped in many ways to diffuse the debate about asymmetries in Brazilian race relations.

The context of the turn of the millennium also helped to diffuse the antiracism debate among university entrance prep courses. With the approach of the Anti-Racism Conference in Durban in 2001, and with the holding of state and regional preparatory conferences, entities of the black-power movement fortified the pressure they exercised on the federal government, pressuring it to take a clear stance and demanding politicians to address racial inequalities. The government identified the prevestibular courses as an initiative already in operation that could be further strengthened. This discourse reinforced tensions among coordinators of prep courses about the racialized character of their initiative.

The recognition of the university entrance prep courses as an antiracism initiative brings about the interrogation of the presence of racialization of different moments of the construction of the prep course. First, the initiative helps reduce racial asymmetries. The first condition here is that the beneficiaries are, for the most part, Afro-descendants. *Racial belonging* thus emerges as an admission criterion for the selection of students. This was already practiced, even if partially, in the PVNC and the prep courses directly influenced by it; but now this criterion becomes a point of inflection and tension for all free prep courses. Therefore, where such criterion is not practiced, coordinators are forced to justify why they are denied. This discourse, in most cases, is marked by a subordination of race under other manifestations of inequality, such as poverty and income (seen as a different factor, and not as a consequence of differentiation in the paths of individuals and of social groups), belonging to a poor community, going to a public school, and other criteria. These manifestations, according to this discourse, contemplate the racial dimension, which is absolutely questionable. On the other side, if we remember that not too long ago, most of these individuals did not imagine establishing a correlation between racism and inequalities, to now be obliged to use such rhetoric puts them in a situation of questioning, which represents, in itself, a flagrant advancement, especially because of the constant character of this questioning, which brings these individuals to change their position, in a process where greater sectors of society are in favor of racialized policies.

The profusion of discourses about different reasons for exclusion, such as the concentration of wealth and income gaps, did not consider race. This becomes a subject of discussion in an environment where free preparatory courses are agents of intervention for the democratization of education in the country. These agents need to dialogue, negotiate, hybridize, and diffuse the antiracism debate. The enunciation of the founding pillars, which finds expression in the name that each course is assuming, becomes yet another strategic moment of constructing prep courses. Yet even after defining their name, the levels and forms of dialogue and mediation with a racial component remain the object of tension.

The recurring pedagogical challenges also open (even if indirectly) possibilities to address race in other areas. Questions about school dropout rates, attempts at political-cultural consciousness-raising, and pedagogical difficulties in diverse disciplines give rise to creative strategies of overcoming them, thus privileging extra class activities and allowing topics that are not directly related to the university entrance exam. In these moments, the central aim many times is the creation of unity where Afro-Brazilian themes frequently emerge, occasioned, for example, by visits to expositions, museums, theaters, and other cultural opportunities. Even if sporadic, such moments can provide opportunities for tension when the activation of latent problems leads to the diffusion of antiracist messages, and even this does not lead to a complete transformation of the course. Rather, it contributes to the strengthening of the consciousness about racial inequalities and about the necessity to construct policies to address these issues.

Relationship of Free Prep Courses and Racialization

In the previous sections, I listed some moments of the construction of free prep courses where, potentially, but not necessarily, the racial argument emerges. This potentiality alerts us not only to the possibility of constructing discourses of denial and belittling the racial dimension, but also to the obvious possibility of nonemergence of racial arguments in many of the above-mentioned courses. This is possible, as discussed further in Santos (2003b), because prep courses represent a new form of political action that can be mobilized according to different values, purposes, and ideological projects.

In other words, acts and meanings attributed to it by the acting subject appear disassociated and independent from each other, that is, similar acts can result from different, even antagonistic, projects, intentions, desires, and meanings. Despite the inheritance of its birth place next to the black-power movement, the university entrance prep courses multiplied because of their weak ideological pacts, constituting themselves as independent agents in the antiracist struggle and giving margin to the amalgamation and intervention of actors originating from other fields of struggle, which also multiplies the interests and forms of action of these courses.

The visibility achieved by the PVNC during the mid-1990s, including the high social demand and popularity of the university entrance prep courses and the interest of financing agencies linked to the possibility of having a place of practice, training, and amalgamation of political militancy, is a factor that attracts entities and subjects from political parties, unions, and NGOs to the creation of their own free university entrance prep courses. The increases in resources, leaders, legitimacy, and social prestige, and the insertion of prevestibular courses into different social contexts, are all anticipated goals of free university entrance prep courses.

The political dimension (conceived as a field of action and dialogue with institutionalized state apparatus) of the free university entrance prep courses, which became an important social interlocutor, especially in the debate about the democratization of the university, is valued for diverse reasons. For example, there are nuclei that serve as references for political action for local communities discussing and intervening in questions that go beyond the university entrance exam, including educational and racial questions, many times articulated with neighborhood associations and similar entities. There are others that are important references at the city level, establishing dialogues with state agencies, secretaries, and city councils. As well, there are movements of university entrance prep courses that enter into contact with state governments and federal departments mainly to debate current university reform, thus extending their power of intervention to the national scale. Hence, there are nuclei whose agendas and agencies (forums, articulations, and power games in which they participate) are local, regional, and national as well as extending into networks beyond the PVNC, such as Educafro, which is strong in Rio de Janeiro and in São Paulo, but with courses in several states too. Another group is MSU, which offers free university entrance prep courses at the state and federal levels.

The dialogues, arenas, and places occupied by the university entrance prep courses multiply. They penetrate the political scene as important interlocutors, but as an actor presented with multiple and, many times, antagonistic voices. When it comes to the racial question, this is particularly important, because free university entrance prep courses are being recognized as privileged interlocutors with the state, qualified because they are initiatives of affirmative action that emanated from civil society and, in the present setting, have their experiences also recognized as models for the definition of public polities for the social promotion of Afro-descendants. We can list two orders of impacts from this: one regarding the definition of the aspects that constitute the drafting of public policies, and another one concerning the identification of legitimate spokespersons. Both situations provide important feedback in the structuring not only of the courses, but also of the field of antiracism in contemporary Brazil.

The recognition by the Brazilian state of the university entrance prep courses as models of intervention in the field of racial inequalities elevates the courses to the stage of models for public action.[13] This appears with a lot of clarity in the main initiative of the state in this field, the Diversity in the University program of the Department of Education, which with financial support of the Bank of Inter-American Development (BID), financed free university entrance prep courses with a racial focus. The courses, selected through public announcement, had to have at least 50 percent plus one black and/or native students. Beyond that, the initiatives also needed to contemplate activities of social formation and cultural valorization, which are not a part of the university entrance exam. This is an influence of the Culture and Citizenship course. Grades for the test are defined according to the rank of these activities and contents in different disciplines, which was the initial proposal of the PVNC. More than that, the evaluation of the quality of these activities is conditioned by the form in which they teach the cultural and social questions of Afro-descendants (or of indigenous Brazilians, according to the dominant public for each course), which added to the demand that more than half of the beneficiaries be black or indigenous. This demonstrates the racialization of state initiatives. Hence, the topics and beneficiaries are designed to raise issues of race, which, faced with disputes over resources that characterize contemporary social initiatives, takes this discussion to places where it did not exist—despite all the strategies of camouflage, resistance, and denial that are created. To contemplate the racial question, in any form, becomes a fundamental element in the struggle of these courses over state resources, thus extending the dialogue on race to a greater number of contexts.

This configuration of public policies, however, points to another order of processes: outsourcing. Outsourcing is important for execution to the extent not only that the format of state-owned programs is the result of observing actions of social movements, but that it points to the construction of a model of social coordination whereby the state shares decisions and actions with organized entities representing civil society. With this, decisionmaking in the public sphere is redefined, through the establishment of diverse arenas of dialogue and negotiation of an agenda that is not just dynamic, but essentially plural— movements and protagonists intervene (and are legitimized for that) in diverse problems that constitute dialogical fields. In our case, this occurs around the central axis of racial inequalities, and unfolds in interventions in diverse areas, but still in dialogue with other principles of the social fabric. Questions such as university reform, urban policy, and public health policies, among others, are spheres of intervention for those active in antiracism, because they are central points for the reversion of racial inequalities. The democratization of higher education, a central agenda of the free university entrance prep courses, creates a political space of dialogue with the state, and immediately establishes a dispute among agents over the legitimacy to exercise this dialogue, because the fruit of such dialogue will inevitably bear the influences of the ideological constructions of those that have power over the state. Although the privileged interlocutors belong to the field of antiracism (such as the PVNC and Educafro), who press for a racialized approach to all policies, not all interlocutors belong to that movement (for example, MSU), thus weakening the focus on racial inequalities. This also generates friction in the racialization of the university entrance prep courses, which can serve either as a valorization or a belittling of the racial dimension.

Conclusion

The free university entrance prep courses are, at present, a privileged channel for the establishment of racial debates. As spaces for the aggregation and recomposition of multiple identities, the prep courses are structured around weak ideological pacts, which define a wide range of relations with the racial question, from being the main pillar to a condition of latency, ready to emerge at different moments during the daily routine of the courses. The racial theme is also important in structuring elements in the dialogue of these courses with the state, a privileged social channel of coordination.

The fragility of the ideological pacts around which the courses are structured at the same time (1) conditions their high potential to be replicated, (2) destabilizes the construction of a political-ideological apparatus (especially around the racial question), and (3) transforms the courses into potential instruments to serve other interests (which may be economic, political, etc.). Even those courses that do not assume an open antiracism agenda—faced with the inheritances and legacies of the antiracism movements, especially the PVNC and Educafro—function as important spaces for the emergence and consolidation of racial questions and demands. This transforms the free university entrance prep courses into a main agent and disseminator of antiracist activism in contemporary Brazil.

Notes

1. I want to highlight the efforts made by Heringer (2003a) in identifying initiatives of the Brazilian state in the 1990s, as well as the impact of the 2001 World Conference Against Racism.

2. Recent research on racism by the Perseu Abramo Foundation examines differences in the life conditions between blacks and whites that indicate that both groups are equally receptive to governmental intervention. This finding supports the idea that inequality between whites and blacks is due to the lack of public policies aimed at generating opportunities for blacks to better their lives.

3. This strategy allowed a significant number of black militants to enter universities in order to pursue college, master's, and doctorate degrees (Heringer 2003a).

4. The Pastoral Commissions are forms of organizations based on the Ecclesiastical Base Communities. The organization of Black Pastoral Agents was created in 1983.

5. For related and historical details of the prevestibular for blacks and needy students see Santos (2006).

6. My data, collected for the study "Raça e Classe no curso Pré-Vestibular para Negros e Carentes do Rio de Janeiro" (Race and Class in the Preparatory Courses for the Black and Poor of Rio de Janeiro), identified eighty-six nuclei of the PVNC since 1993. The exodus of several nuclei of PVNC should be attributed to discord in the movement and the growth of Educafro (Educação e Cidadania de Afro-Descendentes e Carentes), an NGO founded in 1997 by David Frei, the principal leader in the creation of the PVNC. In 2001, Educafro broke with the PVNC, determined that the nucleus that adhered to it could not be connected to the movement, which provoked a reaccommodation of forces with many nuclei coming together against the other.

7. An allusion to the celebrated work of George Orwell's *Animal Farm,* which is critical of the totalitarianism of communist regimes (especially Stalinism) where a revolution of the farm animals symbolizes a popular revolution against a dictatorial regime in which the tyrant is the pig.

8. Diverse documents of the PVNC interpret the creation of these courses as attempts to change two distortions of society: the low quality of public education in the Baixada Fluminense, which practically eliminated possibilities of access of students of the region to higher education; and the low percentage of black and Afro-descendant students in universities. According to these documents only 5 percent of students in Brazilian universities were black, although the Afro-descendant population was 44 percent of the national total.

9. The notion of political culture here refers to the ideas of Alvarez, Dagnino, and Escobar (2000: 29), who note that it "is significant that social movements . . . [arose] from civil society in Latin America in the last two decades . . . [as] they have developed plural versions of political culture that will go far to re-establish formal liberal democracy. As such, the emergence of redefinitions of concepts such as democracy and citizenship point to directions that confront authoritarian culture by means of attribution of new significance to notions of rights, public and private spaces, forms of sociability, ethics, equality, and difference. These multiple processes of resignification clearly reveal alternative definitions that count against politics. . . . To explore the politics of social movements, we should see politics like something more than a conjunction of specific activities (voting, making campaigns, or lobbying), that occur in clearly delimited institutional spaces such as parliament and political parties; it should be seen as encompassing also struggles of power realized by an ample amount of spaces culturally defined as private, social, economic and so on."

10. Consider that popular education should have a political character, especially as it is targeted at historically excluded groups of society and focuses on questions at the local level of daily life. At the beginning, a discipline called "Aspects of Brazilian Culture" was designed to focus on the diverse aspects of Brazilian culture. Culture is something great, dynamic, that involves all dimensions of life, and the prevestibular should prepare students not only for the test, but for everything, including a life of political struggle for emancipation and the social promotion of the populations to which they belong.

11. Here we refer to some passages of Santos (2003a).

12. *O Azânia* was the *official* news of the PVNC movement. Edited, with frequency albeit irregularity, from 1995 to 1999.

13. There were quarrels among black movements about the array of options of affirmative action, and in determining which other measures would be a priority, with the

goal of increasing university entrance of Afro-descendants. Inside the prevestibulars themselves, a lot pointed to the prevestibular as an end in itself, as well as a means to better public education. There also were discussions to adopt other mechanisms to gain access to universities that did not have the false facade of competition based on merit, such as the vestibular, which was a social filter. It was not a form of gauging the quality of schooling, capacity, or aptitude of candidates. Many popular courses, like a lot of entities of the black movement, are contrary to the adoption of prevestibulars as a public policy, claiming that the state should play a different role.

Part 4

Conclusion

12

After the Racial Democracy

Bernd Reiter and Gladys L. Mitchell

Afro-Brazilian agency is the new focus of scholarly work on Brazil, whether that involves black mobilization, racial identification, or affirmative action. While racism continues to play a role in the lives of Afro-Brazilians, the new research represented in this book reaches beyond analyzing racism. The new aims of scholarly work are many, but the main focus is to examine the differing ways that Afro-Brazilians challenge racism in various aspects of their lives. The challenges to racism do not only come in traditional forms of black activism. NGOs, hip-hop artists, and even courses preparing Afro-Brazilian students for the vestibular now all serve as sites of debate and contestation against racism in Brazilian society. Local community organizations, led by women who self-identify as black and understand that class, race, and gender work together to affect their positions in society, also contribute to fighting against racism.

As Afro-Brazilians gain access to university education and there is an increase in the number of those openly embracing blackness, black agency comes to play a more central role in Brazil's racial politics. Studies that place Afro-Brazilian agency at the center of analysis are thus especially relevant. At the same time that social science moves into new fields of analysis, the concepts and tools to conduct empirical research reflect these new trends and fields of inquiry. Analyzing whiteness and inclusion, instead of blackness and exclusion, provides a new field of inquiry that demands a rethinking of several widely accepted concepts connected to established approaches. While the scholarly gaze has long been turned to examine and analyze people of African descent, political science research has slowly turned its attention to unpacking what whiteness means in Brazilian society. Part 1, "Black Empowerment and White Privilege," does this by analyzing how privilege is defended and examining the various ways Afro-Brazilians embrace their identities while combating racism.

By focusing on whiteness and white privilege, Bernd Reiter clearly shows in Chapter 2, "Whiteness as Capital," the benefits of whiteness on inclusion, rather than simply the disadvantages of blackness. By emphasizing white inclusion, and how hard this inclusion is fought for and defended, we gain insight into how much is at stake for white Brazilians if they forsake their inherited privileges. Social change, we can conclude, will not come easily and without struggle, which is why black agency is of such importance.

White inclusion many times is justified with white supremacy. One of the ways Afro-Brazilians challenge white supremacy and racism is by embracing blackness, as Gladys Mitchell demonstrates in Chapter 3, "Politicizing Blackness: Afro-Brazilian Color Identification and Candidate Preference." Afro-Brazilians who claim black identities, such as *negro* and *preto,* support black politicians more than those who do not identify as such. The implications of this finding are extremely important. Identities are not idle choices. While we realize that Afro-Brazilians can identify as different colors at different moments according to the social situation they find themselves in, the fact alone that a number of Afro-Brazilians are choosing black identities is a significant finding because it points to an important trend. Due to changing racial attitudes, Afro-Brazilians now outnumber white Brazilians, thus leaving behind the status of being a numerical minority.

In many Brazilian states where political power has always been in the hands of traditional, white elites, such a shift is highly significant and consequential. As Mitchell's analysis clearly demonstrates, choosing one's identity is not simply a social choice at certain moments, but a political choice with political implications. It is not that *negros não votam em negros* (negroes don't vote for negro candidates); rather, it is that not all Afro-Brazilians vote for black candidates, but those who embrace blackness do.

Not all Afro-Brazilians interpret acts of racism in the same way. The struggle for inclusion, equality of status, and access to civil rights takes different forms. As Angela Figueiredo shows, middle- and upper-class Afro-Brazilian entrepreneurs struggle with being accepted by white Brazilian society and are oftentimes kept away from enjoying the same leisure spaces as their white counterparts. Because they need to navigate in a world of business connections, where networks and social capital are central to their economic success, many choose to avoid open confrontation with white prejudice. Figueiredo's account demonstrates how deeply such avoidance becomes anchored in the minds and hearts of those having to practice it routinely to succeed. The internalization of racist attitudes Figueiredo finds among black entrepreneurs echoes the writings of Frantz Fanon and reminds us of the psychological costs of such an endeavor. Although viable as an individual strategy to cope with consistent discrimination, Figueiredo's chapter, "Out of Place: The Experience of the Black Middle Class," also makes it plain that such a strategy cannot offer a real solution to all those inflicted and curtailed by racist attitudes and practices.

The challenge of racism is not only present in Afro-Brazilians' everyday lives but also poses unique challenges for Afro-Brazilian politicians. Afro-Brazilian political candidates are treated differently by the media than their white counterparts. Cloves Oliveira's chapter, "The Political Shock of the Year," on Celso Pitta's mayoral win in São Paulo, shows that media coverage of Pitta was much different from that of his competitors. Pitta was not dedicated to Afro-Brazilian issues and did not run as a black candidate. Yet, the issue of race became important when he ran for office. He did not claim to represent blacks, but the media sometimes identified him as a black representative. Further, in Pitta's case, the media treated him differently because of his ethnic background. Despite that for most candidates airtime was given according to how the candidate fared during the campaign, Pitta was given less media attention. Through Oliveira's analysis, it becomes clear that although São Paulo is viewed as a developed and modern city in Brazil, race still plays a role in social and political life. Because Pitta was supported by Paulo Maluf, the mayor who preceded him, he was able to gain popular support. Nonetheless, his tenure as mayor was rampant with cases of scandals, including financial scandals. Pitta's case is important because it is a clear example of what Mark Sawyer (2006) terms *inclusionary discrimination,* where discrimination and racial progressive attitudes coexist.

As Part 1 shows that the problem of racism is still rampant in society, yet Afro-Brazilians make individual efforts to overcome discrimination. A large-scale policy to deal with discrimination has come with the enactment of university affirmative action programs throughout Brazil. It took years of collective organizing at the national and international levels to press the Brazilian state enough to finally take action against all-too-common racialized inequality. Since 2001, affirmative action has become the main tool of the Brazilian state and several of its agencies, ministries, and public universities, to remedy the consistent, and now embarrassing, underrepresentation of Afro-Brazilians in universities and among the higher ranks of public administration. Quotas to regulate access to public universities have by far provoked the most sanguine and controversial public debates about Brazilian racial politics.

In Part 2, "Affirmative Action Contested," Seth Racusen moves beyond analysis and diagnosis and proposes proactive ways to address the problems Brazilian public universities currently face in his chapter, "Affirmative Action and Identity." He acknowledges present-day racism by supporting a system that would ensure that middle-class Afro-Brazilians are prioritized over white Brazilians, who do not suffer from color discrimination. His policy-oriented analysis is included in this volume to point beyond problems and initiate discussions of potential solutions; hence, we hope to spark the exploration of new and innovative ways to address and mend the problems of Brazil's racialized inequities.

Mónica Treviño González's study of the predominantly negative opinions against university quotas—even among those that benefit from it—takes us one step deeper into the puzzle of Brazilian attitudes toward racial categorization and the perceived potential for increased racialization it might produce. In Chapter 7, "Opportunities and Challenges for the Afro-Brazilian Movement," detecting these negative attitudes among Afro-Brazilian students at selected Brazilian universities, González ventures into possible explanations for such a counterintuitive phenomenon, finding it in a lack of effectiveness of black-power movements to counteract the predominant ideology of color-blindness, which has ensured white privilege through the perpetuation of social hierarchies inherited from the past.

"The New Politics of Black Power," the third part of this volume, follows Racusen's view toward the future by critically examining some of the new strategies of black contestation in Brazil. Even though the dismantling of structural racism requires collective and concerted action, its strength and per-vasiveness is not only challenged *from above,* that is, by social-movement pol-itics. Keisha-Khan Perry offers a glimpse at the daily struggles of those at the lowest level of the Brazilian pecking order: poor black women, living in infor-mal *favela* neighborhoods. Small and locally restricted as their struggles may seem, if we believe in the social construction of reality, the challenges of a racialized common sense *from below* are as important and consequential as the concerted efforts mentioned above. They are also not disconnected, and one approach does not rule out the other. In her in-depth analysis of the discursive reproduction of black female *favela* identities, in Chapter 8, "Racialized His-tory and Urban Politics," Perry is able to shed light on the various ways in which race, class, and gender interact in Afro-Brazilian women's lives and how they use these intersectional identities to organize and challenge the hege-monic racial order. In doing so, the black women of the Gamboa de Baixo neighborhood in Salvador, Bahia, are indeed as deeply involved in the remaking of Brazilian common sense and, thus, its everyday reality as are the elites—black and white alike.

Both individual efforts and collective efforts help to combat racism and promote positive images of blackness. Sales Augusto dos Santos's chapter, "Black NGOs and 'Conscious' Rap," on the role of NGOs and rap artists, demonstrates that disseminating problack attitudes is not limited to traditional black-movement organizations. Black NGOs can directly engage with govern-ment entities to promote race-specific policies. Rap artists with problack mes-sages inspire Afro-Brazilian youth to embrace their blackness and not fall prey to the racial democracy myth. Rather than simply viewing their marginalization as a result of class, racially conscious rap artists claim that black marginaliza-tion is the result of both race and class. Because these artists are not mainstream artists, they do not depend on CD sales to whites. Racionais MC was success-ful despite that they did not have the backing of a major recording label. This again demonstrates the power of black agency, as most of the racially conscious rap and hip-hop artists are supported by Afro-Brazilian youth.

Fernando Conceição, however, is skeptical of both black NGOs and cultural activists, even those with visible problack messages. Focusing on Salvador, Bahia, in Chapter 10, "Power and Black Organizing in Brazil," he finds that successful black musicians sometimes simply use problack messages for commercial and individual interests. In doing so, they neglect the very people whom they sing about. Further, when they are co-opted by the government with city governmental posts, they use these positions for themselves, not for the black community. Nevertheless, through Conceição's skeptical analysis, we also become aware that today *blackness* has reached the power to be commodified. In Salvador, Brazil's Black Mecca, blackness has long been recognized for its marketing potential by state-led tourism agencies and is forcefully promoted as a means to attract international tourists. According to Conceição, as blackness is now a commodity to be sold and traded for goods, job opportunities, or money, cultural artists should be held responsible for representing the needs of the Afro-Brazilian community. In this way, Afro-Brazilians can promote positive images of blackness while benefiting the community as a whole. The result is that black empowerment relies on blacks, rather than whites, who may co-opt them by offering financial incentives.

Not all forms of black empowerment are financially driven. Empowerment can take shape in the form of racial consciousness among black youth. Renato Emerson dos Santos's chapter, "New Social Activism," allows us a glimpse at one of the many arenas where black agency finds expression in contemporary Brazil. By examining the role of university prep courses, Santos shows how far the struggle for civil rights and access has indeed spread. These programs are important because they are essentially administered by and to Afro-Brazilians. In a sense, these programs can be considered a type of Afro-Brazilian empowerment as they directly empower youth to become prepared for the vestibular and to then pursue a college education.

Prevestibular courses that include a component on citizenship or courses where racial issues are discussed play a more direct and important role in raising awareness. Nevertheless, these courses are not always easy to administer, for a number of reasons. Students are not always interested in these courses, especially those who have been taught to believe in the myth of racial democracy. Yet, a number of these programs exist, and many are run by the voluntary efforts of Afro-Brazilian youth who have benefited from these programs and now wish to give back to their community. Black activists also are willing to speak to youth about racial issues by teaching such courses.

Taken as a whole, the chapters assembled in this book demonstrate that racism continues to pose serious threats to the quality of Brazilian democracy. Nevertheless, Afro-Brazilian efforts to unveil white privilege and challenge traditional social hierarchies have driven an uncomfortable wrench into Brazilian hegemonic self-understanding. Due to black agency, Brazilian state and social elites can no longer comfortably claim that Brazil is a racial paradise. No problem can be fixed without acknowledging it first. After almost 400 years of enslaving more people than any other nation on this planet, upholding slavery longer than any country in the Western Hemisphere, 200 years after releasing the remaining millions of the still-enslaved without providing for any kind of integration or reconstruction to heal the wounds of slavery and assist those that suffered through it, and after all this time of pretending that Brazil was a land of racial harmony and of "cordial race relations," finally Brazilians seem ready and willing to reexamine the images and myths they hold about themselves. The works collected in this book provide ample proof of how hard and difficult an endeavor this is. It is with great regret and resistance that most Brazilians ready themselves to let go of one of their core beliefs, namely that their country is a racial paradise.

This is not surprising. The foundational myth of the racial paradise served the interests of the Brazilian state by forging a sense of unity and nationalism able to bridge the potentially divisive differences among the numerous groups inhabiting the same territory—divided not just by ethnicity, culture, origin, and language, but even more so by extremely unequal access to basic goods and even rights. Any of these divisions could have proven great enough to provoke the formation of factionalism and separatism during the 1930s, and again during the early 1960s. The Brazilian state could easily have broken apart, as the forces to divide the nation were strong and pervasive indeed. But this myth also served the Brazilian people. To all those hitherto excluded and discriminated against, it offered a way to achieve social mobility—even if through much sacrifice and delay. After all, the dream of gradually melting into the emerging *cosmic mestizo* race—which the Mexican thinker José Vasconcelos had heralded in 1925, and his Brazilian counterpart, Gilberto Freyre, had further advocated in 1933—was a far step away from the dominant thinking about race until then, namely the kind of racist determinism sold as science by prominent and respected US, European, and Brazilian intellectuals. Up until the 1930s, and in some parts of the world much later than that, scientific racism had *proven* that civilization and progress were conditioned by race; that is, they were something only white nations could achieve. The darker races, according to the leading social scientists of the time, were unable to ever achieve Western-type civilization, which to them, of course, was the only type of civilization. Nations where black and brown people dominated were thus condemned to eternal backwardness.

Against this thinking, Gilberto Freyre's work was truly revolutionary. His seminal book *The Masters and the Slaves* was first published in 1933, the year Hitler took power in Germany, making sure that racist thought stayed on the scene for another twelve years. According to Freyre, who had studied social anthropology under Franz Boas at Columbia University, some Africans brought to Brazil as slaves were actually superior to their white masters, especially those coming from highly complex West African cultures where they had been exposed to different languages, cultures, and religions. But Freyre's contribution centered not so much on his introduction of the notion of cultural relativism into Brazilian discourse; it was his postulation that mixed people—mestizos and mulattos—represented a happy amalgamation of the characteristics of its three foundational races: white, black, and native. Instead of declaring them ugly and degenerate, as the leading European and US thinkers of the time presented them, Freyre boldly declared that the *metisse* was indeed the most adapted type of human being to life in the tropics. As well, Freyre argued that Brazil was a mestizo nation, a nation where race had become irrelevant, because everybody was mixed to some degree. The Brazilian, to Freyre, was a new and modern human being—born in the New World and the crown of evolution.

To the political elites that had taken over the Brazilian state just three years before Freyre's book appeared, his thinking was exactly what their liberal- and progress-oriented agenda lacked, as it provided a way to overcome old divisions and offered a strong and positive trope under which the Brazilian nation could be brought together. To the masses of Brazilians, less concerned with issues of nationalism than with concrete life chances and age-old barriers to social mobility, Freyre's doctrine of the racial paradise also had something to offer. It provided them with a possible future solution and a road leading away from the trap of being considered "inferior racial stock," and hence unfit for civilizational progress of any kind—if only one that required much effort and strategic action over several generations, as it promised compensation and access only after becoming mestizo. To many former slaves and their descendents, that seemed a far-fetched goal and one that required letting go of some of the core elements that make a people a people—their culture and friends. But at least there seemed to be a way, if not for oneself, then for one's children, if they associated with and married the *right kind of people,* that is, whites, or at least lighter-skinned mulattos. Nevertheless, many people felt as Langston Hughes did when he asked, "What happens to a dream deferred?"

To black Brazilians, then, the dream of respect and equality could not be deferred forever, and letting go of the myth of the racial democracy was but a question of time. Once democracy came back to the country in 1985, it became more and more difficult to explain, understand, and accept that it did not bring improved life chances to Afro-Brazilians. Worse, the new democracy did not offer new hope to the historically excluded; all of a sudden, this lack of hope became more difficult to bear, until the dream deferred finally exploded, giving birth to a new urgency and a new militancy to finally achieve what for so long had been promised.

Yet, finally achieving this goal requires a change in strategy that is difficult to manage for many. Instead of seeking social mobility through symbolic or real whitening, that is, by associating with white Brazilians, marrying white, befriending white, and praising everything and anything white, the new strategy requires black group consciousness, solidarity, and pride. To most Afro-

Brazilians, especially those who have long been able to blend in by stressing their—real or invented—European ancestry, this change of strategy goes against all they have ever learned and perceived as right, successful, and promising. Association with anything black, especially anybody darker than oneself, has always meant social suicide, and Brazilians have been trained for generations to smoothly and elegantly avoid any such association. Several chapters of this book have described and explained the long and arduous efforts of Brazilian black leaders to disseminate this new perspective and anchor it in the minds and hearts of their brothers and sisters.

To white Brazilians, giving up the myth of the racial democracy was and is even harder, because it transforms them into racists. Worse, under the era of the racial democracy, white Brazilians could think of themselves not just as free of racial prejudice, but as whites with soul, that is, *tropical whites*. They were also able to claim access to a world closed to many other whites dominating blacks in other parts of the world: in Brazil, in general, whites were not guilty of brutal lynchings and hate crimes against blacks. They were able to control blacks, yet at the same time they had access to their lifestyles and culture, thus allowing whites to partake in black culture and vernacular. Brazilian whites, thus, had the best of both worlds, and it is not surprising that many struggle to uphold this reality.

Nevertheless, as the myth of the racial democracy crumbles, so does the ideology of white benevolence toward blacks. Understandably, most white Brazilians would prefer not to examine their own values and prejudices toward blacks too closely. Furthermore, giving up the myth not only requires a rethinking of one's own identity; it also implies giving up privileges that were, until now, perceived as normal. Having a black servant, not waiting in line with a large group of nonwhites, being favored at the workplace during hiring, and even the freedom of choosing a partner—all have seemed perfectly normal to white Brazilians ever since Brazilian history was recorded. Worse, to whites, the new scenario does not seem to offer any benefits at all, no matter from what angle it is analyzed. Hence many Brazilian whites struggle hard to defend those privileges they inherited, even more so as they perceive them as normal and as their right. The vehement reactions against affirmative action politics discussed in several chapters of this book provide us with a picture of this struggle over inherited and normalized privilege, as many white Brazilians perceive their access to free university education not as a privilege exercised over centuries and bought with the exclusion of the nonwhite majority, but as their right.

Although this perception predominates, some historically privileged Brazilians have recognized that defending a myth that has been proven to be wrong beyond all doubt is untenable. To truly become democratic and to rescue the dignity of those who have unfairly been privileged, and thus to save the moral groundings of the entire community, more and more Brazilians have begun to face the challenges of instituting a true democracy and to openly address the injustices produced by racism. Exclusion and structural racism do not so much dehumanize the excluded as they degrade those who practice and perpetuate them to their own benefit. The historically excluded stand on a higher moral ground, as their cause is one of seeking justice and democracy. Engaging in this fight ennobles all those that partake in it. Defending historically inherited privilege, on the other hand, has no moral grounding and can only lead into deeper and deeper guilt. Recognizing this allows for a catharsis-like awakening to the tasks that need to be addressed, and it opens the door to the construction of a real democracy in Brazil.

All the contributors to this book are aware of the historical moment Brazil is currently experiencing. Their contributions provide testimony of their awareness of the seriousness of the many tasks ahead. They also allow the reader to realize how broad this discussion really is. None of the contributors to this book are merely engaged in yet another academic exercise. They are, to the contrary, actively involved in a society-wide effort to reimagine the Brazilian nation. And as university professors in a country where the average period of schooling just reached six years, the Brazilian people await the contributions and thoughts of the highly educated. The contributions assembled in this volume also give evidence and provide examples of agency. And different from just a few years ago, this agency is much more colorful than it used to be, as activists have become scholars and scholars activists. It is also much more international. The current stage of discussions does not allow for a prognosis of what will replace the myth of the racial democracy. It does, however, point to the fact that the times of racial democracy are over. The sheer amount of new reflections and analysis leaves no doubt about that. Brazil might finally be able to live up to its eternal promise to be the country of the future, precisely because it is finally willing and able to look critically upon itself. As stated above, no problem can be fixed without acknowledging it first, and Brazil seems finally ready to let go of a long-established tradition of merely pretending to attack its social problems, a tradition so deeply rooted in Brazilian culture that it has produced its own expression: *para inglês ver* (done for the sake of satisfying the Brits). A Brazil ready to face its own problems and shortcomings, not worried anymore what other, "more civilized," nations might think of it, might finally be ready to tackle the many problems it faces. The problem most central to the reinvention of a better, more equitable, and more just Brazil is the problem of racism, and thus addressing it bears the potential of a general catharsis toward a brighter future for more Brazilians.

Acronyms

ABPN	Brazilian Association of Black Researchers
BID	Bank of Inter-American Development
BRASA	Brazilian Studies Association
CEAP	Center for the Articulation of Marginalized Populations
CEDINE	State Council for the Defense of Negro Rights
CEERT	Center of Studies of Work Relations and Inequality
CEFET-BA	Centro Federal de Educação Tecnológica da Bahia
CENARAB	National Center for the Articulation of Afro-Religious Scholars
ENEM	National Exam of Secondary Education
ES	Espirito Santo
ESP	*Estado de São Paulo*
FACEF	Centro Universitário de Franca
FAETEC-RJ	Fundação de Apoio à Escola Técnica do Rio de Janeiro
FAMERP	Faculdade de Medicina S.J. do Rio Preto
FATEC-SP	Faculdade de Tecnologia–São Paulo
FGTS	unemployment benefits
FSP	*Folha de São Paulo*
FUNAI	National Foundation of the Indian
GDP	gross domestic product
HDI	Human Development Index
HGPE	Free Schedule of Electoral Propaganda
IBGE	Institute of Brazilian Geography and Statistics
IPEA	Brazilian Institute for Applied Research in Economics
MNU	Unified Black Movement
MSU	Movement of People without University; Movimento dos Sem Universidade

NEAB	Nucleus of Afro-Brazilian Studies
NEINB-USP	Nucleus of Interdisciplinary Studies of Brazilian Blacks
NGO	nongovernmental organization
PAN	National Party of the Retired
PC do B	Communist Party of Brazil; Partido Comunista do Brasil (PC do B)
PCB	Brazilian Communist Party; Partido Comunista Brasileiro
PDT	Democratic Labor Party
PESB	Brazilian Social Study
PFL	Liberal Front Party
PGT	General Party of Workers
PL	Liberal Party
PMDB	Party of the Brazilian Democratic Movement; Partido do Movimento Democratico Brasileiro
PME	National Employment and Manufacturing Survey
PMN	Party of National Mobilization
PNAD	National Annual Survey of Households; Pesquisa por Amostra de Domicílios
PNUD	United Nations for Human Development
PP	Progressive Party
PPB	Brazilian Progressive Party
PPP	Progressive Popular Party; Partido Popular Progressista
PPS	Popular Socialist Party
PSB	Brazilian Socialist Party
PSD	Party of Social Democracy
PSDB	Brazilian Social Democracy Party
PSL	Liberal Social Party
PSOL	Socialism and Freedom Party
PT	Workers Party
PTB	Brazilian Workers Party; Partido Trabalhista Brasileiro
PTN	National Labor Party
PV	Green Party
PVNC	Prevestibular for Blacks and the Poor; Pré-Vestibular para Negros e Carentes
UEFL	Universidade Estadual de Londrina
UEFS	Universidade Estadual de Feira de Santana
UEG	Universidade Estadual de Goiás
UEMG	Universidade Estadual de Minas Gerais
UEMS	Universidade Estadual de Mato Grosso do Sul
UENF	Universidade do Norte-Fluminense
UEPG	Universidade Estadual de Ponta Grossa
UERJ	Universidade do Estado do Rio de Janeiro
UFABC	Universidade Federal do ABC

UFF	Universidade Federal de Fluminese
UFJF	Universidade Federal de Juiz de Fora
UFMA	Universidade Federal do Maranhão
UFPA	Universidade Federal do Pará
UFPR	Universidade Federal do Paraná
UFRG	Universidade Federal de Rio de Janeiro
UFRGS	Universidade Federal do Rio Grande do Sul
UFSC	Universidade Federal de Santa Catarina
UFSCar	Universidade Federal de São Carlos
UFSM	Universidade Federal de Santa Maria
UNB	Universidade de Brasília
UNESCO	United Nations Education, Science, and Cultural Organization
UNICAMP	Universidade Estadual de Campinas
UNIMONTES	Universidade Estadual de Montes Claros

Bibliography

Agier, Michel. 1992. "Novos Status e Outros Negros: Questões de Identidade entre Trabalhadores Baianos." In *Projeto Classes, Ethnias e Mudanças Sociaís*. Salvador: CRHI UFBA.

Aguero, Felipe, and Jeffrey Stark, eds. 1998. *Fault Lines of Democracy in Post-Transition Latin America*. Miami: North South Center Press.

Aldé, Alessandra. 2004. "As eleições presidenciais de 2002 nos jornais." In: *Eleições presidenciais em 2002 no Brasil: Ensaios sobre mídia, cultura e política*. São Paulo: Hacker Editores.

Aldé, Alessandra, and Heloisa Dias. 1997. "Intervalo Surpresa: Spots Eleitorais na Campanha Municipal de 1996." *Comunicação and Política* 5 (1): 83–100.

Amar, Paul. 2003. "Reform in Rio: Reconstructing the Myths of Crime and Violence." *NACLA Report of the Americas* 37 (2): 37–42.

Ames, Barry. 2002. *The Deadlock of Democracy in Brazil*. Ann Arbor: University of Michigan Press.

Amorim, Lara Santos de. 1997. "Cenas de uma revolta urbana: Movimento hip hop na periferia de Brasília." Dissertação de Mestrado (Master's thesis), Universidade de Brasília, Departamento de Antropologia.

Anderson, Benedict. 1991. *Imagined Communities*. New York: Verso.

Andrews, George Reid. 1991a. *Blacks and Whites in São Paulo Brazil 1888–1988*. Madison: The University of Wisconsin Press.

———. 1991b. "O Protesto Político Negro em São Paulo—1888–1998." *Estudos Afro-Asiáticos* (21): 27–48.

———. 1998. *Negros e Brancos em São Paulo (1888–1988)*. Bauru/São Paulo: Edusc.

Ansolabehere, Stephen, and Shanto Iyengar. 1994. *Going Negative: How Political Advertisements Shrink and Polarize the Electorate*. New York: Free Press.

Arias, Omar G. Yamada, and L. Tejerina. 2004. "Education, Family Background, and Racial Earnings Inequality in Brazil." *International Journal of Manpower* 25 (3–4): 355–374.

Azevedo, Thales de. 1955. *As Elites de Co: Um Estudo Sobre a Ascensão Social*. São Paulo: Cia. Editora Nacional.

———. 1996. *As Elites de Cor Numa Cidade Brasileira: um Estudo Sobre a Ascensão Social e Classes Socais e Grupo de P Prestígio*, 2nd ed. Salvador: EDUFBA.

Bacelar, Jéferson. 2001. *A hierarquia das raças: Negros e brancos em Salvador*. Rio de Janeiro: Pallas.

Bairros, Luiza. 1987. "Pecados no Paraíso Racial: O Negro na Força de Trabalho na Bahia, 1950–1980." Master's thesis, Universidade Federal da Bahia, Salvador.

———. 1991. "Mulher negra: O reforço da subordinação." In P. Lovell, ed., *Desigualdade racial no Brasil Contemporâneo,* pp. 177–193. Belo Horizonte: MGSP.

———. 1996. "Orfeu e Poder: Uma Perspectiva Afro-Americana sobre a Política Racial no Brasil." *Afro-Ásia* (17): 173–186.

Bairros, Luiza, Vanda Sá Barreto, and Nadya Castro. 1992. *Negros e Brancos num Mercado de Trabalho em Mudança.* Série Toques. Salvador: Centro de Recursos Humanos.

Barreto, Viviane. 2003. "Vaga de Pardos Vira Polemica." *O DIA,* May 16. http://www2.uerj.br/clipping, downloaded January 1, 2004.

Barros, Andréa, and Kachani Morris. 1996. "Inesperada Cor Negra da Vitória." *Veja,* November 20.

Batley, Richard. 1982. "Urban Renewal and Expulsion in São Paulo." In Alan Gilbert, Jorge E. Hardoy, Ronaldo Ramirez, eds., *Urbanization in Contemporary Latin America,* pp. 231–262. New York: John Wiley & Sons.

Bento, Maria Aparecida Silva. 1995. "A Mulher Negra No Mercado de Trabalho." *Estudos Feministas* 3: 479–495.

———. 2000. "Racismo no trabalho: O movimento sindical e o Estado." In L. H. Antonio Sergio Alfredo Guimaraes, ed., *Tirando a Máscara: Ensaios sobre o racismo no Brasil,* pp. 325–432. São Paulo: Editora Paz e Terra.

Bevilaqua, Ciméa Barbato. 2005. "A Implantação do 'Plano de Metas de Inclusão Racial e Social.'" Universidade Federal do Paraná, Curitiba. December.

Bhabha, Homi. 1998. *O Local da Cultura.* Belo Horizonte: Ed. UFMG.

Blanco, Merida, 1978. "Race and Face Among the Poor: The Language of Color in a Brazilian Barrio." Ph.D. diss., Stanford University, California.

Bourdieu, Pierre. 1984. *A Social Critique of the Judgment of Taste.* Cambridge: Harvard University Press.

Bourdieu, Pierre, and Loic Wacquant. 1999. "The Cunning of Imperialist Reason." *Theory, Culture, and Society* 16 (1): 41–58.

———. 2002. "Sobre as Artimanhas da Razão Imperialista." *Estudos Afro-Asiáticos,* Número Especial, 1 (24): 15–33.

Bracey, Christopher A. 2006. "The Cul-de-Sac of Race Preference Discourse." *Southern California Law Review* 79 (September): 1231–1325.

Brandão, M. 2001. "Assim caminha a baianidade." In *Província da Bahia* 12. Salvador.

Brubaker, Rogers. 2004. *Ethnicity Without Groups.* Cambridge: Harvard University Press.

Burdick, John. 1998. "The Lost Constituency of Brazil's Black Movements." *Latin American Perspectives* 25: 136–155.

Burity, Joanildo. 2001. "Identidade e Múltiplo Pertencimento nas Práticas Associativas locais." *Série Textos para Discussão,* n. 108. Recife: Fundação Joaquim Nabuco.

Butler, Judith. 1998. "Merely Cultural." *New Left Review* 227 (January–February): 33–43.

Butler, Kim D. 1998. *Freedoms Given, Freedoms Won: Afro-Brazilian in Post-Abolition São Paulo and Salvador.* New Brunswick: Rutgers University Press.

Caldeira, Teresa P. R. 2000. *City of Walls: Crime, Segregation, and Citizenship in São Paulo.* Berkeley: University of California Press.

Caldwell, Kia Lilly. 2000. "Racialized Boundaries: Women's Studies and the Question of 'Difference' in Brazil." *Estudos feministas.*

Cano, Ignacio. 1998. "The Use of Lethal Force by Police in Rio de Janeiro." *Boletim do ISER* (April). Rio de Janeiro.

Cardoso, Edson. 1996. "O Avanço dos Bonecos." *O Estado de São Paulo,* October 11.

Cardoso, Marcos Antônio. 2002. *O Movimento negro em Belo Horizonte: 1978–1998.* Belo Horizonte: Mazza.

Carneiro, Sueli. 1995. Gênero, Raça e Ascenção Social. *Estudos feministas* 3: 544–552.
———. 1999. "Black Women's Identity in Brazil." In R. Reichmann, ed., *Race in Contemporary Brazil: From Indifference to Inequality*, pp. 217–228. University Park: Pennsylvania State University Press.
———. 2000. "Raá e Etnia no Contexto da Conferíncia de Beijing." In Jurema Werneck, Maisa Mendoná, and Evelyn White, eds., *O Livro da Sa: De das Mulheres Negras, Nossos Passos Vím de Longe*, pp. 247–256. Rio de Janeiro: Pallas/ Criola.
Caros Amigos. Ed. n. 3, Setembro 1998.
Carvalho, Jose Jorge de. 2005. "Usos e Abusos da Antropologia em Contexto de Tensão Racial: O caso das cotas para negros na UNB." *Horizontes Antropologicos,* Year 11, N. 23, January/June: 239–240.
Castro, Mary Garcia. 1996. *Family, Gender, and Work: The Case of Female Heads of Household in Brazil (States of São Paulo and Bahia—1950–1980).* Ph.D. diss., University of Florida.
Castro, Mônica. 1993. "Raça e Comportamento Político." *Dados* 36: 469–491.
Castro, Nadya, and Vanda Sá Barreto. 1992. "Os negros que dão certo." In *Anais do XVI encontro ANPOCS,* mimeo. Caxambui: ANPOCS.
Castro, Nadya Araújo, and Antonio Sérgio Guimarães. 1992. "Desigualdades raciais no mercado e nos locais de trabalho." In *XVII International Congress of the Latin American Studies Association,* mimeo. Los Angeles: Latin American Studies Association.
Chaia, Vera, et al. 2002. "São Paulo: Embate partidário, mídia e comportamento eleitoral." In Flávio Silveira, ed., *Estratégia, mídia e voto: a disputa eleitoral em 2000,* pp. 17–47. Porto Alegre: EDIPUCRS.
Cohen, Cathy J., and Michael C. Dawson. 1993. "Neighborhood Poverty and African American Politics." *American Political Science Review* 87: 286–302.
Cohen, Cathy, Kathleen Jones, and Joan Tronto. 1997. *Women Transforming Politics: An Alternative Reader.* New York: New York University Press.
Collins, Patricia Hill. 1989. "A Comparison of Two Works on Black Family Life." *Journal of Women in Culture and Society* 14: 875–884.
———. 1990. *Black Feminist Thought: Knowledge, Consciousness, and the Politics of Empowerment.* New York: Routledge.
Cordeiro, Maria Jose de Jesus Alves. 2007. "Tres Anos de Efetiva Presença de Negros e Indigenas Cotistas nas Salas de Aula da UEMS: Primeiras Analises." In Andre Augusto Brandão, ed., *Cotas Raciais no Brasil: A primeira avaliação.* Coleção Politcas da Cor.
Dávila, Jerry. 2003. *Diploma of Whiteness: Race and Social Policy in Brazil, 1917–1945.* Durham: Duke University Press.
Davis, Darien. 1999. *Avoiding the Dark.* Brookfield: Ashgate.
Davis, Mike. 2006. *Planet of Slums.* New York: Verso.
Degler, Carl N. 1971. *Neither Black nor White: Slavery and Race Relations in Brazil and the United States.* New York: Macmillan.
Diamond, Larry. 1999. *Developing Democracy: Toward Consolidation.* Baltimore: Johns Hopkins University Press.
Dias, Heloisa. 1995. "Mídia e Política: A Cobertura de O Globo e a Eleição Municipal no Rio de Janeiro em 1992." Master's thesis, Instituto Universitário de Pesquisas do Rio de Janeiro.
Downs, Anthony. 1957. *An Economic Theory of Democracy.* New York: Harper and Row.
Du Bois, W. E. B. 1999. *As almas da gente negra.* Rio de Janeiro: Lacerda Editores.
Dunn, Christopher. 1994. "A Fresh Breeze Blows in Bahia." *Americas* 46: 28.

Dyer, Richard. 1986. *Heavenly Bodies: Film Stars and Society.* New York: St. Martin's Press.

Dzidzienyo, Anani. 1971. *The Position of Blacks in Brazilian Society.* London: Minority Rights Group.

Erickson, Kenneth. 1977. *The Brazilian Corporative State and Working Class Politics.* Berkeley: University of California Press.

Espinheira, Gey. 1989. "Pelourinho: A hora e a vez do Centro Histórico." *Centro de Estudos e Ação Social* 119: 35–45. Salvador.

Evans, Arthur S., Jr. 1995. "The Transformation of the Black Middle Class." In Arthur J. Vidich, ed., *The Middle Classes: Life-Styles, Status, Claims and Political Orientations,* pp. 215–237. New York: New York University Press.

Evans, Peter, Dietrich Rueschemeyer, and Theda Skocpol. 1985. *Bringing the State Back In.* Cambridge: Cambridge University Press.

Executive National da Marcha Zumbi (ENMZ). 1996. *March Against Racism for Citizenship and Life.* Brasília.

Feldman, Roberta, Susan Stall, and Patricia A. Wright. 1998. "'The Community Needs to Be Built by Us': Women Organizing in Chicago Public Housing." In *Community Activism and Feminist Politics,* pp. 257–274. New York: Routledge.

Felinto, M. 1997. "O Homem Invisível." *República* 1 (4): 38–42.

Fernandes, Florestan. 1972. *O negro no Mundo dos Brancos.* São Paulo: Difel.

———. 1978. *A Integração do Negro na Sociedade de Classes.* São Paulo: Editora Ática 2.

Figueiredo, Angela. 2002. *Novas Elites de Cor: Estudo Sobre os Profissionais Liberais Negros de Salvador.* São Paulo: Annablume/UCAM.

———. 2003. "Novas elites de cor: A Classe Média Negra Não Vai ao Paraíso: Trajetórias." *Perfis e Identidade entre os Empresários Negros.* Ph.D. diss., IUPERJ, Rio de Janeiro.

Figueiredo, Marcus F. 2000. "Mídia, mercado de informação e opinião pública." In C. Guimarães, ed., *Informação e democracia,* pp. 39–46. Rio de Janeiro: EdUERJ.

Figueiredo, Marcus, et al. 2002. "Rio de Janeiro: Cesar versus Conde e a Nova Política Carioca." In Flavio Silveira, ed., *Estratégia, Mídia e Voto: A Disputa Eleitoral em 2000,* pp. 249–289. Porto Alegre: Edipucrs.

Figueiredo, Marcus, et al. 1997. "Estratégias de Persuasão Eleitoral: Uma Proposta Metodológica para o estudo da propaganda eleitoral." *Opinião Pública* 4 (3): 109–120.

Fontaine, Pierre-Michel. 1985. *Race, Class and Power in Brazil.* Los Angeles: Center for Afro American Studies, University of California–Los Angeles.

Ford, Christopher A. 1994. "Administering Identity: The Determination of 'Race' in Race-Conscious Law." *California Law Review* 82.

Foucault, Michel. 1995. *Discipline and Punish.* New York: Random House.

Fraser, Nancy. 1989: *Unruly Practices: Power, Discourse, and Gender in Contemporary Social Theory.* Minneapolis: University of Minnesota Press.

———. 1997. *Justice Interrupt us.* New York: Routledge.

———. 1998. "Heterosexism, Misrecognition and Capitalism: A Response to Judith Butler." *New Left Review* 228 (March/April): 140–149.

Frazier, E. Franklin. 1975. *Black Bourgeoisie: The Rise of a New Middle Class in the United States.* London: Collier Macmillan.

Freyre, Gilberto. 1933. *Casa Grande e Senzala.* Rio de Janeiro: José Olímpio.

———. 1986. *The Masters and the Slaves: A Study in the Development of Brazilian Civilization.* 2nd English language ed. University of California Press.

Fry, Peter, and Yvonne Maggie. 2004. "Cotas raciais: Construindo um pais dividido?" *Econômica* 6 (1): 151–161. Rio de Janeiro.

————. 2007. "Politica Social de Alto Risco." In Fry et al., eds., *Divisões perigosas: Políticas raciais no Brasil contemporâneo.* Rio de Janeiro: Cilização Brasileira.

Fry, Peter, Yvonne Maggie, Marcos Chor Maio, Simone Monteiro, and Ricardo Ventura Santos, eds. 2007. "Introduction." *Divisões perigosas: Políticas raciais no Brasil contemporâneo.* Rio de Janeiro: Cilização Brasileira.

Galanter, Marc. 1984. *Competing Equalities: Law and the Backward Classes in India.* Oxford University Press.

Giddens, Anthony. 1989. *A constituição da sociedade.* São Paulo: Martins Fontes.

Goés, José de. 2001. "Opinião: Cotas Raciais e Políticas Afirmativas." *O Globo,* 14 December 2001

Gomes, Joaquim Barbosa. 2003. "O debate constitucional sobre as ações afirmativas." In R. E. dos Santos and F. Lobato, eds., *Ações Afirmativas: Políticas Públicas contra as Desigualdades Raciais,* pp. 15–57. Rio de Janeiro: DP and A Editora.

Gonzalez, Lelia. 1985. "The United Black Movement: A New Stage in Black Political Mobilization." In Pierre-Michel Fontaine, ed., *Race, Class and Power in Brazil,* pp. 120–134. Los Angeles: Center for Afro-American Studies, University of California–Los Angeles.

Gregory, Steven. 1998. *Black Corona: Race and the Politics of Place in an Urban Community.* Princeton: Princeton University Press.

Guha, Ranajit. 1994. "The Prose of Counter-Insurgency." In N. B. Dirks, G. Eley, and S. B. Ortner, eds., *Culture/Power/History: A Reader in Contemporary Social Theory.* Princeton: Princeton University Press.

Guimarães, Antonio Sergio. 1995. "Racismo e anti-racismo no Brasil." *Novos Estudos* 43: 26–44.

————. 1997. "Racismo e Restrições dos Direitos Individuais: A Discriminação 'Publicizada.'" *Estudos Afro-Asiáticos* 31: 51–78.

Habermas, Jürgen. 1984, 1989. *The Theory of Communicative Action.* Boston: Beacon Press.

————. 1998. *Between Facts and Norms.* Cambridge: MIT Press.

Hagopian, Francis. 1996. *Traditional Politics and Regime Change in Brazil.* New York: Cambridge University Press.

Hanchard, Michael. 1994a. "Black Cinderella? Race and the Public Sphere in Brazil." *Public Culture* 7: 165–185.

————. 1994b. *Orpheus and Power: The Movimento Negro of Rio de Janeiro and São Paulo, Brazil, 1945–1988.* Princeton: Princeton University Press.

————, ed. 1999. *Racial Politics in Contemporary Brazil.* Durham: Duke University Press.

Harris, Cheryl I. 1993. "Whiteness as Property." *Harvard Law Review* 106: 276–291.

Harris, Marvin. 1964. *Patterns of Race in the Americas.* New York: Walker.

————. 1970. "Referential Ambiguity in the Calculus of Brazilian Racial Identity." *Southwestern Journal of Anthropology* 26 (Spring): 1.

Hasenbalg, Carlos A. 1979. *Discriminação e Desigualdades Raciais no Brasil.* Rio de Janeiro: Graal.

————. 1996a. "Racial Inequalities in Brazil and Throughout Latin America: Timid Responses to Desguised Racism." In Elizabeth Jelin and Eric Hersber, eds., *Constructing Democracy: Human Rights, Citizenship and Society in Latin America.* Boulder: Westview Press.

————. 1996b. "Entre o mito e os fatos: Racismo e relações raciais no Brasil." In Marcos Chor e Santos Maio and Ricardo Ventura, eds., *Raça, Ciência e Sociedade.* Rio de Janeiro: FIOCRUZ/CCBB.

Hasenbalg, Carlos, and Nelson do Valle Silva. 1988. *Estrutura Social, Mobilidade e Raça.* Rio de Janeiro: IUPERJ.

———. 1992. *Estrutura Social, Mobilidade e Relações Racias.* Vertice.

———, eds. 2003. *Origens e destinos: Desigualdades social ao longo da vida.* Rio de Janeiro: Topbooks.

Heringer, Rosana. 1999. "Addressing Race Inequalities in Brazil: Lessons from the United States." Working Paper Series. Washington: Latin American Program, Junior Scholars Training Program; Woodrow Wilson International Center for Scholars, 237: 56–81.

Heringer, Rosana. 2003a. "Promoção da igualdade racial no Brasil: 2001–2003." *Tempo e Presença,* 330 Suplemento Especial.

———, ed. 2003b. *Sonhar o futuro, mudar o presente: Diálogos Contra o Racismo, por uma Estratégia de Inclusão Racial no Brasil.* Rio de Janeiro: IBASE.

———. 2003c. "Governo Lula: Primeiras Realizações, Novas Expectativas." Suplemento Especial. *Tempo e Presença* 25 (330).

Hernandez, Tanya Kateri. 1998. "'Multiracial' Discourse: Racial Classification in an Era of Color-Blind Jurisprudence." *University of Maryland Law Review* 57.

Hirsch, Fred. 1976. *Social Limits to Growth.* Cambridge: Harvard University Press.

Hirschmann, Albert. 1992. *O. A Retórica da Intransigência: Perversidade, Futilidade, Ameaça.* São Paulo: Companhia das Letras.

Holston, James. 1991. "The Misrule of Law: Land and Usurpation in Brazil." *Comparative Studies in Society and History* 33: 695–725.

———. 2008. *Insurgent Citizenship: Disjunctions of Democracy and Modernity in Brazil.* Princeton: Princeton University Press.

Holston, James, and Teresa Caldeira. 1998. "Democracy, Law, and Violence: Disjunctions of Brazilian Citizenship." In Felipe Aguero and Jeffrey Stark, eds., *Fault Lines of Democracy in Post-Transition Latin America,* pp. 263–297. Miami: North South Center Press.

Horowitz, Donald. 1985. *Ethnic Groups in Conflict.* Berkeley: University of California Press.

Hunter, Tera. 2008. *To 'Joy My Freedom: Southern Black Women's Lives and Labors After the Civil War.* Cambridge: Harvard University Press.

Imbassahy, Antônio. 2000. "Símbolo da Bahia." *Notícias do Patrimônio.* Salvador: Informativo do Instituto Histúrico e Artístico Nacional//Ministério da Cultura.

Jamieson, Kathleen H. 1992. *Dirty Politics: Deception, Distraction, and Democracy.* New York: Oxford University Press.

Jenkins, Laura Dudley. 2004. "Race, Caste, and Justice: Social Science Categories and Antidiscrimination Policies in India and the United States." *University of Connecticut Law Review* 36: 747.

Jeter, Jon. 2003. "Affirmative Action Debate Forces Brazil to Take Look in the Mirror." *Washington Post,* June 16.

Johnson, Ollie, III. 1998. "Racial Representation and Brazilian Politics: Black Members of the National Congress, 1983–1999." *Journal of Interamerican Studies and World Affairs* 40: 97–118.

Kachani, M. 1996. "A aposta de Maluf." *Veja* 4 (9): 20–23.

Kelley, Robin. 1997. *Yo' Mama's Disfunktional! Fighting the Culture Wars in Urban America.* Boston: Beacon Press.

Lacarrieu, Monica. 2000. "No Caminho Para o Futuro, A Meta e o Passado: A questão do patrimônio e das identidades nas cidades contemporâneas." Paper presented at the Fifth International Conference of the Brazilian Studies Association, Recife, Brazil.

Lamont, Michele, and Virag Molnar. 2002. "The Study of Boundaries in the Social Sciences." *Annual Review of Sociology* 28: 167–195.

Landry, Bart. 1988. *The New Black Middle Class.* Berkeley: University of California Press.

Leal, Maria. 1994. "Amargo Labor." In *A Tarde Cultural.* 5/21.

Lefebvre, Henri. 1996. *Writings on Cities.* Malden, MA: Wiley-Blackwell.

Leong, Nancy. 2006/2007. "Multiracial Identity and Affirmative Action." *Asian Pacific American Law Journal* 12 (Fall /Spring). University of California–Los Angeles.

Lesser, Jeffrey. 1999. *Negotiating National Identity: Immigrants, Minorities, and the Struggle for Ethnicity in Brazil.* Durham: Duke University Press.

Lima, Márcia. 1997. "A Eleição de Celso Pitta: Relações Raciais e Contexto Político." *Questões de Raç: Seleção de Notícias da Imprensa Brasileira sobre Relações Raciais* 8 (March–April).

Linz, Juan J., and Alfred Stepan. 1996. *Problems of Democratic Transition and Consolidation.* Baltimore: Johns Hopkins University Press.

Lovell, Peggy A. 1999. "Women and Racial Inequality at Work in Brazil." In M. Hanchard, ed., *Racial Politics in Contemporary Brazil.* Durham: Duke University Press.

Luhmann, Niklas. 1996. *Social Systems.* Stanford: Stanford University Press.

Machado, Elielma. 2007. "Acompanhamento e Monitoramento das Politicas de Ação Afirmativa nas Universidades Brasileiras." *Desiguldade e Diversidade* 1: 139–160.

Maggie, Yvonne, and Peter Fry. 2004. "A reserva de vagas para negros nas universidades brasileiras." *Estudos Avanzados* 18 (50): 67–80.

———. 2007. "Politica Social de Alto Risco." In Fry et al., eds., *Divisões perigosas: Políticas raciais no Brasil contemporâneo.* Rio de Janeiro: Cilização Brasileira.

Mainwaring, Scott, et al. 2000. "Conservative Parties, Democracy and Economic Reform in Contemporary Brazil." In Kevin Middlebrook, ed., *Conservative Parties, the Right, and Democracy in Latin America.* Baltimore: Johns Hopkins University Press.

Mainwaring, Scott, ed. 1997. *Presidentialism and Democracy in Latin America.* New York: Cambridge University Press.

Mainwaring, Scott, and Timothy R. Scully, eds. 1995. *Building Democratic Institutions: Party Systems in Latin America.* Stanford: Stanford University Press.

Maio, Marcos Chor. 2001. "UNESCO and the Study of Race Relations in Brazil: Regional or National?" *Latin American Research Review* 36 (2): 118–136.

Maio, Marcos Chor, and Ricardo Ventura Santos. 2005a. *Horizontes Antropologicos* 11 (23) (January/June).

———. 2005b. "Politicas de Cotas Raciais, os 'Olhos da Sociedade' e os Usos da Antopologia: O Caso do Vestibular da Universidade de Brasília." *Horizontes Antropologicos* 11 (23) (January/June): 181–214.

Mancini, P., and D. L. Swanson, eds. 1996. *Politics, Media and Modern Democracy.* Westport, CT: Praeger Publishers.

Martins, Roberto. 2003. *Desigualdades Raciais e Políticas de Inclusão Racial: Um Sumário da Experiência Brasileira Recente.* CEPAL.

Martins da Silva, L. F. 2003. "Ação Afirmativa e Cotas para Afro-descendentes: Algumas Considerações Sociojurídicas." In Renato E. dos Santos and Fátima Lobato, eds., *Ações Afirmativas: Políticas Públicas contra as Desigualdades Raciais,* pp. 59–73. Rio de Janeiro: Laboratorio das Politicas Publicas (LPP/ UERJ), DP&A Editora.

Meade, Teresa A. 1997. *Civilizing Rio: Reform and Resistance in a Brazilian City 1889–1930.* University Park: The Pennsylvania State University Press.

Mitchell, Gladys. 2006. "Political Opinion, Racial Attitudes and Candidate Preference Survey."

——. 2009. "Afro-Brazilian Politicians and Campaign Strategies: A Preliminary Analysis." *Latin American Politics and Society,* forthcoming.

Mitchell, Michael. 1977. "Racial Consciousness and the Political Attitudes and Behavior of Blacks in São Paulo, Brazil." Ph.D. diss., Indiana University.

Mohanty, Chandra Talpade. 2003. *Feminism Without Borders: Decolonizing Theory, Practicing Solidarity.* Durham: Duke University Press.

Montegenro, Erica. 2007. "Cota Racial: Aprovadadas mudanças na UNB." *Correio Brazilense, Jornal Irohin,* October 2.

Moura, Clovis. 1988. *Sociologia do Negro Brasileiro.* São Paulo: Atica.

——. 1994. *A Dialética Radical do Brasil Negro.* São Paulo: Editora Anita.

Munanga, Kabengele. 1994. "Identidade, cidadania e democracia: Algumas reflexões sobre os discursos anti-racistas no Brasil." In Mary J. Paris Pink, ed., *A Cidadania em Construção: Uma reflexão Transdisciplinar.* São Paulo: Cortes.

Nahuz, Carolina, and Adalberto Junior. 2008. "UFMA reconhece error em sistema de cotas." *O Imparcial,* March 13.

Nandy, Ashis. 1983. *The Intimate Enemy: Loss and Recovery of Self Under Colonialism.* Delhi: Oxford University Press.

Nascimento, Abdias do. 1989. *Brazil: Mixture or Massacre? Essays in the Genocide of a Black People.* Dover: First Majority Press.

Nascimento, Alexandre. 2002. "Movimentos Sociais e Democracia: Os Cursos Prévestibulares Populares." In Carmo Thum, ed., *Encontro Experiências de Pré-Vestibulares Populares.* Florianópolis/Pelotas: Ed. Universitária UFPel Anais.

Nascimento, Regina Célia Oliveira. 1994. *Trajetória de uma Identidade.* Master's thesis, Universidade de Campinas.

Nascimento, Solano, and Beatriz Velloso. 2001. "A Semana." *EPOCA,* December 16.

Nobles, Melissa. 2000. *Shades of Citizenship: Race and the Census in Modern Politics.* Stanford: Stanford University Press.

Nogueira, Oracy. 1985. *Tanto Preto Quanta Branco: Estudos de Relações Raciais.* São Paulo: T. A. Queiroz.

Novaes, Carlos A. 1996a. "A Geografia do Voto em São Paulo e Contornos Sociais das Preferências do Eleitor." *Novos Estudos CEBRAP* 45: 4–14.

——. 1996b. "O primeiro turno da eleição para prefeito de São Paulo." *Novos Estudos CEBRAP* 46: 21–38.

Oliveira, Cloves Luiz P. 1997. *A Luta por um Lugar: Gênero, Raça, e Classe: Eleições Municipais de Salvador-Bahia, 1992.* Salvador: Serie Toques Programa A Cor da Bahia.

——. 2002. "O negro e o poder no Brasil: Uma proposta de agenda de pesquisa." *Caderno CRH* 36: 49–67. Salvador.

——. 2004. "O que Acontece Quando um Cavalo de Cor Diferente Entra na Corrida? O Painel das Estratégias Eleitorais dos Políticos Afro-Americanos nas Eleições Municipais nos Estados Unidos." *Revista Brasileira de Informação Bibliográfica em Ciências Sociais.* 57: 103–123. São Paulo.

——. 2007. "A Inevitável Visibilidade de Cor: Estudo comparativo das campanhas de Benedita da Silva e Celso Pitta às prefeituras do Rio de Janeiro e São Paulo, nas eleições de 1992 e 1996." Ph.D. diss., Instituto Universitário de Pesquisa do Rio de Janeiro (Iuperj).

Oliveira, Dijaci David de, Sales Augusto dos Santos, and Valéria Getulio de Brito e Silva. 2001. *Violência Policial: Tolerância Zero?* Goiânia, Goibâs, Brasil: Editora UFG.

Oliveira, Ney dos Santos. 1996. *Favelas and Ghettos: The Influence of Race on the Location of the Poor in Rio de Janeiro and New York.* Ph.D. diss., Columbia University, New York.

Pabst, Naomi. 2003. "Blackness/Mixedness: Contestations over Crossing Signs." *Cultural Critique* 54 (Spring).

Paixão, Marcelo. 2003. *Desenvolvimento Humano e Relações Raciais*. Rio de Janeiro: DP &A.

Pang, Eul-Sound. 1979. *Coronelismo e Oligarquias*. Rio de Janeiro: Civilização Brasileira.

Pardue, Derek. 2005. "Putting *Mano* to Music: The Mediation of Race in Brazilian Rap." *Ethnomusicology Forum* 13: 253–286.

———. 2007. "Hip Hop as Pedagogy: A Look into 'Heaven' and 'Soul' in São Paulo, Brazil." *Anthropological Quarterly* 80 (3): 673–708.

Park, Robert. 1942. "Introduction." In Donald Pierson, ed., *Negroes in Brazil: A Study of Race Contact at Bahia*. Chicago: University of Chicago Press.

Pedrão, Fernando. 1992. "O negro na formação econômica na Bahia." In *Anais do seminário O Papel do Negro na Economia Baiana*. FCE/UFBA (mimeo). Salvador.

Pena, Sérgio D. J., and Maria Cátira Bortolini. 2004. "Pode a Genética Definir quem Deve se Beneficiar das Cotas Universitárias e demais Açòes Afirmativas?" *Estudos Avançados* 18 (50).

Petruccelli, Jose Luis. 2002. "Opinião: Cotas de Cidadania." *O Globo,* November 7, Rio de Janeiro.

———. 2006. "Classificação étnico-racial brasileira: Onde estamos e aonde vamos." *REAA Textos para discussão, número 1.* Rede de Estudos de Ação Afirmativa.

Pierson, Donald. 1942. *Negroes in Brazil: A Study of Race Contact at Bahia*. Chicago: University of Chicago Press.

Pinho, Osmundo de Araújo. 2001. "Revolução afrodescendente do século 21." *Tempo e Presença* (319) (September): 17–20.

Pinho, Patrícia de Santana. 2008. "African-American Roots Tourism in Brazil." *Latin American Perspectives* 35 (3): 70–86.

Piper, Adrian. 1992. "Passing for White, Passing for Black." *Transition* 58 (1).

Pitta, Celso. 2002. *Política e preconceito: A história e a luta do prefeito que enfrentou os poderosos*. São Paulo: Editora Martin Claret.

Posel, Deborah. 2001. "What's in a Name? Racial Categorizations Under Apartheid and Their Afterlife." *Transformation* 47.

Racionais MC'S. 1993. *Raio X do Brasil*. Zimbabwe Records.

———. 1997. *Sobrevivendo no Inferno*. Cosa Nostra Fonográfica.

Racusen, Seth. 2002. "A *Mulato* Cannot Be Prejudiced: The Legal Construction of Racial Discrimination in Contemporary Brazil." Thesis, Department of Political Science, MIT.

———. 2004. "Making the 'Impossible' Determination: Flexible Identity and Targeted Opportunity in Contemporary Brazil." *University of Connecticut Law Review* 36 (Spring): 797.

Ransby, Bárbara. 2005. *Ella Baker and the Black Freedom Movement: A Radical Democratic Vision*. Chapel Hill: The University of North Carolina Press.

Rawls, John. 1999. *A Theory of Justice*. Rev. ed. Cambridge, MA: The Belknap Press of Harvard University Press.

Rebouças, Diógenes, and G. Filho. 1985. *Salvador da Bahia de Todos os Santos no Século XIX*. Salvador: Odebrecht, SA.

Reichmann, Rebecca. 1999. *Race in Contemporary Brazil*. University Park: Pennsylvania State University Press.

Reiter, Bernd. 2009a. *Negotiating Democracy in Brazil: The Politics of Exclusion*. Boulder: First Forum Press.

———. 2009b. "Inequality and School Reform in Bahia, Brazil." *International Review of Education,* forthcoming.

————. 2009c. "Fighting Exclusion with Culture and Art: Examples from Brazil." *International Social Work* 52 (2) (March).

————. 2009d."The Limits of Popular Participation in Salvador, Brazil." *Journal of Developing Societies* 24 (3), forthcoming.

Reiter, Bernd, and Gladys Mitchell. 2008. "Embracing Hip Hop as Their Own: Hip Hop and Black Racial Identity in Brazil." *Studies in Latin American Popular Culture* 27: 151–165.

Reskin, Barbara. 1997. "Affirmative Action in Employment." Washington, DC: American Sociological Association.

Roberts, Dorothy. 1997. *Killing the Black Body: Race, Reproduction, and the Meaning of Liberty.* New York: Pantheon.

Rochetti, Ricardo. 2004. "Not as Easy as Black and White: The Implications of the University of Rio de Janeiro's Quota-Based Admissions Policy on Affirmative Action Law in Brazil." *Vanderbilt Journal of Transnational Law* 37.

Roland, Edna. 2000. "O Movimento de mulheres negras brasileiras: Desafios e perspectivas." In Antonio Sérgio Alfredo Guimarães and Lynn Huntley, eds., *Tirando a máscara: Ensaios sobre o racismo no Brasil.* São Paulo: Paz e Terra.

Rolnik, Raquel. 1994. "São Paulo and the Early Days of Industrialization: Space and Politics." In L. Kowarick, ed., *Social Struggles and the City: The Case of São Paulo.* New York: Monthly Review Press.

Sandoval, Salvador. 1991. "Mecanismos de la Discriminacion Racial em el Trabajo en el Brasil Urbano." *Estudios Sociologicos Cidade de Mexico* 25 (9): 35–61.

Sanjek, Roger. 1998. *Race and Neighborhood Politics in New York City.* Ithaca: Cornell University Press.

Santos, Hélio. 2000."Uma avaliação do combate às desigualdades raciais no Brasil." In Antonio Sérgio Alfredo Guimarães and Lynn Huntley, eds., *Tirando a Máscara: Ensaios sobre o racismo no Brasil.* São Paulo: Paz e Terra.

Santos, Ivair, and Carlos Alberto dos Medeiros. 2001. "Opinião: Privilégios Ameaçados." *O Globo,* December 21.

Santos, Marcio André de O. dos. 2006. "Mutações políticas e desafios das novas institucionalidades: Os movimentos negros e a luta pela promoção da igualdade racial." IV Congresso Brasileiro de Pesquisadores Negros. Texto apresentado no Grupo de Trabalho: Ações Afirmativas, Estado e Movimentos Sociais. Salvador, 13–16 set.

Santos, Milton. 1987. "Modernidade e Memória." In W. C. Ribeiro, ed., *Milton Santos: O País Distorcido,* pp. 24–26. São Paulo: Publifolha.

————. 1996. *Território e Sociedade: Entrevista com Milton Santos.* São Paulo: Editora Fundação Perseu Abramo.

Santos, Renato Emerson dos. 2003a. "Agendas e agências: A construção do movimento pré-vestibular para negros e carentes." In Iolanda Oliveira and Petronilha B. Silva, eds., *Identidade negra: Pesquisas sobre o negro e educação no Brasil.* Rio de Janeiro: ANPED; São Paulo: Ação Educativa.

————. 2003b. "Racialidade e novas formas de ação social: O pré-vestibular par negros e carentes." In Renato E. dos Santos and Fátima Lobato, eds., *Ações Afirmativas: Políticas públicas contra as desigualdades raciais.* Rio de Janeiro: DP and A Editora.

————. 2005. "Pré-vestibulares populares: Dilemas políticos e desafios pedagógicos." In José Carmelo Braz Carvalho, Hélcio Alvim, and Renato Pontes Costa, eds., *Cursos Pré-vestibulares Comunitários: Espaços de mediações pedagógicas.* Rio de Janeiro: Ed. PUC-Rio.

————. 2006. "Agendas and Agências: A espacialidade dos movimentos sociais a partir do Pré-Vestibular para Negros e Carentes." Niterói: Tese de doutorado apresentada ao Programa de Pós-Graduação em Geografia da Universidade Federal Fluminense.

Santos, Sales Augusto dos. 2000. *A Ausência de uma Bancada Suprapartidária Afro-Brasileira no Congreso Nacional (Legislatura 1995/1998).* 2 vols. Brasília: Centro de Estudos Afro-Asiaticos.

———. 2003. "Ação Afirmativa e Mérito Individual." In Renato E. dos Santos and Fátima Lobato, eds., *Ações Afirmativas: Políticas Públicas contra as Desigualdades Raciais,* pp. 83–125. Rio de Janeiro: Laboratorio das Politicas Publicas (LPP/UERJ), DP&A Editora.

———. 2006. "Who Is Black in Brazil? A Timely or a False Question in Brazilian Race Relations in the Era of Affirmative Action?" *Latin American Perspectives* 33 (4): 30–48.

———. 2007. *Movimentos Negros, Educação e Ação Afirmativa.* Ph.D. diss., Departamento de Sociologia, Universidade de Brasília, June.

Santos, Sales Augusto dos, and Nelson Olokafá Inocêncio da Silva. 2006. "Brazilian Indifference to Racial Inequality in the Labor Market." *Latin American Perspectives* 33 (4): 13–29.

Santos, Theresa. 1999. "The Black Movement: Without Identity There Is No Consciousness or Struggle." In L. C. a. R. Johnson, ed., *Black Brazil: Culture, Identity, and Social Mobilization,* pp. 23–30. Los Angeles: University of California Press.

Saukko, Paula. 2002. "Studying the Self: From the Subjective and the Social to Personal and Political Dialogues." *Qualitative Research* 2 (2): 244–263.

Sawyer, Mark. 2006. *Racial Politics in Post-Revolutionary Cuba.* New York: Cambridge University Press.

Schwarcz, Lilia Moritz. 2003. "Not Black, not White: Just the Opposite, Culture, Race and National Identity in Brazil." Working Paper CBS-47-03. University of Oxford, Centre for Brazilian Studies.

Schwartzman, Simon. 1999. "For a de Foco: Diversidade e Identidades Étnicas no Brasil." *Novo Estudos CEBRAP* 55: 83–96.

Scott, David. 1999. "The Archaeology of Black Memory: An Interview with Robert A. Hill." *Small Axe: A Caribbean Platform for Criticism* 5 (March): 80–150.

Selden, Steven. 2000: "Eugenics and the Social Construction of Merit, Race, and Disability." *Journal of Curriculum Studies* 32 (2): 235–252.

Sheriff, Robin E. 2001. *Dreaming Equality: Color, Race, and Racism in Urban Brazil.* Piscataway: Rutgers University Press.

Showbizz. 1998. ed. 155, junho.

Silva, Benedita da. 1999. "Race and Politics in Brazil." In L. C. a. R. Johnson, ed. *Black Brazil: Culture, Identity, and Social Mobilization,* pp. 17–21. Los Angeles: University of California Press.

Silva, Nelson do Valle, and Carlos A. Hasenbalg. 1992. *Relações raciais no Brasil Contemporaneo.* Rio de Janeiro: Rio Fundo Editora.

Simpson, Amelia 1993. *Xuxa: The Mega-Marketing of Gender, Race, and Modernity.* Philadelphia: Temple University Press.

Skidmore, Thomas. 1974. *Black into White: Race and Nationality in Brazilian Thought.* New York: Oxford University Press.

———. 2002. "Raízes de Gilberto Freyre." *Journal of Latin American Studies* 34(1).

Smith, Barbara. 2000. *The Truth That Never Hurts: Writings on Race, Gender, and Freedom.* New Brunswick: Rutgers University Press.

Smith, Tom W. 1997. "Measuring Race by Observation and Self-Identification." *GSS Methodological Report No. 89.* National Opinion Research Center, University of Chicago.

Soares, Glaucio Ary Dillon, and Nelson da Valle Silva. 1987. "Urbanization, Race, and Class in Brazilian Politics." *Latin American Research Review* 22: 155–176.

Soares, Lucila. 2004. "Retrato em Preto e Branco: Cotas para negros na UnB põe fogo na discussão sobre o acesso ao ensino superior." *Veja* 37 (16): 75.

Souza, Amaury de. 1971. "Raça e Política no Brasil urbano." *Revista de Administração de Empresas* 11: 61–70.

Sowell, Thomas. 2004. *Affirmative Action Around the World: An Empirical Study.* New Haven: Yale University Press.

Stepan, Nancy. 1991. *The Hour of Eugenics: Race, Gender, and Nation in Latin America.* Ithaca: Cornell University Press.

Sudbury, Julia. 1998. *"Other Kinds of Dreams": Black Women's Organizations and the Politics of Transformation.* New York: Routledge.

Sugrue, Thomas J. 1996. *The Origins of the Urban Crisis.* Princeton: Princeton University Press.

Tajfel, Henri, and J. C. Turner. 1986. "The Social Identity Theory of Intergroup Behavior." In S. Worchel and W. G. Austin, eds., *Psychology of Intergroup Relations.* Chicago: Nelson-Hall.

Tavares, Luís Henrique Dias. 2001. *História da Bahia.* 10th ed. Salvador: Edufba.

Teixeira, Moema de Poli. 1998. *Negros em Ascensão Social: Trajetórias de Alunos e Professores Universitários no Rio de Janeiro.* Ph.D. diss., Rio de Janeiro PPGAS/ Museu Nacional.

Telles, Edward E. 2002. "Racial Ambiguity Among the Brazilian Population." *Ethnic and Racial Studies* 25 (May).

Telles, Edward. 2003. *Racismo à Brasileira: Uma Nova Perspectiva Sociológica.* Rio de Janeiro: Relume Dumará.

———. 2004. *Race in Another America: The Significance of Skin Color in Brazil.* Princeton: Princeton University Press.

Trouillot, Michel-Rolph. 1995. *Silencing the Past: Power and the Production of History.* Boston: Beacon Press.

Turra, Cleusa, et al. 1995. *Racismo Cordial: A Mais Completa Analise sobre o Preconceito de Cor no Brasil.* São Paulo, SP: Editora Atica.

Twine, France Winddance. 1998. *Racism in a Racial Democracy: The Maintenance of White Supremacy in Brazil.* New Brunswick: Rutgers University Press.

Valente, Ana Lúcia E. F. 1986. *Política e Relações Raciais: Os Negros e às Eleições Paulistas de 1982.* São Paulo: FFLCH-US.

Vargas, João. 2004. "Hyperconsciousness of Race and Its Negation: The Dialectic of White Supremacy in Brazil." *Identities: Global Studies in Culture and Power* 11: 443–470.

Venturi, Gustavo, and Vilma Bokani. 2004. "Queda do preconceito: real ou retórica?" *Revista Teoria e Debate* 59.

Verger, Pierre. 1987. *Fluxo e Refluxo.* Salvador: Corrupio.

Viana Filho, Luiz. 1988. *O Negro na Bahia.* Rio de Janeiro: Nov Fronteira.

Vizeu, Rodrigo. 2008. "Sistema de entrevistas para comprovar condição de Negro para aprovação no sistema de cotas da UnB estreia com criticas." *O Globo,* March 10.

Wagley, Charles. 1952. *Race and Class in Rural Brazil.* Paris: UNESCO.

Werneck, Jurema. 2008. "Of Ialodes and Feminists: Reflections on Black Women's Political Action in Latin América and the Caribbean." *Cultural Dynamics* 19 (1): 99–113.

Wiarda, Howard. 1981. *Corporatism and National Development.* Boulder: Westview Press.

———. 2003. *The Soul of Latin America.* New Haven: Yale University Press.

Winant, Howard. 1992. "Rethinking Race in Brazil." *Journal of Latin American Studies* 24: 173–192.

———. 1999. "Racial Democracy and Racial Identity." In Michael Hanchard, ed., *Racial Politics in Contemporary Brazil,* pp. 98–115. Durham, NC: Duke University Press.

———. 2001. *The World Is a Ghetto: Race and Democracy Since World War II.* New York: Basic Books.

———. 2006. "Race and Racism: Towards a Global Future." *Ethnic and Racial Studies* 29 (5).

Wright, Talmadge. 1997. *Out of Place: Homeless Mobilizations, Subcities, and Contested Landscapes.* Albany: State University of New York Press.

Yang, Tseming. 2006. "Choice and Fraud in Racial Identification: The Dilemma of Policing Race in Affirmative Action, the Census, and a Color-Blind Society." *Michigan Journal of Race and Law* 11 (Spring).

Young, Crawford. 1994. *Ethnic Diversity and Public Policy: An Overview.* Geneva: United Nations Research Institute for Social Development.

Zaluar, Alba. 1994. *Condomínio do Diabo.* Rio de Janeiro: Editora Raven.

Zinn, Maxine Baca. 1989. "Family, Race, and Poverty in the Eighties." *Journal of Women in Culture and Society* 14: 856–874.

The Contributors

Fernando Conceição is 2008–2009 visiting professor at the Latin America Institute at the Freie Universität in Berlin, Germany. He is professor of communication in the Department of Communication at the Federal University of Bahia, where he teaches graduate and undergraduate classes. His research focuses on communication and politics, media and ethnicity, and culture and society.

Angela Figueiredo is associate professor of anthropology at the Recôncavo da Bahia University (URB) in Cachoeira and coordinates a course at the International Factory of Ideas (CEAO/UFBA). Her areas of interest are black identity, racism, whitening, social mobility, the black middle class, gender relations, body politics, sexuality, and the prevention of HIV/AIDS.

Mónica Treviño González is a course lecturer in the interdisciplinary studies program at McGill University, Montreal, Quebec. Her research focuses on race relations, identity politics, social movements, democratization, state–civil society relations, and the political economy of development.

Gladys L. Mitchell is a visiting research fellow at the Social Science Research Institute at Duke University, Durham, North Carolina. Her research focuses on Afro-Brazilian racial identification, candidate preference, voter choice, and race in electoral politics.

Cloves Luiz Pereira Oliveira is associate professor at the State University of Feira de Santana and a researcher associated with the Color of Bahia Program at the Federal University of Bahia and the DOXA Laboratory at the University

Institute of Research of Rio de Janeiro. His research interests are political communication, political participation, race, gender, and electoral strategies.

Keisha-Khan Y. Perry is assistant professor of African studies and anthropology at Brown University, Providence, Rhode Island. She is currently completing a book based on her ethnographic research on black women's neighborhood activism for land rights in Salvador, Bahia, Brazil.

Seth Racusen is associate professor of political science and criminal justice at Anna Maria College, Paxton, Massachusetts. His research has focused on the mutual construction of law, identity, and nation.

Bernd Reiter is assistant professor of political science at the University of South Florida, Tampa. His research focuses on citizenship, nationalism, democracy, racism, and exclusion.

Renato Emerson dos Santos is associate professor at the State University of Rio de Janeiro. He was the director of the Association of Brazilian Geographers (AGB) from 2006 to 2008. His principal areas of study are social movements, urban geography, the internal organization of cities, university affirmative action, and the prevestibular for black and economically disadvantaged students.

Sales Augusto dos Santos is a member of the University of Brasília's Nucleus of Afro-Brazilian Studies (NEAB/UnB) and editor of *Affirmative Action and the Fight Against Racism in the Americas* (2005). His research focuses on racism, race relations in Brazil, affirmative action policy, racial discrimination, and higher education.

Index

About the Book

As the popular myth of racial equality in Brazil crumbles beneath the weight of current grassroots politics, how will the country redefine itself as a multiethnic nation? *Brazil's New Racial Politics* captures the myriad questions and problems unleashed by a growing awareness of the ways in which racism structures Brazilian society.

The authors bridge the gap between scholarship and activism as they tackle issues ranging from white privilege to black power, from government policy to popular advocacy, and from historical injustices to recent victories. The result is a rich exploration of the conflicting social realities characterizing Brazil today, as well as their far-reaching political implications.

Bernd Reiter is assistant professor of political science at the University of South Florida. **Gladys L. Mitchell** is a visiting research fellow at the Social Science Research Institute at Duke University.